AFRICAN LITERATURE TODAY

13 Recent Trends in the Novel

A review
Editor: Eldred Durosimi Jones
Associate Editor: Eustace Palmer

Editorial Assistant: Marjorie Jones

HEINEMANN
LONDON · IBADAN · NAIROBI

AFRICANA PUBLISHING COMPANY
NEW YORK

Heinemann Educational Books
22 Bedford Square, London WC1B 3HH
PMB 5205 Ibadan PO Box 45314 Nairobi
EDINBURGH MELBOURNE AUCKLAND TORONTO
HONG KONG KUALA LUMPUR SINGAPORE NEW DELHI
JOHANNESBURG KINGSTON TRINIDAD

Published in the United States of America 1983
by Africana Publishing Company
a division of Holmes & Meier Publishers, Inc.
30 Irving Place
New York, NY 10003
Library of Congress Card No 72–75254

ISBN 0-8419 0804-4 (cased)
ISBN 0-8419 0805-2 (paper)

British Library Cataloguing in Publication Data

Recent trends in the novel – (African Literature
Today; 13)
1. African fiction (English) – History and criticism
I. Jones, Eldred   II. Palmer, Eustace
III. Series
823   PR9344

ISBN 0-435 91646 7 (cased)
ISBN 0-435 91647 5 (paper)

Set in 10pt Melior by Unicus Graphics Ltd., Horsham
Printed and bound in Great Britain by
Biddles Ltd., Guildford, Surrey.

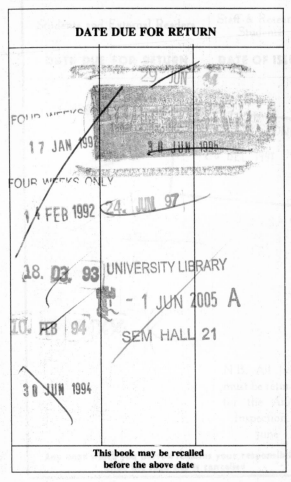

AFRICAN LITERATURE TODAY

Recent Trends in the Novel

AFRICAN LITERATURE TODAY
Edited by Eldred Durosimi Jones
In the same series

Editor: Eldred Durosimi Jones
Associate Editor: Eustace Palmer

FUTURE ISSUES

ALT 14 already in preparation will be a comparative number: *Africans and Non-Africans Looking at Africa.*

ALT 15 will focus on poetry and articles are invited on new African poets as well as on the established writers, particularly where new approaches to the latter illuminate their work.

ALT 16 is planned around women and African Literature and will seek to examine the output of women writers, portrayals of women in Literature and reactions to them. It is hoped that women critics will feature largely though not necessarily exclusively in this number.

The deadline for the submission of articles for *ALT 14* has already passed. That for *ALT 15* is January 1983, and for *ALT 16*, January 1984.

Proposals for articles should be sent with a brief summary to the Editor, Professor Eldred Durosimi Jones: Principal's Office, Fourah Bay College, University of Sierra Leone, P.O. Box 87, Freetown, Sierra Leone.
All articles should be well typed preferably on A4 paper and double spaced. References to books should include the author or editor, place, publisher, date and the relevant pages.

Contents

Contents

REVIEWS

Editorial

African Literature Today 13 returns to the subject of the novel. This is in itself a recognition of the importance of the novel genre in African literature. No other branch of African literature is growing at a faster rate, as the most cursory glance at the lists of the Heinemann African Writers Series or the Longman Drumbeat Series will readily testify. No other branch seems to elicit greater critical interest. To a much larger extent than drama or poetry the novel reflects the experiences of the African peoples from pre-colonial times to the present post-independence phase when so many of our writers are engaged in the task of hammering out new values and pointing the way towards the reconstruction of our societies. It was highly significant that most of the articles contributed to *African Literature Today* 10 (the number that celebrated the tenth anniversary of *African Literature Today*) were about the novel

But while *ALT* 10 was concerned with an exhaustive critical reassessment of the major literary landmarks up to that point, *ALT* 13 looks at the latest trends in the development of the African novel or at those aspects of the more established works which have hitherto received scant critical attention.

One of the most significant trends in the development of the African novel in recent years is the emergence of a very powerful feminist streak — the rise into prominence of a number of highly accomplished and articulate women novelists like Buchi Emecheta, Mariama Bâ* and Rebeka Njau; the redoubtable Ama Ata Aidoo has at last also turned her attention to the novel form. Various theories can be adduced to explain the comparative dearth of female novelists on the African literary scene; and the feminists will no doubt be ready with their own predictable explanation. The fact remains that the female contribution to the African novel has

* Since this editorial was written, Mariama Bâ has died in Dakar, Senegal.

hitherto been meagre. Up to the early 1970s, Bessie Head and Flora Nwapa were virtually the only female voices that were heard, and they were soon drowned by the much more powerful and insistent voices of the males. It seemed for a while that the field of African fiction, like so many other areas of African life, would unfortunately become a male preserve. The appearance of this new crop of female novelists promises to upset all that. Their work, which is very much concerned with the condition of women in traditional and contemporary African society, also promises to challenge quite seriously the cosy view of the traditional African woman cheerfully accepting her lot. These female novelists present heroines who seriously question the accepted system; and articles in this issue by Eustace Palmer and Femi Ojo-Ade examine the depth and intensity with which they present the female point of view.

The Nigerian Civil War made a searing impact on the consciousness, not just of Nigerians, but of Africans as a whole. To the entire continent it served as a paradigm of the agonizing teething problems African countries have to experience in the process of readjustment and in the attempt to resolve their more catastrophic colonial legacies. The African writer who has made it his business not only to record the process of change, but also to serve in his own peculiar way as an agent of change, was bound to react very sensitively to this traumatic conflict. Consequently the Nigerian Civil War has given rise to a whole corpus of new novels by names such as Chukwuemeka Ike, Eddie Iroh, Cyprian Ekwensi, I. N. C. Aniebo, John Munonye, Andrew Ekwuru and Isidore Okpewho. These novels are of varying quality. Some do not rise much above the level of reportage; others, like Okpewho's *The Last Duty*, are highly significant and accomplished works of art. Dr V. G. Ola's article on 'Identity Crisis in the Tragic Novels of Okpewho' does much towards elucidating the peculiar quality of this major novel as well as assessing the general contribution of one of Africa's most erudite and promising novelists.

Kole Omotoso is another young Nigerian novelist whose work, in a sense, marks an interesting departure from the mainstream of the African novel. As Odun Balogun points out in his article, he has been busy hammering out a personal aesthetic geared to the needs of his chosen audience – a populist readership. Omotoso writes about ordinary people for ordinary people, and he has deliberately tailored his art to suit their needs. Perhaps the criticism of African literature, like the criticism of several other literatures, has posited much too rigid boundaries between 'populist' and 'highbrow' fiction. The kind of work Omotoso has been doing is very significant and it is to be hoped that Dr Balogun's article marks the beginning of a serious evaluation of his work.

On the other side of the continent the dominant preoccupation of the East Africans still seems to be the social and political consequences of independence. And here we note with sorrow the death of the highly talented Robert Serumaga whose novel *Return to the Shadows* predicted so graphically and with such telling accuracy the turmoil that would overwhelm his native Uganda as various forces jockey for position and compete for political supremacy. The East Africans seem to be strongly aware of how sour the fruits of independence have become, of the prominence of the new breed of black imperialists, of the widespread sense of deprivation and the lack of adequate educational and occupational opportunities, of the glaring inequalities, of the corruption of the weak and innocent and the destruction of the human spirit. This is an area that the young Kenyan Meja Mwangi, in particular, has made his chosen territory, as Elizabeth Knight's timely article points out.

Southern African fiction has not featured very much in the pages of *African Literature Today* for several reasons. In the first place South African censorship laws affected the publication of African works adversely. A good deal had to be produced underground and smuggled out of the country, and whatever was produced inside South Africa itself was largely inaccessible to outsiders. Secondly, the war in Zimbabwe and that country's own peculiar racial and political problems prior to its recent independence similarly militated against the production of African literature. However, there are new signs that southern African works are becoming more and more accessible. The dynamism of Rex Collings has brought the work of a new generation of South African writers like Sepho Sepamla and Wilson Katiyo to our attention. The Ravan Press has also been doing good work in this regard and Stephen Gray's *Southern African Literature: An Introduction* is one of the new critical works enhancing our understanding of that branch of African literature. With the end of the war in Zimbabwe and the installation of a black majority government, a new literary self-confidence can be expected in that country, but already writers like S. Nyamfukudza (*The Non-Believer's Journey*) and Dambudzo

Marechera (*The House of Hunger*) have pointed the way ahead. Nyamfukudza's novel suggests that we are to look forward to a number of Zimbabwean novels based on the war of liberation. Dambudzo Marechera, for his part, created quite an impact at the Bonn Book Fair, and Mbulelo Mzamane's article on the prize-winning *The House of Hunger* attempts to demonstrate the artistry that led to such wide acclaim. Norman Jones's useful article on some other southern African novelists like Mungoshi, Samkange, Nadine Gordimer and Doris Lessing places the work of these writers in context and throws much needed light on a rather neglected area.

The articles on the more established figures of Achebe, Soyinka, Ngugi, Oyono and Armah take a fresh look at certain aspects of their work that it is all too easy to take for granted. Numerous comments have been made about the verbal density and the consequent 'difficulty' of Soyinka's language in *The Interpreters* and *Season of Anomy*. But few commentators have taken the trouble to analyse this linguistic complexity in as great detail as Niyi Osundare has done in his article in this issue. If we say Soyinka is difficult, it is extremely useful to know exactly why he is difficult and Osundare's effort is an important breakthrough in this regard.

An important recent trend in the African novel has been the search, by writers like Armah, Ngugi and Soyinka, for alternative societies to replace the current depraved ones to be found everywhere on the continent. Faced with the imminent disintegration of African contemporary society, these writers exhort us to go back to our origins to see whether we can learn lessons that could be used in the reorganization of our societies. In almost every case the answer involves a Marxist form of organization. But in presenting their alternatives these writers resort to the use of myth, and Okpewho's seminal and provocative article on Armah demonstrates how that writer uses traditional myth 'by abandoning it', by showing how inadequate it is to cope with the problems of contemporary life.

The African novel emerges from all these studies as a dynamic vital entity capable of responding to change, and with a tremendous capacity for change and development.

Myth and Modern Fiction: Armah's *Two Thousand Seasons*

Isidore Okpewho

In a recent article I recommended what may be called a *qualitative* definition of myth. I chose to see the tales of the oral tradition as belonging in a continuum in which they enjoy various degrees of contiguity one with the other. One side of the continuum is marked by the element of fact, the other side by the element of fantasy or fiction. Every tale will be located on this continuum depending on the proportional relationship that it demonstrates between one element and the other. It soon becomes clear that the further away a tale moves from the world of real-life experiences into that of fantasy, the more it liberates itself from the bondage to historical time and thus addresses itself to larger philosophical questions of existence. Myth, therefore, I have argued, is that quality of fancy that informs the symbolistic or configurative powers of the human mind in varying degrees of intensity. In that sense we are free to call any narrative of the oral tradition *a* myth, so long as it gives due emphasis to fanciful play.[1]

If a myth is a quality that marks tales of the oral tradition in proportion to their liberation from the constraints of time and experience, then surely we can identify this mythic quality in modern fictional works according as they are indebted to the received material of the oral tradition in content and/or in form?

A number of African writers have shown a certain Proustian nostalgia for roots, and a review of the various uses they have made of the oral narrative traditions of the continent would reveal the following tendencies. The first may be labelled *tradition preserved* in the sense that the writers concerned have done little more than translate the indigenous tale into a modern European language like English with few liberties, or at most restructured the tale into what they consider a more representative (formally or stylistically) mode. Examples are J. P. Clark's two presentations of the Ozidi tradition,[2] Taban lo Liyong's 'The Old Man of Usumbura and His Misery',[3] and Bessie Head's 'The Deep River'.[4] A second tendency may be called *tradition observed* in the sense that the writers have simply woven the themes and techniques of the oral narrative tradition around the experiences of protagonists created by them; their stories, that is, are little more than a pastiche of folk tale episodes built around a more or less contemporary hero. Examples are the tales of Fagunwa's hunter-narrator Akara-Ogun[5] and Tutuola's drinkard.[6]

The above two tendencies reveal a marked bondage to tradition. Here and there we may find a technical or idiomatic device that strains to appeal to modern educated taste or else a moralistic outlook and contextual references that advertise a relevance to contemporary society. But on the whole the writers have not allowed themselves much imaginative freedom from the received material of the oral narrative tradition. The writers in our next two categories, however, are as marked by a sense of present-day socio–political imperatives as the writers in the above categories are by their archival awe, so to speak, for the time-honoured ways. We thus come to a third tendency which may be called *tradition refined*. The classic example in this regard can be seen in the creative work of Wole Soyinka. Here the tales in their old forms are gracefully abandoned and, by some process of creative alchemy, drained of their enduring essences. One major reason for this is that the tales of the oral tradition are told largely to delight the audience: traces of this element of entertainment can be seen in Fagunwa's *Ogboju Ode*, where the author at the start invites his readers to see the tale in the light of a veritable *agidigbo* musical performance, and the narrator concludes the tale by hoping that it has delighted the audience. But Soyinka conceives his creative work against the background of the painful socio–political morass of his African society and indeed the world at large. His work is imbued with a certain revolutionary spirit; the element of idyllic delight has had to give way to a tone of painful criticism. Soyinka has therefore scoured the Yoruba oral narrative tradition to derive a figure who would represent the painful dualities of existence and the revolutionary urge to grapple persistently with the mess of society and menace of existence. In the creative output of Wole Soyinka the revolutionary essence of the Ogun figure has spanned both those works that are more or less intended for local cultural consumption (for example, *A Dance of the Forests*) and those that embrace a larger cultural universe, as in his novels[7] and *The Bacchae of Euripides.*

However far afield Soyinka strays in his mythic vision of the human predicament, he is nevertheless firmly tethered to a recognizable body of traditional tales that constitute his solid guide. This body of tales defines or is defined by an integral world-view which is distinctly Yoruba though it may have parallels across the world. There is first a local ethnic vision, which is then projected on the world or humanity at large.

But what happens when the ethnic base is not as limited as that from which Soyinka takes off? What happens when the writer's sensibility is guided not so much by a cultural outlook defined by a known setting and an equally known body of tales, as by the vision of a culture yet to be evolved or in the process of evolving? In the absence of any definitive body of tales, will the writer not be forced to create a new mythology to suit the new cultural outlook? Even when the writer is dealing with the mythology of a known group of people, will he not engage in a programmatic rejection of its well-advertised ideas if he finds they do not suit the new vision of society that he advocates on the basis of urgent social imperatives? These are the kinds of questions we have to confront in dealing with the younger generation of African writers who are guided by a certain revolutionary conscience and do not think the old mythology provides sufficient answers for the problems of contemporary African society. In their works we find an intensification of the critical spirit, an urge to overhaul the foundations on which the old social outlook was erected, and consequently an energy directed at creating a new mythology that would offer for the projected or emergent society a firmer road to self-realization than could be found in the older traditions. We may therefore wish to call the tendency here revealed *tradition revised.* Perhaps no recent work better demonstrates this urge to review the old mythic tradition and furnish new hopes than Armah's *Two Thousand Seasons.*[8]

It must be admitted right away that so far as revolutionary zeal is concerned Soyinka precedes and has in many ways inspired the new generation of writers. In embracing the figure of Ogun rather than Chaka as the true guide in Africa's confrontation with the menaces of racialism and other forms of domination,[9] Soyinka demonstrates a firm awareness of the needs and aspirations of contemporary African society, whether or not all Africans are prepared for a physical confrontation. And in dismissing as shortsighted the Obatala view of life as a sacrosanct whole or harmony,[10] Soyinka reveals a willingness to question some of the premises of the traditional mythology. But he nevertheless continues to revere that tradition and to use it as the basis for his recommendations on contemporary life and his proposals for contemporary action. The new radical writers simply do not think Soyinka has gone far enough. Some of them have embraced the Marxist–Socialist outlook as the only real solution to Africa's present socio – political problems. From this point of view, the old tales are dismissed outright as indices of the intellectual infancy of the race – where the oppressors of the race would like it to remain – or else as devices by which the ruling class of the traditional society perpetually kept the masses in servitude. What is needed now is a programmatic replacement of these tales and their symbols by new ones, or at least a thorough reassessment of the parameters of the old mythology so as to reassert the rights and claims of elements of the society who have been for too long dispossessed. Whether as whole tales or as metaphors, therefore, tales about gods and heroes and other superior beings have no room in the new radical outlook, because they help to perpetuate an unjust order and do not take due account of the urgent problems of contemporary society. Something else must be put in their place without, to be sure, abdicating any of that imaginative power on which their system was founded.

In a large sense this radical quest for a new order of reality and a new direction for the old imaginative energy recalls the efforts of certain American writers who saw themselves very much at a similar turning point in cultural and political history to that at which the present generation of African writers clearly finds itself. Walt Whitman accepted the fundamental imaginative fire that inspired the myths of the Old World, but rejected the tales themselves as well as the figures who people them (gods, nymphs and what-not) because they did not go very well with the emerging democratic and pragmatic outlook of the America of his time. In his recent book Richardson tends to underestimate the mythic impulse and to exaggerate the *religious* fervour in Whitman's poetry, but he clearly grasps the essence of the poet's attitude to the old tales when he says:

> In place of myth Whitman gives us symbols, images of man himself, a
> new religion of humanity, and prophecy. It is hard to see how any poet
> could make a greater or more affirmative use of myth than Whitman did
> by the very process of abandoning it.[11]

William Faulkner was forced to make a similar adjustment in his relationship to the older mythic tradition, which, to counter the feeling of degradation resulting from defeat in the Civil War, saw the old South as essentially noble in spirit and the martial defeat itself as a vindication rather than a condemnation of a just ethical code. Living in an age when the South needed badly to open its eyes to the social picture that was slowly but clearly emerging, Faulkner found he could not accept unconditionally the old illusions about fundamental nobility; in his novels he has created the mythical society of Yoknapatawpha in which the genteel morality of the Sartorises competes on equal terms with the amoral pragmatism of the Snopeses, both classes huddled inextricably together in a melting pot simmering with a sense of guilt from the systematic dehumanization of Indians and Negroes. For Faulkner, the Yoknapatawpha myth is a more realistic picture of contemporary Southern society. In response to critics who have continually seen Faulkner as a fervid defender of the old Southern tradition, Irving Howe has rightly pointed out:

> The truth is that he writes in opposition to this myth as well as in acceptance of it, that he struggles with it even as he continues to acknowledge its power and charm. As he moves from book to book, turning a more critical and mature eye upon his material, the rejection of an inherited tradition acquires a much greater intellectual and emotional stress than its defense. At no point, neither in his early romanticizing nor his later moral realism, is Faulkner's attitude toward the past of the South a simple or fixed one.[12]

In *Two Thousand Seasons* Armah gives due acknowledgement to the power and charm of the African oral tradition; but he will have none of that social stratification that the tales put forward. What we have in the book is a tale in the oral style all right, but one that is intensely critical rather than eulogistic or designed to please, one that rejects the present social history of Africa as unrepresentative of its true character and so projects us, in true prophetic fashion, to a vision of an Africa that is free of its shackles and guided by an ideology or religion – 'the way' – on which the race was nurtured from time immemorial. The tone of the novel is nasty and for the most part downright intemperate – as Soyinka himself has observed, 'the humane sensibility tends to recoil a little';[13] but nobody who has encountered the flagellating prose of the classic Faulkner will pretend that the language of such intense self-reassessment can be anything like good music.

Two Thousand Seasons is a rolling survey of the history of Africa (here given the name of one of its mythical ancestors, Anoa) from a nebulous past to a visionary future. It tells of a people tormented every step of the way by the menace of 'the white death', which is Armah's standard phrase for the various shades of colonial domination – religious, cultural, economic and what have you. The story starts with a wistful memory of a peaceful and congenial land, so welcoming and 'giving' that it is totally unaware of the demonic intent of Arabs (here called 'predators') who come seeking hospitality. With the Arab conquest comes the alien god of Islam and a growing threat to the cherished ways of the people – a 'way of death' steadily infiltrating the traditional 'way of life'. After a bitter confrontation the people of Anoa weigh their chances and decide to leave their original home (somewhere on the fringes of the Sahara). But in their new land the people begin to realize that the Arabs have indeed infiltrated the traditional outlook. For there now grows an uncharacteristic hunger for privileges and social prestige, as demonstrated by the rise of the institution of monarchy; the old way of reciprocity is now being supplanted by a selfish instinct for absolute power and exclusive authority. A certain divisiveness thus comes upon the people, which makes it easy for the next group of colonizers (white hordes from over the seas whom Armah calls 'destroyers') to entrench themselves. Under the notorious and damnable king Koranche, the people begin to lose every shred of liberty they ever had, the white men ensuring the continued co-operation of the king with gifts of worthless jewellery and alcohol as well as armed protection against the growing resentment. The end of all this is the enslavement of the people; a spiritual process materializes into a physical reality, as the traditional rites designed to usher the flower of Anoa's youth into full social maturity succeed only in conducting them into the slave ships of the white destroyers. But there is, in spite of all this, a handful of citizens who still remember 'the way', whose vision and sanity have not totally succumbed to the menace of 'the white death'. One of these is the wise councillor Isanusi, who is forced into exile by the overwhelming degeneracy of the land and its leaders but whose apostasy ultimately yields good results. For the enslaved youths, now on their voyage to the land of the destroyers, combine courage with imagination to overpower their slavers and black stooges ('askaris') and so turn the ship back towards home, with a handy store of ammunition won in successive confrontations with hordes of slavers. The struggle for the total liberation of the land of Anoa has effectively begun. The youths finally link up with Isanusi in his jungle hideout, and after a series of lightning operations the land is firmly rid of white destroyers and the puppets they have propped up for their advantage. The story ends with an appeal to future generations for continued watchfulness and an exhortation to that reciprocity and communalism that will ensure the permanence of 'the way' long after the chroniclers of it have passed away:

> Soon we shall end this remembrance, the sound of it. It is the substance that continues. Soon it will end. Yet still, what a scene of carnage the white destroyers have brought here, what a destruction of bodies, what a death of souls!
>
> Against this what a vision of creation yet unknown, higher, much more profound than all erstwhile creation! What a hearing of the confluence of all the waters of life flowing to overwhelm the ashen desert's blight! What an utterance of the coming together of all the people of our way, the coming together of all people of the way. (p. 206)

Two Thousand Seasons is a racial epic. In tracing the mythic quality of the novel, we may best begin by discussing Armah's debt to the oral tradition from which the narrative genre of the epic ultimately derives. The narrative voice of the novel is that of 'remembrance' or chronicling; so to a large extent we are right in seeing the entire performance (such as it is) in the light of the classic legends of the Sunjata type. But we soon realize that the two lines run only parallel to one another, largely because many of the stylistic techniques that Armah borrows from the oral tradition are far less attuned to delight than they are to sadness and criticism: instead of a historical song of glory, that is, what we get is a song of sad condemnation – though it ends with the promise that better days await the race with the elimination of the troubles plaguing it. We have a good deal of repeated phrases, but where in most oral traditions there is a lyrical feeling to these repetitions and an urge to please the ear, in Armah's novel there is either a condemnatory ring to them ('Woe to . . .', 'Prince Bentum, renamed Bradford George') or else a harsh admonitory din so as to burn the message indelibly into the reader's mind (as in the interminable repetition of 'our way', 'the way' throughout the book).

The rhetorical flavour of several passages in the book also leans only faintly towards the oral tradition. The numerous exclamations of 'Hau!' recall analogous instances in the heroic narrative of what may be called a *sense of moment*, by which the narrator highlights the magnitude of a spectacle or the significance of an event.[14] But

here in Armah the alert seems restricted to a painful emphasis on
the immensity of the horrors or tragedies that the black race has
experienced at successive stages of its history. The novel is indeed
strikingly economical in its eulogistic use of the rhetorical voice.
Where the oral narrator would with all due rhetorical *élan* dwell at
considerable length on events that call for glorification, Armah's
narrator dismisses such events with only a flourish of rhetorical
questions so that the reader is not diverted by cheap adulation from
the urgent task that lies ahead. The following passage is notable for
the way it almost makes light of a series of successes won by the
liberators at the earlier stages of their confrontation with the
destroyers and their puppets:

> But of the thousand days of work behind us which shall we call back for
> remembrance now? Shall we remember the days of waiting, days that in
> our eagerness began to seem unending, the days of waiting for the
> predators' long boats on the brown river Osu, far to the falling from the
> first home of our survival, Ullimboka's cave? Or shall we recall the
> single day of the liberating ambush that followed another patient wait?
> Or the day another predator, closer here, driving humans to slaughter,
> counting already in his head the things he stood to gain, found himself
> staring straight into the unblinking eyes of our avenging justice? Shall
> we remember the white destroyers' surprise when askaris they thought
> they had newly found brought against them the living force of a
> violated people's anger?[15] (pp. 174–5)

There are many occasions when our narrator's spirit is tempted to
seek release in an extended lyrical flourish, but it is sternly checked
because the job needing to be done is an arduous one and all that is
permitted is a handful of wistful lines. 'The promise of a praise
song', we are told, 'will pass swiftly; we shall not halt the main
remembrance long' (p. 56).

But nothing in the entire narrative marks its departure from the
style of the oral tradition quite as much as the narrative voice and
the nature of the empathy that it allows itself. One of the notable
marks of the oral narrative is the prominence of the single artistic
personality, the manner in which the narrator assumes a certain
proprietorship over the events that he recreates and seeks full
recognition, from the audience, of his merits as a performer. The
various versions of the Sunjata legend show the narrators making
every effort to let us know who they are and what their
backgrounds are. In the Innes collection[16] Bamba Suso lets us know
that it was his grandfather who brought the *Kora* (harp-lute) from
the land of the spirits and introduced it to Mandinka culture, and

the following portrait of a figure who can be no other than Mansa
Musa I of Mali:

> Have we forgotten the stupid pilgrimage of the one surnamed – o,
> ridiculous pomp – the Golden: he who went across the desert from his
> swollen capital twenty days' journey from where we lived; he who went
> with slaves and servants hauling gold to astonish eyes in the desert?
>
> Have we forgotten how swiftly the astonishment he aimed in his
> foolishness to generate turned to that flaming greed that brought us
> pillage clothed in the idiocy of religion? We have among us even now
> humans with a reputation for wisdom in the knowledge of our people
> who yet remember that journey of an imbecile as if its gigantic wastage
> meant some unspoken glory for our people. The aftermath of that moron
> journey was the desert white men's attack on us. (p. 62)

It is not only acknowledged historical figures that Armah divests
of the false glory that the traditions have put upon them. He also
directs his attack on the heroic stereotype of the figure credited
with superhuman powers and achievements that can be conceived
only in the 'idiocy' – to borrow Caudwell's sneer – of the fictive
imagination. Armah dates such a tradition to the infiltration of
black culture by the Arabs and their agents:

> Children walked among us believing secretly there had been an age of
> giants and doers of great deeds now gone, and that these doers of great
> deeds had been their fathers' fathers. They heard secret, nostalgic tales
> of a time when a brave man had no need to do the careful, steady work of
> planting, watching, harvesting, but could in one sudden, brilliant flash
> of violent energy capture from others all the riches he craved, then like a
> python lie lazy through the length of coming seasons, consuming his
> victim profit. (p. 32)

The treatment of the development of Anoa, the female ancestor
from whom the race takes its name, gives us a good instance of the
divergence between Armah and the oral tradition in the portrayal
of the heroic personality. What we see in Anoa is little more than a
realistic picture of a child prodigy – nothing of that fanciful
language that surrounds the figures of Sunjata, Kambili, and so on.
Here too is a character shaped more by a communal instinct than by
the selfish urge for self-glorification, attuned more to peace than to
the clamour of heroic action. Thus, when she does master the art of
hunting:

> She further discomfited her teachers by reminding them that aggressive
> hunting was against our way, that the proper use of hunting skills
> should be for halting the aged lion seeking human prey in its dangerous
> impotence, for stopping the wild hog prowling about the growing farm,

for teaching his sidelong hyena to keep its distance, not for wanton
pleasure (pp. 14–15).

We may wonder how honest such a picture is; but anyone who can
perceive the heavily Islamic flavour in the Mandinka epics will
scarcely wonder why Armah is convinced that the indigenous
African view of personality *must* be different and that such
exaggerated portraits of heroism must date from foreign contact.

Any theory of diffusion of tales and their motifs will naturally
run against the counter-theory of the psychic unity of mankind. In
the light of his general condemnation of the corruption, by the
foreign white elitist culture, of the healthy communalism of Africa,
Armah will be the last to put the indigenous black mind on a level
with that which conceived the 'grotesque' images of Arab culture.
But it is in his attack on the Christian theology that Armah reveals
his summary rejection of the supernatural community or machinery on which much traditional African mythology and religion
rest. Speaking of the missionary who comes to Anoa as the third in
the line of 'white destroyers', the collective narrator mocks his
Christian doctrine as fables fit only for juvenile, uninitiated minds:

> We told the white missionary we had such fables too, but kept them for
> the entertainment of those yet growing up – fables of gods and devils
> and a supreme being above everything. We told them we knew soft
> minds needed such illusions, but that when any mind grew among us to
> adulthood it grew beyond these fables and came to understand that
> there is indeed a great force in the world, a force spiritual and able to
> shape the physical universe, but that that force is not something cut off,
> not something separate from ourselves. It is an energy in us . . . (p. 96)

In espousing the animistic basis of the African world-view
Armah seems closer to the sage Ogotemmeli[21] than to Soyinka, who
clearly accepts the hierarchical relationship between divinity and
humanity as a first principle in his derivation of the essences
guiding the Yoruba world-view. We may recall that terrible
moment in the battle of Ire when the frenzied pleas of the people are
unable to stop the bloodthirsty god from his indiscriminate
carnage: 'Too late came warning that a god/Is still a god to men'.[23]
However, Ogotemmeli incorporates his animistic logic within a
broad mythological sketch of the creation of the universe and the
emergence of Dogon religious ideas. But even such traditions of
origin, presented in a scheme of images that have no basis in
objective reality, Armah would dismiss as the product of the
'idiocy' of foreign sanction:

What we do not know we do not claim to know. Who made the earth and when? We have no need to claim to know. Many thoughts, growing with every generation, have come down to us, many wonderings. The best have left us thinking it is not necessary for the earth to have been created by any imagined being. We have thought it better to start from sure knowledge, call fables fables, and wait till clarity. (p. 3)

In abjuring the fanciful imagery of traditional mythology and embracing objective reality, Armah is at pains — very much like Walt Whitman — to stress the urgency of historical experience and the contemporary scene in shaping the density of the race. In a more recent publication of his, a sympathetic review essay on Thomas Mofolo's 'historical epic' *Chaka*, Armah tries very hard to excuse the fanciful language of that classic but does not hesitate to be critical where he thinks 'the author has twisted historical fact'.[23] There is a certain naivete in any attempt to separate 'poetry' from 'history' in the material of the oral narrative tradition (on which Mofolo's *Chaka* has been constructed), but Armah is anxious here to see the cultural progress of the black race conducted only by recognizable historical figures. Accordingly, *Two Thousand Seasons* is peopled by characters (both good and evil) taken mostly from contemporary African culture and political history as well as (understandably) such African 'historical' classics as *Chaka*. On the positive side we have the following figures leading the struggle for black liberation (no doubt the conjectures have the support of Armah's historicist conscience): on p. 155 (Wole) Soyinka, renowned creative writer and essayist; Kimathi, Dedan (from the struggle for Kenyan independence as celebrated in Ngugi's novels); (Abiola) Irele, Nigerian scholar; (Atukwei) Okai, Ghananian poet, and so on. From the historical traditions of the Zulu of southern Africa Armah has also taken the names Isanusi (p. 73 and *passim*), the witchdoctor in Mofolo's *Chaka*; Nandi (p. 125), Chaka's mother; Noliwe (p. 54), Chaka's beloved whom he had to sacrifice for power, and so on. On the negative side we have characters — the 'ostentatious cripples' and stooges of the white men — who dangerously echo the names of present-day African leaders with whose policies and lifestyles Armah obviously does not agree: Bokasa, Senho (p. 28), and, most prominent of all, Kamuzu (p. 155 and *passim*). There are also terrible portraits of figures who invite uneasy connections with contemporary leaders from the Arab world: Hussein, Hassan and Faisal (pp. 21-2).

The recourse to 'history' in this work is overwhelming, and that leads us to a significant question: is it possible for a work that deliberately renounces the major techniques as well as the premises of traditional mythopoiesis to achieve a mythical character? One way to answer this question would be to identify the fundamental means of myth-making. It should be clear that an attachment to historical, time-bound reality robs a tale of its chances of yielding an abstract, transcendent message, and that the true mythic quality of tales of the truly fanciful kind lies in their flight from time-bound circumstances and their employment of the medium of symbol and mimesis. By his attachment to history, therefore, Armah may seem to have given up any need or desire for a symbolic reading. This would have been true but for the amazing *scope* that he has given to this historical survey, in creative art, of the black experience – and scope is one of the real mainstays of myth-making. What Armah has done in his book is to identify one transcending concept – 'the way' – stretch it over a massive landscape of time, within which the various stages of the black historical experience can be seen only as symbolic illustrations of the imminence of 'the way'. To be sure, the slave trade was a real historical experience; but within the massive canvas of the story it serves primarily as one in a series of pointers to the superior claims of 'the way' over the horrors of the 'white death'. So, too, with the initiation ceremony. It is a cultural fact in traditional African society; but when characters chosen from diverse ethnic communities are put through the ceremony in one community, then obviously the ceremony has only a symbolic value as a preparation for coping with one of the series of struggles that will confront the citizens in this society out of time and place. A single historical moment or cultural act has achieved a semiotic value in the illustration of a chosen idea. *Two Thousand Seasons* thus fulfils one of the fundamental functions of myth, which is to transmute reality into fancy through the medium of symbolism.

In the larger ethnic setting he gives to the story Armah has combined his sense of scope with another important element in mythopoiesis: escape from the limitations of contemporary reality by the creation of a different and higher order of reality. This must sound paradoxical, considering the effort that Armah makes here to identify closely with objective or historical reality and eschew the fantastic imagery of the oral narrative tradition. But it is quite clear to Armah that the socio–political realities of contemporary Africa are deplorable and unreflective of what he considers to be the indigenous way of life. Something must be done to correct that fragmentation which has caused the black race to lose grasp of its traditional sense of values. As a solution, Armah has created a fictional black society embracing as many ethnic groups as possible from the plethora of peoples in sub-Saharan Africa: among the band of liberators, Isanusi is Zulu, Kimathi is Gikuyu, Soyinka is Yoruba, and so on. Besides, most of these characters come from different walks of life; but no matter, since the liberation of the race is a mass struggle requiring the participation of everyone whatever his ethnic or occupational background.

Armah's political vision here is no different from that of those who have espoused the concept of an 'African personality' or of a brand of socialism that makes full use of the communalistic outlook of traditional African society. Each of these apologists is convinced that Africa would be much better off psychologically and gain a more meaningful place in the international community if it were to recover and affirm the collective conscience on which its traditional code of values was built. Again, how feasible or honest is such an effort, given the tremendous changes that have taken place over time, changes that the Marxist–Socialist, with his diachronic view of social reality, is not the least qualified to appreciate? The question was perhaps better put by one recent critic of the idea of African socialism, whose reservations may be used as a valid comment on the vast ethnic geography that Armah has subsumed for his fiction:

> For the important question here is, how are we to integrate the traditional system within a social structure which has been transformed? Is African socialism meant to be village communalism 'writ large' or some new system that will take into account the complex nature of a modern state, and the fact that the citizen belongs no longer to a restricted community held together by blood ties and religious sanctions, but to a secular and more embracing social system?[24]

Whether or not we agree with Armah's socialist recommendations in this novel, it seems clear that he has achieved by a new medium and within a new context what traditional mythology has constantly done, which is to transport the society that supports it away from the painful constraints of the present into a happier state of affairs. This of course makes nonsense of Caudwell's condemnation of the motivations of those oral artists who will themselves into a more comfortable existence. For as long as that 'connected' will which Armah belabours in the story has not materialized, the vision of the black race he projects into the future is no less a product of wish-fulfilment than the portrait of a privileged existence that temporary griots project into the past.

Here as in the oral narrative tradition the sensitive use of language aids the force of suggestiveness and projection in the myth-making process. As the revolutionary zeal of the liberators grows, the word 'connected' is repeated at an ear-splitting pitch and a frequency that aptly matches the intensity of that growth. Against such a force of connectedness the efforts of the white destroyers and their agents among the people can be seen to be thoroughly doomed. We can thus imagine what chances a handful of slavers stand against their numerous captives, as in the following account of the five slave-trading boats going up the river Osu:

> Each long boat carried a hundred men – more, maybe thirty more. The captives sat below their captors, their bodies immobilized from the thighs down by rigid planks of young bamboo tied in measured bundles across the width of each boat. Only the captives worked at the oars. The predators stood over them and swung their whips at them as the spirit moved them, whips made of iron chain, not leather; or they simply rested in the shade of shelters on the boats. Each boat carried ten predators. Only ten . . . (p. 176)

What can ten men do against a hundred men who though held down in body are filled with a fierce sense of 'connected' purpose? By dressing his projective vision in such sensitive language, Armah makes the prospects of black liberation that much brighter.

The visionary quality of Armah's tale is also reinforced by the fact that his concept of 'the way' is unlocated in any specific time or place. It is unlocated in time because the narrator knows only that it has been a living heritage of the race from an indeterminate past, a past that it is pointless to probe (p. 1). It is also unlocated in place because the builders of the race have had to be constantly on the move from one abode to another, preferring to sever their all-too-tenuous link with a narrow piece of earth than lose the enduring virtues of 'the living way' to the soul-destroying tendencies of 'the white death'. In this Armah's ideology bears a strong kindship with 'destroyer' evangelism. The final chapter of the book – entitled 'The Voice' – is a veritable appeal from a voice in the wilderness[25] exhorting the race to embrace a way of life that ensures for them the only true salvation. Very much as Christ urged his followers, the voice here exhorts all black men to abandon all family ties and all sentimental connection with home in favour of something more rewarding and more enduring. Whether he likes it or not, the socialist vision that underlies the concept of 'the way' bears a strong relation to Judaeo-Christian myth and dogma.

Armah takes his visionary programme one step further, and in this way perhaps he gives us something a little more than traditional myths do: the potential for victory over the forces of destruction is actually realized. The children of Anoa – the black race – are not simply promised liberation; they are given, or rather they actively win, effective liberation from all forms of enslavement and are then exhorted to keep the faith. This is clearly as revolutionary as a writer can be in his portrait of the predicament of his people: he not only offers the programme for effective revolution but he actually presents the goal as won. 'Do something, sir,' the griot Dembo Kaunte tells the host of his performance of the Sunjata tale. 'Life consists of doing something.'[26] What we have here is simply the promise that action will win contemporary society everlasting glory and immortalization in song. True, the ideals are timeless, but the griot's mind operates against the background of a bygone era whose glories contemporary society has only a fighting chance of matching. There is something equally tentative in Soyinka's bringing together of the figures of Chaka and Ogun in *Ogun Abibiman*. President Samora Machel of Mozambique declares a state of war against Rhodesia: Soyinka's sketch of the meeting of the figures of history (Chaka) and myth (Ogun), and the consequent ascendancy of the latter, is simply a reification of the belligerent posture assumed by Machel and does no more than offer us a prospect of victory. In constructing his vision with figures consciously chosen from present-day society as well as from the past, Armah shows the goals of self-realization and victory to be far more attainable than Soyinka and traditional mythology seem to do.

We can thus clearly appreciate Armah's relation to the oral narrative tradition: it is essentially one of a combination of respect and irreverence. He accepts the stylistic and mythopoeic apparatus of the oral culture, but demonstrates that its attitude is considerably inadequate for coping with the problems of contemporary society. Traditional mythology seems to do no more than wistfully recall the ideals on which society could draw for a meaningful self-realization; but Armah pushes the projection further by presenting society in the actual process of realizing its desired goals with the human as well as ideological resources at its disposal. If we may once again echo Richardson's assessment of Walt Whitman, it is hard to see how a writer could make a greater or more affirmative use of traditional myth than Armah does by the very process of abandoning it.

The aim of this paper has been to measure Armah's *Two Thousand Seasons* against the record of modern African writers who have tried to incorporate the African oral narrative legacy into their creative thinking. If we can see a correspondence between the modern writer's flight from bondage to the received material of the oral tradition and the traditional narrator's flight from the constraints of time and experience, then we shall to a large extent have grasped the meaning of that quality of fancy which we have earlier identified as myth: the mythical force of a creative work which looks to tradition depends essentially on the degree to which it embraces the *spirit* of fanciful play encouraged by the tradition with the consequent attenuation of the *stuff* or material provided by that tradition.

We can see the progressive growth in this freedom of the fancy. Even in Clark's play *Ozidi*, which may be taken as an epitome of the cosmetic job on tradition, the weakness of the imaginative freedom can be seen in the fact that, fourteen years after the publication of the play, no producer has had the courage to put in on. This is because the play makes certain technical demands that evoke an affecting picture in the oral narrative performance but are simply impossible to execute within the terms of practical dramaturgy: for instance, the scene in which the old wizard Bouakarakarabiri is shown standing on his head and gripping Ozidi with his feet (pp. 41–3) is no mean threat to the actor's life and limb!

In Fagunwa we can acknowledge a greater element of imaginative licence. He has made a random selection of elements of the oral tradition and rechannelled this selection into the scheme of experiences of a fresh personality, Akara-Ogun; with him, therefore, the myth-making legacy does enjoy a certain increase and we may even agree with Irele in putting him in the company of contemporary writers like Kafka who put a primacy on the larger metaphysical context in which human character operates.[27] But that his work is still firmly bonded to tradition is shown by its rather episodic structure: the career of Akara-Ogun is simply a string of experiences that recalls more the oral narrator's emphasis on independent narrative incidents than the modern writer's oppressive endeavour to paint a monolithic picture of character. Fagunwa's work may therefore more usefully be seen within the context of the oral tradition than of modern efforts in creative writing.[28]

A very different picture emerges when we move to Soyinka. Here the presence of the contemporary socio–political scene is as overwhelming as it is subdued in both *Ozidi* and *The Forest of a Thousand Daemons*. Here too we take leave of the tales in their old forms, because the writer is thoroughly attached to the more contemporary modes of creative writing. So the tales in their old forms are dropped; only their figures are adopted for the essences or values that they embody. With these writers the creative imagination is allowed far more freedom. New tales are told – not the old ones in a new arrangement – though the old messages endure. And with this imaginative licence goes a new temperament suited to the painful socio–political climate: the urge to please, which is the mark of the traditional performer, now gives way to the compulsion to disturb the conscience of the reader/ audience so that he may be enlisted in the painful duty to change society. The mythopoeic art in its old form cannot help contemporary society to achieve these goals.

The inadequacies of the oral tradition are more fully highlighted by Armah. In Soyinka we still feel a considerable attachment to the tradition. The myth-making imagination is still not quite free, because everything continues to be seen within the recognized parameters of a few mythic figures if not one (Ogun). What is more, in Soyinka we feel a certain despair in the knowledge that man is doomed to an irredeemable cycle of errors. The disposition here is nearly a closed one; there is room for continued struggle, but all we can achieve is a painful awareness of our limitations as men. This is so because the entire human experience is seen through the eyes of a *given* mythic figure (Ogun) who embodies the essence of continued strife and tragic wisdom. But Armah creates his own myth of a society with an undifferentiated ethnicity working towards a goal that is presented as won; he has been able to do so because he has taken full leave of the old tales and the prejudices they embody, thus bestowing on the new myth a character as prospective as the old myth was wistful. This point was well grasped by Professor Michael Echeruo when, in his inaugural address here at Ibadan, he declared that 'Armah is to us what Faulkner was to the American South: a Jeremiah without Jehovah.'[29] Though the prospective vision respects the deep-seated religious conscience and metaphysical urges of the race, it is not pronounced on the authority of any well-advertised pantheon. Here the fancy is at its freest.

At this point we may wish to expand the definition of myth which we gave earlier. It is that quality of fancy that informs the symbolistic or configurative powers of the human mind at varying degrees of intensity; its principal virtue is that it tends to resist all constraint to time and experience to the end that it satisfies the deepest urges of a people or of mankind. Such a definition helps us to unite the kind of imaginative effort that goes on in oral narratives like the Sunjata legend with that in a novel like *Two Thousand Seasons*.

Our emphasis on the aesthetic element of imagination or fancy is significant. In concrete terms, of course, *a* myth will continue to mean a tale of the oral tradition that lays stress on imaginative play. But when we identify a work as a 'mythical novel' it need do no more than employ the mythopoeic technique and ends characteristic of the oral tradition; it does not necessarily have to attach itself to recognized mythic figures, because such a dependence immediately limits the possibilities of meaning or critical interpretation. This is perhaps the major difference between Soyinka on the one hand and writers like Armah on the other who have chosen to stand back somewhat from the known figures of traditional mythology. Soyinka has defined for us the seminal qualities of the god Ogun and has declared his attachment to this figure; the result of this is that every time we read a work by Soyinka we immediately begin to look for the Ogun sensibility behind it – especially the opposition between creation/life and destruction/death, and the way in which this may be mediated. The same may be said of James Joyce, John Barth and other writers who have openly modelled various characters in their works after well-worn mythical figures and motifs. There may be a complexity in the texture of such works; the pieces may be thrown about. But once they are reassembled the key to the puzzle has been found and the possibilities of interpretation and debate are severely limited if not entirely closed. This is apparently what Richard Chase means in his use of the term *paramyth*:

> The danger is to seize upon one facet of the myth, one ghost precipitated from the artistic whole, and suppose that this *is* the myth or the explanation of the myth. A philosophical concept, a moral allegory, a symbol seized upon, cut off from the living whole – this is what I should call a *paramyth* ... To see one form in the whole to the exclusion of others is to see a paramyth.[30]

This is essentially what Soyinka has done in his reduction of Yoruba mythology under the overriding personality of Ogun. Though we applaud the ingenuity with which he transmutes the facts of contemporary life within the symbolic parameters of traditional mythology and the intellectual excitement that we get from deciphering his references, we can say no more for his career in this connection than is contained in the following judgement from Chase:

> We should rather say that a poem which out of present emotional necessity . . . becomes mythical and then fuses itself with an old myth is a truly mythological poem – but that it does not need the old myth to become mythical.[31]

There can be no greater endorsement of that metaphysical quality which Armah shares with traditional mythology: a power of projection that bestows a sense of fulfilment and reassurance.

Beyond Armah, what? With a writer like Armah in *Two Thousand Seasons* we come to the end of works that may be broadly described as 'mythical', in so far, that is, as there is no projecting beyond the future. Now, the counterpart of, say, the mythical novel is the realistic novel. Here the pressure of historical reality or contemporary experience is so strong that the sense of projection steadily gives way to the urge towards documentation even with the utmost figurative skill. The *mythic* quality does not, of course, entirely disappear. For even though we miss the recourse to personalities and stylistic devices characteristic of the oral narrative tradition, we may still discover the odd (archetypal) motif, as Charles Nnolim does in Oyono's *Une Vie de Boy*;[32] or the mission of collective self-fulfilment, as in the fiction of Ngugi; or perhaps the phenomenon of opposition and mediation which Lévi-Strauss has recognized as the mythic mind's peculiar way of gaining self-reassurance.[33] The mythic quality ultimately reduces to a minimum with those writers (for example, Ekwensi, as some have established) in whom the imaginative power does not rise to appreciable configurative heights and whose works are consequently not far from bland naturalism or the journalistic report. This is perhaps as far as the writer can go in his bondage to historical reality. There may be such a thing as imaginative journalism, but that is only the phantom of myth hovering insecurely in an atmosphere dominated by time-bound reality. With journalistic literature we re-enter that zone of constraints which we have seen as characteristic of (a) the oral narrator's bondage to historical fact, and (b) the modern writer's loyalty to the well-worn material of the oral tradition.

NOTES

1. *See* Isidore Okpewho, 'Rethinking Myth', *African Literature Today*, no. 11, 1980, pp. 5–23.
2. J. P. Clark, *Ozidi: A Play*, London, Oxford University Press, 1966; and *The Ozidi Saga*, Ibadan, Ibadan and Oxford University Presses, 1977.
3. Taban lo Liyong, *Fixions and Other Stories*, London, Heinemann (AWS 69), 1969, pp. 2–10.
4. Bessie Head, *The Collector of Treasures*, London, Heinemann (AWS 182), 1977, pp. 1–6.
5. D. O. Fagunwa, *Ogboju Ode Ninu Igbo Irunmale*, translated by Wole Soyinka as *The Forest of a Thousand Daemons*, London, Thomas Nelson, 1968.
6. Amos Tutuola, *The Palm Wine Drinkard*, London, Faber, 1952; Westport, Conn., Greenwood, 1953.
7. Especially *Season of Anomy*, London, Rex Collings, 1973.
8. Ayi Kwei Armah, *Two Thousand Seasons*, Nairobi, East African Publishing House, 1973; London, Heinemann, 1979; Chicago, Third World, 1980.
9. See Wole Soyinka, 'And After the Narcissist?', *African Forum*, no. 2, 1966, pp. 53–64.
10. See Soyinka, *The Interpreters*, London, Andre Deutsch, 1965, p. 155; Heinemann (AWS), 1970; New York, Africana, 1972.
11. Robert D. Richardson, Jr, *Myth and Literature in the American Renaissance*, Bloomington, Indiana University Press, 1978, p. 164.
12. Irving Howe, *William Faulkner: A Critical Study*, New York, Vintage Books, 1951, p. 26. For one of those views of Faulkner as a traditionalist, see George Marion O'Donnell, 'Faulkner's Mythology' in Robert Penn Warren (ed.), *Faulkner: A Collection of Critical Essays*, Englewood Cliffs, Prentice-Hall, 1966, pp. 23–33.
13. Wole Soyinka, *Myth, Literature and the African World*, Cambridge, Cambridge University Press, 1976, p. 111.
14. See Isidore Okpewho, *The Epic in Africa*, New York, Columbia University Press, 1979, pp. 212–20.
15. Even when our 'rememberer' dwells at length on the account of an achievement – as in the destruction of the lecherous Arabs (chapter 2) – it is usually with a touch of tragic awareness rather than of celebration and self-congratulation as in the oral tradition.
16. Gordon Innes, *Sunjata: Three Mandinka Versions*, London, School of Oriental and African Studies, 1974.
17. Charles Bird et al., *The Songs of Seydou Camara*: vol. 1. *Kambili*, Bloomington, African Studies Centre, Indiana University, 1974.
18. Christopher Caudwell, *Illusion and Reality*, London, Lawrence and Wishart, 1946, pp. 41–2, Woodstock, N.Y., Beckman, 1973.

19. See especially the last two versions of Innes' *Sunjata*.
20. On Mansa Musa I's journey to Egypt and the spread of Islam, see Nehemiah Levtzion, 'The Early States of the Western Sudan to 1500' in J. F. Ade Ajayi and Michael Crowder (eds), *History of West Africa*, vol. 1, London, Longman, 1971, pp. 152–3; New York, Columbia University Press, 1976 (2nd ed.).
21. See Marcel Griaule, *Conversations with Ogotemmeli*, London, Oxford University Press, 1965.
22. Wole Soyinka, *Idanre*, London, Methuen, 1967, p. 78.
23. See Ayi Kwei Armah, 'The Definitive Chaka', *Transition*, no. 50, October 1975 – March 1976, pp. 10–13.
24. Frank Niger, 'Reflections on the New African Myths', ibid. no. 50, p. 72.
25. Notice we are told that 'in the best darkness of that night a voice crossed Anoa, a voice clear, unhurried yet secret still, and untrappable. It was a voice speaking to the people . . .' (p. 297).
26. Innes, op. cit., p. 269
27. See Abiola Irele, 'Tradition and the Yoruba Writer', *Odu*, no. 11, 1975, 83ff.
28. For Fagunwa's shortcomings as a novelist, see further Abiodun Adetugbo, 'Form and Style', in Bruce King (ed.), *Introduction to Nigerian Literature*, Lagos, Evans Brothers and University of Lagos, 1971, p. 174.
29. M. J. C. Echeruo, *Poets, Prophets, and Professors*, Inaugural Lecture delivered at Ibadan University, Ibadan, 29 October 1976, mimeo, p. 17.
30. Richard Chase, *Quest for Myth*, Baton Rouge, Louisiana State University Press, 1949, p. 106.
31. Ibid., p. 112.
32. Charles Nnolim, 'Jungian Archetypes and the Main Characters in Oyono's *Une Vie de Boy*', *African Literature Today*, no. 7, 1975, pp. 117–22.
33. Claude Lévi-Strauss, *Structural Anthropology*, London, Allen Lane, 1968, pp. 220–9; New York, Basic Books, vol. 1, 1963, vol. 2, 1976.

Words of Iron, Sentences of Thunder: Soyinka's Prose Style

Niyi Osundare

Were Kola, the profound painter in *The Interpreters*, to give Soyinka a place on his canvas, he would most probably represent him as a rugged wordsmith whose forge casts words with cryptic hardness, packed into sentences whose compactness strikes like a thunderbolt. Like Ogun his patron god, Soyinka plies the deep jungle of words where daemonic sentences confuse the reader and frustrate his wanderings, and metaphors take on the baffling proteanness of the chameleon.

Consequently, the critical and stylistic hallmark of Soyinka's writing is its 'obscurity'. Undergraduate literature students write countless essays trying to unravel the mystery of Soyinka's prose, many declaring it unreadable after giving up on the first page of *The Interpreters*. Critics too complain. For example, Ossie Enekwe cites obscurity of diction as one of the 'traits pernicious to his [Soyinka's] fiction'.[1] Biodun Jeyifo goes beyond Enekwe to identify the two chief sources of Soyinka's obscurity as 'the pantheon of gods, deities, and supernatural beings and archetypal characters who people his work in recurring fashion' and 'the elaborate internal, often hermetic language which yields a seemingly inexhaustible panoply of poetic symbols and conceptions'. This obscurity, Jeyifo adds, is compounded by Soyinka's privatization or appropriation of traditional themes and motifs and their verbalization in an idiom that is almost equally private and recondite. Reading Soyinka thus becomes a battle not only with his personalized pantheon, but also with words and phrases unleashed from his private and almost esoteric lexicon.[2]

A lot of other observations have been made about Soyinka's obscurity, some of which hardly go beyond the level of intuitive, 'metaphysical' generalization, lacking as they do an explicit linguistic substantiation of their critical claims.[3] This article intends to go beyond the truism of 'Soyinka's obscurity'; it seeks to identify and examine the linguistic and stylistic sources of this obscurity in an effort to throw light on some of the lexical and syntactic predilections that make Soyinka's fiction so tough and forbidding. The texts examined are *The Interpreters* and *Season of Anomy*, the only two novels yet by Soyinka.

Words of Iron

Soyinka is essentially a poet. His writings – whether drama, essay, or journalism – are complicated by the kind of cryptic and ruthlessly condensed language that dominates his poetry. The first source of obscurity in Soyinka's prose is the extensive use of what one may call mixed metaphor. A good example of this comes from the opening paragraph of the Second Part of *The Interpreters*:

> The rains of May become in July slit arteries of the sacrificial bull, a million bleeding punctures of the sky-bull hidden in convulsive cloud humps, black overfed for this one event, nourished on horizon tops of endless choice grazing, distant beyond giraffe reach. Some competition there is below, as bridges yield right of way to lorries packed to the running-board, and the wet tar spins mirages of unspeed-limits to heroic cars and their cargoes find a haven below the precipice. The blood of earth-dwellers mingles with blanched streams of the mocking bull, and flows into currents eternally below earth. The Dome cracked above Sekoni's short-sighted head one messy night. Too late he saw the insanity of a lorry parked right in his path, a swerve turned into a skid and cruel arabesque of tyres. A futile heap of metal, and Sekoni's body lay surprised across the open door showers of laminated glass around him, his beard one fastness of blood and wet earth.[4]

To apply the reductionist strategy of paraphrase, what this passage is saying is that Sekoni died in a motor accident. But Soyinka says this in the most cryptic manner and creates a setting that situates the event within the mesh of his private mythology. A metaphysical correspondence is forged between rain falling and blood flowing:

The *rains* of May *become* in July *slit arteries* of the *sacrificial bull*. Perhaps the most vital word here both lexically and syntactically is 'become'. Lexically, it is the purveyor of transition, a concept central to Soyinka's metaphysics and philosophy; syntactically, it serves as the predicator that affirms the change between the subject ('the rains') and the subjective complement ('slit arteries . . .'). This leaves us with the semantic question: how can 'rains' become 'slit arteries'? The idea of sacrifice, a recurrent theme in Soyinka, comes to mind. The disparate ideas 'yoked by violence together' thus find a meeting ground in sacrifice, as can be seen in this diagram:

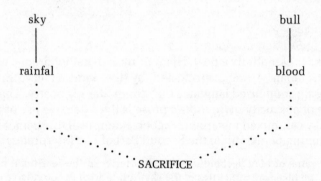

(Corollary: The showers of May become a deluge in July, like blood gushing from the slit throat of a sacrificial bull.)

The chief source of difficulty in this passage is the austere economy with which the metaphor of the rain and that of the bull have been fused within a single sentence, resulting in unusual collocations such as 'sky-bull' and 'cloud humps' which may be called mytho-lexemes. Ideas and metaphors rapidly coalesce so that in the end, Soyinka erases the phenomenological distinction between the rain cloud and the black, overfed bull. In Soyinka's mythological pasture, both cloud and bull are 'nourished on horizon tops . . . distant beyond giraffe reach'. Other things undergo a bizarre mixture in the passage: 'The blood of earth-dwellers mingles with blanched streams of the mocking bull', and in the end, Sekoni's head is 'one fastness of blood and wet earth'. On a wider plane, Sekoni himself can be seen as a bull sacrificed to the maddening frustrations of a dangerously inefficient society.

Shorter examples of such scrambled metaphors abound in Soyinka's fiction:[5]

(i) Metal on concrete *jars* my *drink lobes* (*I*, p. 7).

(ii) The *trumpet stabbed the night* in one last defiant note, and the *saxophone slunk* out of sight, a wounded *serpent* diminishing in obscene *hisses* (*I*, p. 15).

(iii) late *corn stalks* dragging their *heads* on the *copper lap* of *floods* (*I*, p. 221).

(iv) And outwards from the black edges of the moveable *proscenium* which *framed* him [Joe Golder], an archaic *figure* disowned from a family *album* (*I*, p. 245).

(v) Cowed by superstition they might *sow* a live *cow* in their backyards but they raised a *crop* of armed *serpents* when the need arose (*SOA*, p. 133).[6]

(vi) ignored by an eloquence of eyes (*SOA*, p. 268).

In (i) the alimentary and the auditory are yoked together through the quaint collocation of 'jar' and 'drink lobes'. The problematic lexical item here is 'drink', which disturbs the usual collocation of 'jar' and 'lobe' (meaning 'ear'). But an understanding of Sagoe's peculiar sensibility establishes a private and personal logic for this unusual collocation: the sound that jars his 'drink lobes' (meaning 'guts') passes through his normal 'lobes' (ears). The collocation 'drink lobes' so indigenous to Sagoe cryptically summarizes his character as a hard-drinking but intelligent and sensitive person who jokingly locates the seat of his sensibility in his guts.

In (ii) the trumpet is endowed with the power of a dagger, while the saxophone is compared to a snake. The latter comparison is particularly ingenious: Soyinka exploits all the similarities in appearance, movement and sound between a saxophone and a snake. The tapering sound of the saxophone parallels the faint hisses of a wounded snake slinking out of sight. (The sibilant phenome 's' common to both 'saxophone' and 'snake' also compels attention.)

The metaphoric twist in (iii) is further compounded by the personification of the basic lexical items: corn stalks have 'heads' which they 'drag', and floods have 'laps' with a 'copper' (reddish-brown) complexion.

Example (iv) shows Soyinka at his most etymologically profound. By building up a collocation between 'proscenium', 'framed', 'figure' and 'album', he reactivates in one poetic swoop the traditional nickname of the proscenium stage as the 'picture frame'.

In (v) the almost surrealistic collocation of sow + cow-
+ raised + crop + serpents is an awesome indication of the
'anomy' that dominates human life and activity in Soyinka's
second novel. The similarity here between what is sown and what
is reaped is informed by a kind of moralistic and metaphysical
metaphor. Throughout *Season of Anomy*, the lexical item 'sow'
collocates with frightful seedlings:

> The sowing of any ideas (p. 23).
> sowing the wind and reaping the whirlwind (p. 24).
> death sowed by these false farmers (p. 128).
> And Batoki sowed a forest of bayonets (p. 139).
> Plant the horns (p. 178).

The first of the above expressions is seemingly innocuous until we
learn two lines later that the young seedling may need to be
protected by 'violent means'.

The last example, (vi), defeats expectation by collocating 'eyes'
(+ visual) with 'eloquence' (+ sound).

In all these examples, Soyinka's 'short cut of metaphor imprisons
features, ideas, and personalities in a brief phrase'.[7] Soyinka's
metaphoric eye hardly sees anything less than double; his words
weave disparate ideas together like 'threads in an intricate
tapestry'.[8] These, without doubt, are characteristics of good writing
anywhere in the world. But what makes Soyinka especially
difficult is the fact that a good number of his metaphors and idioms
derive from his personal musings and private mythology. A
reasonable understanding of Soyinka demands a more than casual
acquaintance with his mytho-lexicon. Another lexical predilec-
tion that has contributed to the difficulty of Soyinka's prose is his
extensive use of compound words. It may be argued, of course, that
compounding has become a lexical fad in a twentieth century of
'nounspeak' and 'nounfreight', but Soyinka uses compounds in a
way that boosts the baffling compactness of his prose. We may
examine his compounds under two broad categories – simple and
multiple. Simple compounds are those consisting of not more than
two free morphemes, while multiple are those containing more
than two. Simple compounds are further divisible into unhyphe-
nated and hyphenated. A diagrammatic illustration will elucidate
the categorization further:

COMPOUNDS

Simple

unhyphenated	hyphenated
cloudburst (*I*, p. 22)	thigh-high (*I*, p. 7)
centrepiece	root-strands (*I*, p. 9)
houseboat (*I*, p. 23)	mud-dark (*I*, p. 10)
outsplash (*I*, p. 246)	mid-swallow (*I*. p. 37)
tunesmith (*SOA*, p. 86)	fore-brush (*I*, p. 37)
scapeclan (*SOA*, p. 170)	sweat-slippery (*I*, p. 117)
	after-crisis (*I*, p. 201)
	earth-bull (*SOA*, p. 18)

Multiple

sit-down-strike (*I*, p. 76)
back-to-the-bush (*I*, p. 97)
book-and-shovel (*I*, p. 97)
Nat-King-greasy-Cole (*I*, p. 110)

What is collapsed into single compounds here are potentially longer expressions and structures:

thigh-high = as high as the thigh (spatial)
mid-swallow = in the middle of the act of swallowing (process-oriented)
sweat-slippery = slippery as a result of sweat (causative)
fore-brush = before the brush (temporo–sequential)
centrepiece = the piece of the centre (genitival–locative)

Such compounds help Soyinka achieve a tremendous economy of expressions, and since a compression of words is ultimately a compression of ideas, compounding entails a frugality that slows down the pace of reading comprehension. Furthermore, compounding aids Soyinka's irrepressible penchant for neologism; for example some of the formations above have a Soyinkaesque freshness: 'scapeclan', 'tunesmith', 'rootstrands', 'earth-bull', 'Nat-King-greasy-Cole'. The formation 'earthbull', for instance, has a mytho-lexical affinity with 'sky-bull' which we encountered above. Compounding is so common in Soyinka that it catches the attention of even his most cursory reader; for example, there are eight compound formations on page 2 of *Season of Anomy*, four on page 10, seven on each of pages 12 and 13, five on page 14, and six on page 15. Compounding brings out the poet in Soyinka, helps him to the shortest cut to ideas, and encourages him to take liberties with the lexis and structure of language.

Soyinka also saves words by the use of what may be called condensed or indirect similes. By this method, he explodes upon the reader the forceful similarity of the two things being compared by omitting the conjunction 'like'. Let us consider a few examples:

(i) The beer reversed direction and Lasunwon's nostrils were / twin nozzles of a fireman's hose (sic) (*I*, p. 15).

(ii) Bandele fitted himself, / wall gecko, into a corner (*I*, p. 16).

(iii) The air was / a horn of straight palm wine on a ten-day fast (*I*, p. 52).

(iv) There was a stampede of elephants on the stairs (*I*, p. 135).

(v) Egbo's eyes were / / outheld on black cuspids, embers on the end of a blacksmith's tongs (*I*, p. 249).

We may fill in the omissions in (i) to (iii) with 'like' and that in (v) with 'as if', but the result will be expressions that are rather too common and too unpuzzling for Soyinka, the word-pruner. Sentence (iv) is the most remorselessly compressed of all, and its compression is unnecessarily misleading and confusing; for those responsible for the 'stampede' are not 'elephants', but human beings compared to elephants. Sentence (ii) is structurally intriguing. The omission of the 'like' conjunction and its replacement by commas before and after 'wall gecko' give the latter nominal word group a kind of appositive quality. On the whole, the omission of the 'like' and 'as if' conjunctions tends to make these sentences structurally equative (x is y) whereas they are semantically comparative (x is like y). This is another common stylistic terrain for Soyinka, which is nothing but a 'baffle-ground' for the reader.

Cascades of words and ideas throng Soyinka's head, and in putting them on paper, he fuses, yokes and integrates, often bringing violently together those things the world has learnt to place apart. This explains the highly allusive nature of his writing. A number of such allusions often come through direct similes:

(i) his [Alhaji Sekoni's] haji mantle blown about his shoulders like the *mane of Lear on an asphalt heath* (*I*, p.98).

(ii) *Like sand-elves in Ogboju Ode*, the mob materialised with every step (*I*, p. 115).

(iii) And Bandele held himself unyielding, like the *staff of Ogboni* (*I*, p. 244).

(iv) Bandele, old and immutable *as the royal mothers of Benin throne*, old and cruel as *the Ogboni* in conclave pronouncing the Word (*I*, p. 251).

To realize the full import of these similes, one must know the other half of the compared pair: Lear's heath, Fagunwa's sand-elves in *Ogboju Ode*, the Ogboni cult, and the royal mothers of Benin. The nominal word group 'asphalt heath' in (i) is particularly intriguing. The deliberate anachronism involved here results in temporal as well as semantic discollocation: there is hardly anything like asphalt heath, and even if there were, it could not have existed in Lear's (Shakespeare's) time. Crisis of understanding arises when the reader does not share the same mythological and literary universe which produces Soyinka's allusions.

Because of Soyinka's Christian background, his works contain biblical references and metaphors. In *The Interpreters*, Lazarus and Barabbas share (or claim to share) certain similarities with their biblical countertypes; the flood that occurred during the interpreters' visit to Lazarus's church brings echoes of the Flood in Genesis, an echo amplified by the change of Barabbas's name to Noah. There is reference to Jacob and Esau (p. 102), while Sagoe calls Dehinwa 'damned Jael' (p. 67). In *Season of Anomy*, there are references to 'ten pieces of gold' (p. 110), 'the chariot of wrath' (p. 167) and Herod the heartless infanticide (p. 221). The constant use of the word 'sow' in this novel cannot but remind one of the Sower in the Bible. Thus allusion to the Judaeo-Christian lore confronts the reader with additional problems of understanding and interpretation of Soyinka's mythological network, an elaborate mesh of Yoruba, Graeco-Roman and Hindi (Soyinka tinkers with this latter in *Season of Anomy*) mythologies plus Soyinka's own private abstraction from all these.

Soyinka also narrates in a kind of hyperpoetic opaqueness events that are considered common in everyday life. Egbo's teacher did not beat him ceaselessly, rather he 'wore out canes on him' (*I*, p. 16); Sekoni, instead of simply electrifying Ijioha, would rather 'bathe Ijioha maidens in neon glow' (*I*, p. 29). Nothing illustrates this elaborate periphrasis better than Soyinka's description of the first sexual encounter between Egbo and Simi:

And a lone pod strode the baobab on the tapering thigh, leaf-shorn, and high mists swirl him, haze-splitting storms, but the stalk stayed him

> ... parting low mists in a dark cave ... in darkness let me lie, in
> darkness cry ... (I, p. 60)

If, according to Eldred Jones, Soyinka indulges in this oracular hightalk in order to avoid 'obviousness or prurience',[9] the price for such priggishness is the obfuscation of an ordinary event and the bafflement of the reader. The only lexical item that directly refers to coitus in the above passage is 'thigh'; the reader has to sweat – and guess – his way through the others: 'a lone pod' may be referring to the penis, while the 'baobab ... leaf-shorn' stands for Simi's naked body. Soyinka moves from the arboreal metaphor in this first portion of the passage to the subterranean in the second. The vagina now becomes a 'dark cave' with 'low mists'. And, of course, the dotted blanks that permeate the passage are delegated to say what the author would rather not mention. Such impenetrable indirectness may be tolerable in a book of poems; in prose, it is unnecessarily tough and forbidding.

Sentences of Thunder ...

The opaqueness that characterizes Soyinka's lexical items naturally affects his syntax: the structure in which those lexical items are ordered and arranged. Soyinka exerts great economy on structure, bent, as he is, on always finding the shortest cut to his expression. Consequently some of his sentences are graphological rather than grammatical, a device he shares with a good number of modern writers, particularly D. H. Lawrence and James Joyce.[10] The typical Soyinka sentence reminds one of a dry pod whose seeds are so closely packed that they cannot shake or move about.

One of his strategies for achieving such tightness of structure is what may be called narrative ellipsis. This is most prominent in the dialogue sections of his narrative:

(i) *Sagoe was moaning:* 'I must lie down flat on my belly ...
   Dehinwa wearily: 'Oh Sagoe ...' (I, p. 21).
(ii) *Kola laughed,* 'You want him to do that right now?'
   And Bandele, 'When we leave here we'll go to the office ...'
   (I, p. 208).

In both examples, the illocutionary–narrative cue 'said' has been omitted, replaced by a cataphoric colon in (i) and the anticipatory comma in (ii). The result is a lexico–syntactic compression that portrays Soyinka as a writer who is as stingy with words as he is with structure.

In a number of places, Soyinka mentions the names of speakers at the beginning of a dialogue and omits them in subsequent exchanges:

> Egbo moved his head gently . . . as if he meant to clear it.
> 'I am confused,' he admitted.
> 'Why?'
> 'I cannot accept this view of life . . .'
> 'I think it is very clever.'
> 'I said nothing about that.'
> 'It works . . . .' (*I*, pp. 232–3)

Narrative economy seems to have backfired here as it becomes difficult towards the end of the dialogue to know who is saying what. The reader must flip back the pages to retrieve the speakers, as it were, and this puts an unnecessary strain on his reading attention.

Because of the way words and ideas seem to throng Soyinka's consciousness, he sometimes piles up a series of sentence fragments (the type referred to above as graphological sentences). This syntactic device is more frequent in *Season of Anomy*, probably due to the more reportorial nature of the narrative. Let us look at an example:

> Camwood vistas on chalk. Walls in dark-gritty daubings of camwood, chalked doors and doorsteps, wide swathes of chalk below the camwood against beaten clayey earth. Rushes of red barley in the fences, chalk belts on massive tree trunks, posts, bamboo piers and the store houses of the waterfront. (p. 8)

Notice that there is not a single finite verb in these sentences. Predication seems not to have been Soyinka's concern, but objects, articles and artefacts, which are laundry-listed in the manner in which they strike the writer–observer's eye.

The cascade of words quite often gathers greater volume as it plunges over the steep rock of more grammatical sentences:

(i) Doormen, newsvendors, thugs, market women, street pedlars, colonels, smugglers, catechists, highway robbers and students shook their heads and said there was dirty business about (*SOA*, p. 62).

(ii) With Iriyise unbound, unearthed, salvaged, transformed and created, a grand design for the Cocoa campaign had crystalized in the flash of their first encounter . . . (*SOA*, p. 94).

The seriation and listing above come close to what is called *accumulatio* in rhetoric.[11] The items, which are partly pleonastic, display Soyinka the wordmonger at his weakest.[12] Listing in the two examples has an interesting effect on syntax. The subject of (i) is made up of thirteen lexical items (all nouns) and one grammatical item ('and'); in (ii) the frontally placed non-finite participial clause (functioning as adjunct in the whole sentence) consists of five seriated past participal verbs. The reader gallops through these series with hardly enough time to comprehend one item before encountering another.

Perhaps the most notorious syntactic cause of obscurity in Soyinka's prose is the run-on nature of many of his sentences. Like those of Henry James and James Joyce, many of Soyinka's sentences are psychological sentences, not guided by the grammar book's rubric on punctuation with its rigid commas and full stops, but directed by the pulses of the mind and the rhythms of consciousness. Let us illustrate with two samples.

   (i) On the day, the Final Day of that public airing of flesh, reconditioned wrinkles, artificial spots, deodorated pores, lightening creams and obituary scalps – thus Zaccheus christened wigs – on that day of breastful optimism, the favourite was missing (*SOA*, p. 61).

   (ii) And Kola, who tried to see it all, who tried to clarify the pieces within the accommodating habit of time, felt, much later, in a well-ordered and tranquil moment, that it was a moment of frustration, that what was lacking that night was the power to shake out events one by one, to space them in intervening standstills of the period of creation (*I*, p. 244).

Sentence (i) has an A (Adjunct) – S (Subject) – P (Predicator) – SC (Subjective Complement) structure:

Adjunct
On the . . . optimism

Subject
the favourite

Predicator
was

Subjective Complement
missing

This is an example of a left-branching sentence with a sprawling frontally placed adjunct. The adjunct itself is a conglomeration of word groups comprising:

(a) a prepositional word group: On *the* day, with 'the day' as the completive element of the preposition.

(b) a lengthy nominal group functioning as explanatory adjunct to the completive element of (a): 'the Final Day . . . wigs', which consists of recurrent prepositional groups ('of that public airing of flesh'), and a series of elliptical prepositional groups – (of) 'reconditioned wrinkles', (of) 'artificial spots', (of) 'deodorated pores' and so on.

(c) a rankshifted (minor) sentence functioning as a parenthetical interruptor within the larger sentence (– thus Zaccheus christened wigs –).

(d) a prepositional group partially reiterating the first one in the major sentence: 'on that day of breastful optimism'.

We encounter all these structures before finally arriving at the subject and other elements of the clause. Prepositional group (d) above is particularly striking: it is sneaked in to bridge the structural and semantic gap between the initial adjunct and the subject, a device similar to a scheme of addition called epanalepsis in rhetoric.

While sentence (i) comprises mainly a network of word groups, sentence (ii) is a web of rankshifted clauses. Its skeletal structure is SPAC:

Subject
Kola

Predictor
felt

Adjunct
much later, in a well-ordered . . .

Complement (direct)
that it was a moment of frustration . . .

As in sentence (i), there is a lot of interruption between clause elements. For example, between the real subject (Kola) and the main predicator (felt), there are two seriated relative clauses:

(a) 'who tried to see it all.'

(b) 'who tried to clarify the pieces . . .'.

Between the predicator and the complement there are also interruptions:

- (c) a modified temporal adjunct: 'much later'.
- (d) a prepositional group functioning as adjunct in the main clause: 'in a well-ordered and tranquil moment'.

The direct complement is a couple of rankshifted noun clauses:

- (e) 'that it was a moment of frustration'.
- (f) 'that what was lacking . . . was the power to shake out events . . .'
- (g) a non-finite infinitive clause seriated with the one embeded in (f): 'to pace them in intervening standstills . . .'.

As must be evident from this syntactic analysis, most of Soyinka's sentences are hypotactic (complexly subordinated) and convoluted, with a kind of Carlylesque intricacy. They are characterized by highly interrupted structures that slow down the eye and hamper comprehension. Because the predicator, which is supposed to reveal what the subject is or does, is placed so far away from it, the actor tends to slip away before the mind reaches the action. The reader feels tortured and is forced into yawning despair.

Conclusion

Opinions vary about the justification of obscurity in Soyinka. While critics like Ossie Enekwe believe that it is a source of 'chaos' in Soyinka's novels,[13] others like Isidore Okpewho acclaim it as a mark of genius.[14] In a rather belletrist vein, Okpewho argues that 'Soyinka has never pretended that a novel like *Season of Anomy* is suitable for secondary school children'; but we are not told whether the same reasoning explains why university graduates in English find Soyinka's novels virtually impenetrable. It may be true, as Okpewho has submitted, that 'difficult writing' is not 'bad writing' but do we then conclude that difficult writing is *good* writing?

The fact has got to be admitted that Soyinka is the most prolific but most inaccessible writer in English in Nigeria today, a genius largely circumscribed within university lecture halls and senior staff seminar rooms. The concern of this article has been to throw light on some of the linguistic and stylistic causes of the obscurity of Soyinka's prose.

NOTES

1. Ossie Enekwe, 'Wole Soyinka as a Novelist', *Okike* 9,1975, pp. 72-86.
2. Biodun Jeyifo, (forthcoming), 'Soyinka Demythologized: Notes on a Materialist Reading of *A Dance of the Forests, The Road* and *Kongi's Harvest.*'
3. Louis T. Milic, 'Metaphysics in the Criticism of Style', *College Composition and Communication*, xvii, 1966, pp. 124-9.
4. Wole Soyinka, *The Interpreters*, London, Andre Deutsch, 1965. Heinemann (AWS 76), 1970, p. 155. All further page references are to this edition.
5. In the following extracts *I* — *The Interpreters; SOA* — *Season of Anomy.*
6. Wole Soyinka, *Season of Anomy*, London, Rex Collings, 1973. All further page references are to this edition.
7. Eldred Jones, 'Introduction to *The Interpreters*, op. cit., pp. 1–6.
8. Niyi Osundare, 'The Poem as a Mytho-Linguistic Event: Study of Wole Soyinka's "Abiku".' Paper presented at University of Ibadan, 1980.
9. Jones, op cit., p. 5.
10. John Russell, *Style in Modern British Fiction*, Baltimore, John Hopkins University Press, 1978.
11. Robert Cluett, *Grossly Speaking: Twelve Dozen (More or Less) Rhetorical and Stylistic Terms*, Toronto, York University. In mimeo, 1976, p. 1.
12. Soyinka's love of words has been erroneously attributed to his Yoruba origin by Bernth Lindfors, 'Characteristics of Yoruba and Ibo Prose Styles in English', *Folklore in Nigerian Literature*, New York, Africana, 1973, pp. 153–75, one of the proponents of tribalist criticism of African literature, a new literary virus which, if not killed outright, will spread the plague of chauvinism and balkanization over Africa's intellectual universe. We must treat the writer on his own merit, not as a kind of atavistic tribal archetype.
13. Enekwe, op. cit., p. 85.
14. Isidore Okpewho, 'African Fiction: Language Revisited', *Journal of African Studies*, vol. 5, no. 4, 1978, pp. 414–26.

The Feminine Point of View: Buchi Emecheta's *The Joys of Motherhood*

Eustace Palmer

> God, when will you create a woman who will be fulfilled in herself, a full human being, not anybody's appendage?[1]

The African novel has until recently been remarkable for the absence of what might be called the feminine point of view. This has been partly due to the dearth of female African novelists. Those few voices, like Flora Nwapa, who attempted to present portraits of African womanhood from a female point of view are, to say the least, muted.[2] The presentation of woman in the African novel has been left almost entirely to male voices – Achebe, Amadi, Ngugi, Ousmane Sembene, Laye, Beti, Armah and Soyinka – and their interest in African womanhood, even in the case of Ousmane Sembene, has had to take second place to numerous other concerns. These male novelists, who have presented the African woman largely within the traditional milieu, have generally communicated a picture of a male-dominated and male-oriented society, and the satisfaction of the women with this state of things has been, with the possible exception of Ousmane Sembene, completely taken for granted. Achebe, Ngugi and others have portrayed women who complacently continue to fulfil the roles expected of them by their society and to accept the superiority of the men. From the pages of these novelists as well as from the views of some sociologists it could be inferred that the traditional African woman does not feel that the acceptance of her man's dominance necessarily diminishes her; on the contrary she sees her femininity as consisting precisely in her cheerful acceptance of and willingness to fulfil her allotted role. Critics like Iyasere, basing their case on a study of Achebe's novels, have even suggested that the superficial impression of a male-dominated society must be set against the entrenchment, in these societies, of the powerful 'female principle.'[3] The impression conveyed, then, is of an ordered society with women playing a secondary but cheerfully accepted and important role.

The emergence recently of a number of accomplished female African novelists – Rebeka Njau, Mariama Bâ and Buchi Emecheta – seriously challenges all these cosy assumptions. The picture of the cheerful contented female complacently accepting her lot is replaced by that of a woman who is powerfully aware of the unfairness of the system and who longs to be fulfilled in her self, to be a full human being, not merely somebody else's appendage. Buchi Emecheta's powerful novel *The Joys of Motherhood* presents essentially the same picture of traditional society as the novels of Achebe, but the difference lies in the prominence in Emecheta's novel of the female point of view registering its disgust at male chauvinism and its dissatisfaction with what it considers an unfair and oppressive system.

Buchi Emecheta presents a traditional society in which the roles of men and women are very sharply defined:

> You are to give her children and food, she is to cook and bear the children and look after you and them . . . A woman may be ugly and grow old, but a man is never ugly and never old. He matures with age and is dignified. (p. 71)

The heroine Nnu Ego and her creator sternly reject this traditional concept which consigns the woman to cooking, providing comfort for her husband's bed and bearing children. In a society that lays so much premium on children as the means of ensuring the continuity of the family and the clan, a woman's femininity seems to consist precisely in her ability to bear children. Correspondingly, an inability to conceive is regarded, not merely as a misfortune, but as a sign of wickedness: 'When a woman is virtuous, it is easy for her to conceive' (p. 31). So deep-seated is this feeling, that Nnu Ego herself, having just lost her baby, claims in her agony that she is not a woman any more. Nnu Ego who has been so strongly aware of society's injustice towards the female kind is forced by her misery and the intimidation of society to accept that her loss of motherhood means loss of womanhood, and appropriately she makes the exclamation in a masculine voice and the chorus of countrymen agrees that 'a woman without a child for her husband was a failed woman' (p. 62).

Clearly, the man is the standard and the point of reference in this society. It is significant that the chorus of countrymen say, not that a woman without a child is a failed woman, but that a woman without a child *for her husband* is a failed woman. There is very little concern for Nnu Ego's personal feelings and her individual suffering; she is merely a tool for the procreation of her husband's children and her worth as an individual depends on her success in performing certain functions for her husband and keeping his name free from blemish. When Nnu Ego just fails to commit suicide, no one bothers to enquire about the personal circumstances and the mental torture that must have led to such an attempt; their concern is for the respectability of Nnu Ego's husband: 'You mean you have a baby at home and you come here disgracing the man who paid for you to be brought into this town?' (p. 62). That men are the standard is authenticated by the fact that in this society the senior wife is expected to be strong, to behave more like a man than a woman. Women are clearly the underdogs, and they are supposed to be content if their man merely sleeps with them even if he fails to discharge his other obligations. Nnu Ego feels the full injustice of the arrangements as she looks at her husband Nnaife – he looks younger than his age while she looks and feels very old after the birth of only three children.

In the novels of Achebe and others the father's responsibility to choose a husband for his daughter is calmly taken for granted. In *The Joys of Motherhood* Emecheta makes the reader feel fully the misery to which such an arrangement can lead. The role played by Nnu Ego's father, Agbadi, in bringing about his daughter's disaster should not be minimized. Through his insistence on choosing a serious and not a handsome man for Nnu Ego's second husband, even though his friend Idayi tries to warn him about the need to change with the times and accept a modern man, he picks on the feckless Nnaife, the first sight of whom disgusts Nnu Ego beyond bearing. But he is generally supported by his clan, for to them a woman cannot possibly hate a man chosen for her by her people.

The issue of polygamy in Africa remains a controversial one. The received African wisdom seems to be that polygamy has distinct social and economic advantages, that its practice in the traditional milieu does not necessarily result in the erosion of the status and dignity of the woman and that it is perfectly accepted and welcomed by both men and women. A completely different

picture, however, emerges from *The Joys of Motherhood*. What
Emecheta stresses is the resulting dominance, especially sexual, of
the male, and the relegation of the female into subservience,
domesticity and motherhood. The usual picture of polygamous
wives who calmly agree to share their husband and show no signs
of jealousy is completely negated here. Indeed, *The Joys of
Motherhood* presents one of the most compelling studies of
jealousy from the female point of view in the whole history of the
African novel. Both Nnu Ego and the second wife Adaku are
pathologically jealous of each other, suspicious of each other's
motives and envious of the success of the other's children; and each
one is on her guard lest the other might harm her own children. The
happy polygamous household does not obtain here.

In spite of the author's angry glare it is possible to glean from the
novel the economic and social reasons that must have given rise to
polygamy. Thus the arrangement whereby Nnaife inherits all his
elder brother's wives on the latter's death seems to ensure both
sexual and economic provision for the wives within the traditional
set-up. It therefore seems to make sound sense. But the author
concentrates on the misery and deprivation polygamy can bring;
far from being an economic panacea, it can lead to economic
disaster. And while the traditional woman might accept it placidly,
Nnu Ego, who has become somewhat alienated during her sojourn
in Lagos, is powerfully aware of its disadvantages, and through her
we are made to see the misery that polygamy can bring, particularly
in the urban situation. It might of course be objected that even in
the novel itself polygamy survives triumphantly in the traditional
milieu within which it was meant to operate originally, and that
the strains begin to appear only when it is translated to the urban
situation where the stresses of urban life – the scramble to ensure a
decent standard of living and the consequent erosion of the
husband's authority – would inevitably result in its deathknell
anyway. The objection is valid, and one might perhaps argue that it
is unfair of Buchi Emecheta to make a judgement of polygamy
based on the urban experience. But Emecheta is generally
concerned with the fate of women, not merely with an analysis of
polygamy, and in the drift from the rural traditional to the urban
area polygamy has been translated in many African societies, with
grim consequences for not a few women.

The preoccupation in African societies with the continuity of the
line means, not just a desire for children, but a preference for sons.
Sons are quite clearly at a premium in the society Emecheta

presents. One of the older neighbours in an attempt to get Nnu Ego to behave properly says: 'now you are a mother – not of daughters who will marry and go, but of good-looking, healthy sons' (p. 119). And after Adaku's quarrel with her co-wife Nnu Ego she is made to feel inferior and given the impression that she has no business to complain even though she is clearly in the right. The reason for this apparent injustice is, of course, that Nnu Ego has sons, while Adaku has none:

> 'Don't you know that according to the custom of our people you, Adaku, the daughter of whoever you are, are committing an unforgivable sin?' Nwakusar reminded her. 'Our life starts in immortality and ends in immortality. If Nnaife had been married to only you, you would have ended his life on this round of his visiting earth. I know you have children, but they are girls, who in a few years' time will go and help build another man's immortality. The only woman who is immortalising your husband you make unhappy with your fine clothes and lucrative business.' (p. 166)

This is as blatant a statement of the male chauvinist position as can be found in the whole of African literature. The feeling that the woman has no independent existence or dignity of herself but must always be considered in relation to her husband, that her main role in life is ensuring the immortality of her husband by bearing him male offspring, and that it is the wife who is to blame, who has in fact condemned her husband to loss of immortality if the couple fail to have male offspring, that if she does not have male children she has no right to do anything, however innocent, which would irritate the co-wife who is immortalizing her husband by bearing male children, is sexist, repellent and almost simple-minded. But one can see how Emecheta revels in this kind of statement because it enables her to make an important propagandist point.

This traditional preference for sons leads to some strange consequences since it has disturbing effects on the psyches of not just the women but some of the men as well. The great chief Obi Ummuna, who has no sons, all but converts his daughter Ona, Nnu Ego's mother, into a boy, dedicating her to the gods to produce children in his name and ensure the continuity of his line. He refuses to allow her to marry, because she would then become someone else's appendage, merely producing children to ensure, not his, but another man's immortality. He thus clings to Ona and treats her like a boy, and the consequence is that Ona develops clear masculine traits of character. For instance, shortly after Ona's pregnancy is discovered, Agbadi her lover is forced to say to her:

'You see, you won't even allow yourself to be a woman. You are in the first weeks of motherhood, and all you can do is think like a man . . .' (p. 24). Emecheta has created some unforgettable early scenes in this novel which present the constant tussle between the high-spirited Ona and her no less spirited lover Agbadi. In this contest of wills the male Agbadi, great hunter, warrior and lover, famous for his achievements in the masculine pursuits of this male-oriented society, and renowned for his ability to tame spirited women, is out to assert his dominance and his masculinity over the female, but she who has publicly at least renounced the feminine role is doing her best to resist this. There are moments when the impression comes through that Ona is making a deliberate effort to smother the genuinely feminine within her in order not to appear to capitulate to this assertive and supremely egoistic male partner. At one point during Agbadi's illness 'Ona felt like gathering him in her arms and singing to him, as one would do to a baby' (p. 15). Traditional society would regard this as a very feminine impulse, but Ona remembers her self-control and smothers the impulse. Her conduct is the psychological consequence of her upbringing and the attitudes of her male-oriented society, but the author uses her to register a protest against the stereotypes normally associated with women.

Any notion of the polygamous male operating in traditional society as a reasonable and considerate being is completely dispelled by Emecheta's presentation. Agbadi who not only has several wives but openly encourages a concubine as well betrays a callous indifference to the suffering that his philandering causes his legitimate wives:

> 'You are wrong, Idayi, to suggest she might be sore or bitter just because last night with Ona I amused myself a little. Agunwa is too mature to mind that. Why, if she behaved like that what kind of example would that be to the younger wives?' (p. 22).

It is of no concern to him that his dangerous illness has caused his wives great mental agony and taken a severe toll of their physical stamina; he can with great equanimity start dallying with his concubine the moment he is rescued from the jaws of death. It is this irresponsibility which leads to his eldest wife's death, for she collapses with shame and despair on hearing her husband 'giving pleasure to another woman in the same courtyard where she slept' (p. 21). And if we are to take the supernatural machinery of the novel seriously, then it is possible to argue that this act of Agbadi's leads indirectly to his daughter's disasters, for it is the reluctant slave who is killed and buried with his wife that becomes Nnu Ego's *chi* and continues to plague her, first with childlessness, and then with children who bring her nothing but pain.

Nnu Ego's first husband Amatokwu betrays a callousness and lack of consideration for the female's feelings that are even worse than Agbadi's. On discovering Nnu Ego's barrenness he tells her brutally that she has to make way for a new wife, and as though to emphasize that a woman's main function is the propagation of her husband's line, he virtually turns her out into the fields and degrades her to the level of an unpaid labourer. Denying her even her basic conjugal rights he exclaims: 'I am a busy man. I have no time to waste my precious male seed on a woman who is infertile. I have to raise children for my line' (p. 32). And when the new wife bears a son the unscrupulous Amatokwu breaks all the traditional taboos by showing a preference for the nursing mother and calling her into his hut even before she weans her baby. And being a male he is allowed to get away with it. Emecheta's point apparently is that the traditional arrangements lead to chauvinism and irresponsibility in the male. Even Nnu Ego's witless new husband Nnaife, who is totally lacking in dignity, displays this irresponsibility when his second wife Adaku leaves him; he makes up for his humiliation by deciding to claim his right in his dead brother's other wife, and he later decides to take yet another wife – a sixteen-year-old girl – heedless of the economic and social consequences. Later when their children misbehave, Nnaife unfairly blames it all on poor Nnu Ego who has done her best to keep the family together. However, the author's determination to show up the males as irresponsible and unreasonable interferes somewhat with her characterization of them. Their irresponsibility is exaggerated to the point of unrealism. It is difficult, for instance, to accept Nnaife's conduct towards the end of the novel as plausible. It must be admitted that while her portrayal of the women is excellent, Emecheta's success with the men is something less than total.

What gives this novel its peculiar quality is the unashamed presentation of the woman's point of view. This comes out not merely in the powerful evocation of Nnu Ego's misery but even in the narrator's own omniscient comments. And on the occasions when Nnu Ego registers her complaints against the system we can be sure that it is Emecheta speaking through her. When for instance, Nnu Ego pleads with her husband: 'Is it my fault that I did not have a child for you? Do you think I don't suffer too?' (p. 32), we can be sure that she speaks for the author and all women. When Nnu Ego reflects that she was a prisoner, imprisoned by her love for her children, imprisoned by her role as a senior wife, it is surely the author making her propagandist point about the fate of mothers and the evils of the polygamous situation, and she is meant to express the views of all wives in similar circumstances. When Nnu Ego cries: 'God, when will you create a woman who will be fulfilled in herself, a full human being, not anybody's appendage ... When will I be free?' (pp. 186–7), she is bemoaning the fate, as far as the author is concerned, of all womankind and uttering their desire for total emancipation. Of course the note of propaganda becomes even stronger when the author steps out of the narrative and condemns the existing arrangements in her own voice:

> Agbadi was no different from many men. He himself might take wives and then neglect them for years, apart from seeing that they each received their one yam a day; he could bring his mistress to sleep with him right in his courtyard while his wives pined and bit their nails for a word from him (p. 36).

The author's bias gives itself away in statements such as 'men being what they are ...'. And even when she seems to be presenting an objective scene the bias is barely concealed by the sarcasm.

Some supporters of women's liberation often point to the fact that woman herself has been subjected to centuries of brainwashing and that even when she begins to show some resistance she finds it difficult to discard the stereotypes immediately. This certainly seems to be the case with Nnu Ego and possibly even with her creator in *The Joys of Motherhood*. On the one hand Nnu Ego, disgusted by her condition and that of women in general, can say:

> 'I am beginning to think that there may be a future for educated women. I saw many young women teaching in schools. It would be really something for a woman to be able to earn some money monthly like a man.' (p. 189)

And yet Nnu Ego is full of revulsion at the way in which she considers western men spoil their women by giving them the independence that she herself is secretly yearning for. The fact that western men allow their women to smoke is utterly abhorrent to her. We notice, of course, that the man is still the point of reference; it is the man who is blamed for spoiling the woman, for *allowing* the woman to smoke. Although she feels that women are harshly treated even in traditional society and that men have too great an advantage, Nnu Ego still subscribes to the traditional concept of manliness; she prefers men to look and behave like men and not like women. This surely implies that she accepts that men are supposed to be strong, masterly and masculine while women are docile, and that an unmanly man would be like a woman. She often refers to her second husband Nnaife as a woman; for one thing he does women's work, since he is a washman in the white man's household. She considers that marriage to Nnaife, that 'jelly of a man', would be like marriage to a middle-aged woman. On the other hand, in spite of the male chauvinist Amatokwu's degradation and brutalization of her she considers that he measures up to the standard her culture had led her to expect of a man:

> 'How would he react if he were forced by circumstances to wash for a woman, a skinny shrivelled-up one with unhealthy skin? He would surely refuse. That was the sort of man to respect.' (p. 72).

What Nnu Ego fails to realize is that a system which tolerates that kind of man and which holds that only women should do the washing, will also tolerate the brutalization and degradation of women. Nnu Ego cannot eat her cake and have it too. Her traditional society has produced in her a woman who is almost a schizophrenic, who yearns for liberation and for fulfilment as a woman, while still respecting the traditional concept of manliness. If men are bedevilled by stereotypes, some of the women are also.

Emecheta's chosen method of narration is ideally suited to her theme. Granted that she was interested in a full presentation of the woman's position it was perhaps inevitable that she would tell the story almost exclusively from the heroine's point of view. In this novel we see almost entirely with Nnu Ego's eyes and from her point of view. The other characters are presented as they appear to her occasionally limited consciousness. This has resulted in a very full and powerful portrait of the heroine, though the others, especially the males, are rather sketchy. The story also demanded almost total sympathy for the heroine, and the device therefore of using her consciousness as a reflector of events was a sound one. For excellent though Nnu Ego is in most respects, and much as we feel the poignancy of her suffering, she does have her weaknesses. If this story had been told, for instance, from the point of view of Adaku, her co-wife, or Nnaife her second husband, it might have taken on a different colouring and Nnu Ego would have appeared much less attractive than she is. Consider, for instance, her reaction to the arrival of Adaku, one of the two wives that her husband

Nnaife has inherited from his elder brother. Nnu Ego is, of course, understandably shocked by the unheralded arrival of this new co-wife, an undesirable addition for a woman who has been used to having her husband all to herself. But then tremendous sexual jealousy supervenes as Nnu Ego observes the peace, satisfaction and good looks radiated by this young woman and her equally well-rounded child, and compares them with her own worn, haggard and ageing features: 'She hated this type of woman, who would flatter a man, depend on him, need him' (p. 118). She then proceeds in consequence to treat Adaku with the most incredible discourtesy. Nnu Ego's conduct may be psychologically plausible, but it is still impolite. The incident, reported from Adaku's point of view, would have made Nnu Ego seem a model of discourtesy. In fact it is clear that the biased Nnu Ego is quite wrong in her estimate of Adaku's conduct, for far from being a woman who would flatter a man, depend on him, need him, Adaku turns out to be a remarkably resourceful young woman who is capable of branching out on her own, defying her husband and succeeding in a male-oriented world. Later that same night when the delighted Nnaife takes Adaku to his bed Nnu Ego's agony and jealousy lead her to place what must surely be a completely distorted construction on Adaku's conduct:

> It was a good thing she had prepared herself, because Adaku turned out to be one of those shameless modern women whom Nnu Ego did not like. What did she think she was doing? Did she think Nnaife was her lover and not her husband, to show her enjoyment so? She tried to block her ears, yet could still hear Adaku's exaggerated carrying on. Nnu Ego tossed in agony and anger all night, going through in her imagination what was taking place behind the curtained bed. Not that she had to do much imagining, because even when she tried to ignore what was going on, Adaku would not let her. She giggled, she squeaked, she cried and she laughed in turn, until Nnu Ego was quite convinced that it was all for her benefit. (p. 124)

Clearly these thoughts are not Emecheta's, but Nnu Ego's registering impressions as the goings-on behind the curtain impinge on her consciousness. The unbiased reader can see that nothing in Adaku's conduct suggests that she is shameless or doing anything wrong.

Similarly Nnu Ego behaves just as badly to a visiting relation of Adaku's simply through envy of the woman's prosperous appearance:

> *And look at her*, Nnu Ego thought angrily, *look at the expensive shoes*

she is wearing, look at that headtie, and even a gold chain — all this just
to come and see her relative Adaku, and in this rain! God, the cost of
that headtie! Whatever she paid for it would feed me and the children
for a whole month. And she is the daughter of a nobody! Yet look at me
the daughter of a well-known chief, reduced to this . . .
Nnu Ego watched her, mouth still covered, her body shaking.

The woman looked up and asked, 'Are you all right, Nnaife's wife?
Why do you look at me like that? I am not your enemy, eh? Why are you
looking at me like that, as if you don't want to see me? I have come all
the way from Obalende, the other side of Lagos Island, and there was no
word of welcome from you—'

'Shut up! Shut up and go away! You can't stand here. My baby is
crying — go away!' Nnu Ego's voice was so loud that it was more
thunderous than the rain. 'Come in, children, it's raining.' The little
ones came in and Nnu Ego banged the door shut. (pp. 163–4)

Even the author herself is aware that Nnu Ego is behaving
unreasonably: 'As the months passed, Nnu Ego began to act in this
way. She did everything she could to make Adaku jealous of her
sons' (p. 162). And in a well-placed omniscient comment she
describes Nnu Ego thus:

Nnu Ego was like those not-so-well-informed Christians who, promised
the Kingdom of Heaven, believed that it was literally just round the
corner and that Jesus Christ was coming on the very morrow. Many of
them would hardly contribute anything to this world, reasoning 'What
is the use? Christ will come soon.' They become so insulated in their
beliefs that not only would they have little to do with ordinary sinners,
people going about their daily work, they even pitied them and in many
cases looked down on them because the Kingdom of God was not for the
likes of them. (p. 162)

Looked at from another point of view Nnu Ego might even appear
lacking in resourcefulness. With a bit more drive and initiative she
could have used the money sent her by Nnaife from the war front to
establish herself in trade as her co-wife Adaku successfully does.
Her family need not have continued to live in abject poverty and
squalor. Later when she gives her mind to her trade it flourishes,
but the lack of drive becomes apparent once more: 'Her business
was going well because of her large capital, but many a time she
would have liked to relax and not go anywhere, just stay at home
and look after her children' (p. 181). In spite of her yearnings and
her dissatisfaction with her condition and that of women in
general, Nnu Ego lacks the drive that is necessary to give her the
independence she seeks. Deep down she is a conventional woman

who has herself been brainwashed into accepting the conventional stereotypes; she can therefore take refuge in her children. Other women can seek wealth, but she has her children.

On the other hand Adaku, Nnu Ego's co-wife, resolutely rebels against convention and the restrictive nature of an unfair polygamous system and determines to make her own way in this male-dominated world. In spite of the unsympathetic picture of Adaku that comes through Nnu Ego's blinkered point of view, Emecheta really needs Adaku in this novel to make extremely important points about female liberation and emancipation; Adaku is central to the author's design. When she realizes that her husband and his people have no use for her because she has not borne a male child, she makes up her mind to leave, to concentrate on her business and be successful. And with her money she is going to take her daughters out of the conventional feminine situation and treat them as Nnu Ego treats her boys; she is going to stop them going to market and send them to school, for she has a vision of the future in which daughters will be as important as sons and no one, not even Nnaife, is going to marry off her daughters before they are ready. Of course Adaku says she is going to become a prostitute and Nnu Ego and the rest of the clan are scandalized and condemn her for it. But it is obvious that this is said deliberately to annoy Nnu Ego, for Adaku does not, in fact, become a prostitute. Indeed, the kind of woman she turns out to be would abhor prostitution, because it would still mean making a living through men and allowing men to exploit her. Instead Adaku resolutely takes to business and becomes enormously successful not through but in spite of men. She looks to the future, bringing up her daughters like men with the full intention of sending them to college, whereas Nnu Ego's girls have to drop out of primary school after a couple of years in order to give preference to the boys' education. Adaku is forced by circumstances and attitudes towards women to become a forerunner of women's liberation in Africa and the experience is truly liberating for her. Once she leaves Nnaife's household and sets up on her own she looks better, dresses better and is generally happier. Mammy Aby too, though snubbed by society, is able to improve her lot through her independence. She and Adaku are excellent examples to Nnu Ego of what can be achieved.

The plot of the novel and its presentation of the position of women unfolds against the background of drastic change. Indeed, it can be said that it is this change involved in the move from a traditional rural to an urban area that brings to prominence the question of women's rights. In the traditional world prosperity was relatively easy to acquire and men were able to retain their pride and self-confidence and keep the women in their place. Therefore, the men were able to maintain their control over polygamous households. The roles of men and women were sharply defined and accepted by both sexes. The women suppressed whatever uneasiness they might have felt about the traditional arrangements because their men were manly and discharged their role effectively. The move from the rural to the urban world of Lagos, however, means poverty, squalor and degradation and a tremendous erosion in the self-confidence of the male. They exchange respectable traditional occupations such as farming and hunting for menial jobs as labourers, messengers, cooks, servants and washmen. Nnu Ego herself becomes a petty trader – selling cigarettes, matches and oranges – while her husband is a white man's washman, washing women's clothes.

This change from the traditional to the urban situation correlates with a slight modification of the roles of the sexes. The prospect of privation means that the women have to shoulder a large part of the burden of providing for the family, a role that in the traditional system would be performed largely by the men. On occasions, in fact, the women become the sole breadwinners. When Nnaife is unemployed or away at sea or in the war, the task of providing for the beleaguered family devolves on Nnu Ego. This modification of roles implies, in a sense, that the women are becoming more masculine and the men more feminine. Thus Cordelia, Nnu Ego's neighbour, says: 'Men here are too busy being white men's servants to be men. We women mind the home. Not our husbands. Their manhood has been taken from them. The shame of it is that they don't know it' (p. 51). Throughout the novel there is the suggestion that the urban men have lost their masculinity and become increasingly like women. Images of femininity are constantly used in reference to the men, particularly Nnu Ego's husband Nnaife whose femininity registers strongly on his wife's mind. When Nnu Ego first sees Nnaife he is 'a man with a belly like a pregnant cow' (p. 42) and his hair looks like that of a woman mourning for her husband. Similarly Nnu Ego notices that her second son, who looks very much like a girl, has more of Nnaife in him. The fact that Nnaife earns his living by doing women's work – washing clothes – does nothing to enhance his masculinity in the eyes of his wife: 'Oh, dear mother, was this a man she was living with? How could a situation rob a man of his manhood without him knowing it? . . . I want to live with a man, not a woman-made man' (p. 50).

Inevitably, the wives are much more aware of the forces of change in their lives, since these are reflected in the change in their men, and in a sense they are more responsive to change and crave it more than they do; the men on the other hand are unaware of their demasculinization. The women are also aware that these subtle shifts in the roles of the sexes must inevitably mean a corresponding shift in the relationship between men and women. But the men, whose pride, confidence and masculinity have been so significantly eroded, continue to demand the same ancient rights and privileges and insist on the same relations even in this urban environment; and this is the source of the trouble.

Buchi Emecheta has written a novel whose power derives partly from the singlemindedness with which she has presented the female point of view. She makes us feel Nnu Ego's misery very strongly from her early frustration and emotional sterility caused by her barrenness in Amatokwu's household, to her patient stoicism as the latter degrades her, her shock and disgust at the personality of her new husband Nnaife, her inexpressible grief leading to near suicide on the death of her first child, her privation and suffering in the squalor of Nnaife's household and her struggle to eke out a means of livelihood against overwhelming odds, her anguish as Nnaife finally disowns her, blaming her unreasonably for the conduct of the children and her final loneliness as the children she had worked so hard for all but desert her. If we feel so very strongly for Nnu Ego it is partly because Emecheta's technique keeps us so close to her consciousness, forcing us to travel with her as she goes. To say that this novel is written in the first person omniscient would be an oversimplification. For Emecheta does not so much narrate the events, as present experiences and people as they appear to the mind of Nnu Ego. Of course Emecheta reverts to the omniscient in order to present other characters, such as Nwokocha Agbadi, but generally speaking she continues to ensure built-in sympathy for Nnu Ego by making us travel with her. Here is an example:

> She stopped abruptly in her fight. She looked up at the bystanders, her eyes roaming over their heads and not on their faces. She was shocked. Someone in this crowd knew who she was! She had bargained on the fact that Lagos was such a big place, with people of so many different races and backgrounds that it was very unlikely that anyone would know her. She had known she would probably be opposed by some

pedestrians on the bridge, but she had calculated that she would arrive there before it got too busy. She was wrong . . . .

For the first time since Nnu Ego had seen her child there on the mat, tears of shock and frustration flowed down her cheeks. Who was going to give her the energy to tell the world that she had once been a mother, but had failed? How would people understand that she had wanted so desperately to be a woman like everybody else, but had now failed again? *Oh, God, I wish these people, though they mean well, had simply let me be.* (pp. 60–1)

Such a passage demonstrates the skill with which Emecheta can keep us close to Nnu Ego's consciousness. Having travelled all along with Nnu Ego and come to share her point of view we are in almost total sympathy with her and we certainly understand her reasons for wishing to commit suicide. But Emecheta is equally adept at slipping from one mind into another, a technique that E. M. Forster referred to as 'bouncing'. For instance, having presented us in this episode with Nnu Ego's point of view up to the moment she makes her suicide attempt, Emecheta slips easily into the mind of Nwakusor, Nnu Ego's countryman, and his own point of view now qualifies Nnu Ego's showing that suicide might be a rather futile act after all. Similarly, on Nnu Ego's first arrival in Lagos we are riveted to her consciousness as she registers her first impressions of her husband Nnaife; like her we are duly disgusted. But we are almost immediately taken into Nnaife's mind, although in this case Nnaife is treated ironically as he reveals his male chauvinism, his smug self-satisfaction and his egoism. Nevertheless, the technique of 'bouncing', of slipping unobtrusively from one mind to another, results at times in an objective presentation of experience. For instance during a very interesting stage of the relations between Nnaife and his wives, when jealousy between the latter is at its height, Nnu Ego, whose consciousness we have been kept close to up to this point, suspects quite unjustifiably that Adaku will harm her sons through jealousy once her back is turned. Very shortly after this Emecheta bounces us into Adaku's mind to show that she, for her part, also unjustifiably suspects Nnu Ego of playing up to Nnaife:

'The shameless fool,' Adaku said under her breath. 'No wonder she was pregnant again so soon after the twins, because she knew how to sneak behind people's backs and make up to Nnaife.' (p. 13)

Generally, however, it is with Nnu Ego's eyes that we see and the resulting sympathy for her is so strong that it is possible to accuse the author of over-idealization. At times this even borders on sentimentality as in this passage:

> She looked at the crying child again. Why not breastfeed him herself? The mother wouldn't mind, she wouldn't even know. Nnu Ego locked her hut, lay beside the child and gave him her virgin breasts. She closed her eyes as contentment ran through her whole body . . . This became almost the daily pattern and Nnu Ego did not discourage it. One evening she noticed that milk was dripping from her still firm breasts, which were responding to the child's regular stimulation. She ran to the effigy of her *chi* and cried once more: 'Why don't you let me have my own children? Look, I am full of milk. I can't be barren or juiceless as my father said. Why are you so wicked to me?'
>
> Before the baby was scarcely a year old, it became clear that the young wife was expecting another child. Nnu Ego took up the boy's feeding in earnest. She would sing and coo to him and say, 'Why did you not come to me? I cried in the night and longed for a child like you – why did you not come to me?' (p. 34)

Emecheta shows great psychological insight in the penetration of her characters' thoughts. She is particularly good at the presentation of the feminine psyche. Scarcely any other African novelist has succeeded in probing the female mind and displaying the female personality with such precision. The presentation of Nnu Ego's frustration due to her barrenness or her jealousy on the arrival of Nnaife's second wife or her shock and disgust at the appearance of her new husband Nnaife or Adaku's spirited reaction to ill-treatment at the hands of her husband and his clan are all convincingly done. As we have already seen, however, her touch is much less sure with the presentation of the male characters. Nnaife would have been a compelling presentation if his melodramatic attack on his daughter's Yoruba boyfriend were not so psychologically implausible. Similarly it is difficult to imagine that Oshia, Nnu Ego's eldest son, who should have been so powerfully aware of his parents' sacrifice in giving him a decent education, would eventually be so insensitive to their claims and would be so callous and disrespectful in the end. He may have been alienated by his education, but such a change in his character ought to have been demonstrated, or the reader ought at least to have been given an insight into the thought processes leading to such insensitivity. It is even more difficult to believe that Adim who has been closest to his mother could forget her completely when he goes to Canada for further studies. In her attempt to blacken the males in order to show up the poignancy of Nnu Ego's (the representative female's) situation, Emecheta sacrifices psychological plausibility and mars her characterization somewhat.

Unlike most of the male novelists, Emecheta makes very little attempt to Africanize the language she uses. It is of course possible that, following Achebe, we have overstressed the need for the African novelist to modify the metropolitan language he or she is using. *The Joys of Motherhood* demonstrates generally that it is possible for an African novel to be powerful, even though written in unmodified, idiomatic English. However, there are a few occasions in this novel when the adherence to standard English jars and the language fails to communicate the impression of Africans speaking. Here for instance is Nnaife's neighbour giving instructions to his wife Cordelia on the discovery of Nnu Ego's dead baby: ' "That may be being over-dramatic. Just go. Keep calm, and surreptitiously look about for her without raising any alarm until I have told Nnaife. God, this is really awful" ' (p. 66). And this is what Nnaife says when he suspects that something is wrong: ' "No, I'm not in the habit of coming home at odd times. I wish you would be kind enough to tell me what all this hide-and-seek is about" ' (p. 69). Fortunately, these lapses are few.

Emecheta's impressive grasp of detail has resulted in the evocation of some very powerful scenes. The presentation of the setting, both in the traditional and urban environment, is tellingly done. And in a novel that generally presents a grim and sombre picture she can suddenly surprise us with a flash of humour, as in her description of Nnaife or her presentation of the neighbours' reaction to the saga of Nnaife's guitar.

Emecheta's attitude to the supernatural which has such a significant bearing on the story of the novel is ambivalent. On the one hand she shows some scepticism when the medicine man who is called upon to exorcise the spirits playing Nnaife's guitar is shown to be a fraud. But on the other hand the novel seems to demonstrate the power of Nnu Ego's *chi* who continues to plague her either with childlessness or with useless children. The dreams in which her *chi* features have a very important bearing on subsequent events. It would seem, in fact, that Emecheta uses the supernatural to enhance plot rather than as a means of demonstrating the beliefs of the people as Amadi and Achebe do. It is the conception of Ona's daughter Nnu Ego that leads to the death of Agbadi's wife Agunwa and therefore to that of the slave girl. The slave girl consequently punishes Ona and Agbadi by punishing their daughter Nnu Ego. There is some confusion of thought in the suggestion that the slave girl may have been reincarnated in Nnu Ego. As she is being cut down she vows to come back and plague Agbadi's house and it is significant that Ona's pregnancy becomes apparent almost at the same moment of the slave girl's death, and when the child Nnu Ego is born she has an annoying mark on the same spot on which the slave girl was hit. But Nnu Ego does not plague her own family as the slave girl had threatened and in any case we are later meant to believe that the slave girl becomes Nnu Ego's *chi*, not Nnu Ego herself; and it is Nnu Ego who is tormented. This confusion suggests that the supernatural is not rendered convincing on the artistic level. However, this may not have been Emecheta's interest. She merely wanted to use it as an element of plot to spark off a chain of events.

There will be many who will find Emecheta's analysis of the female situation controversial; her presentation may not be able to stand up to sociological scrutiny. But *The Joys of Motherhood* is an imaginative and not a scientific work, and the artist is surely within her rights to exaggerate or even to depart from sociological authenticity. The novel must be judged as a work of art and it is difficult to deny the accomplishment of the artistry.

NOTES

1. Buchi Emecheta, *The Joys of Motherhood*, London, Heinemann (AWS 227), 1979, pp. 186-7. New York, George Braziller, 1979. All further page references are to this edition.
2. See Flora Nwapa, *Efuru*, London, Heinemann, 1966; and *Idu*, London, Heinemann, 1970.
3. Solomon Iyasere, 'Narrative Technique in *Things Fall Apart*', in B. Lindfords and C. I. Innes (eds), *Critical Perspectives on Achebe*, Washington D.C., Three Continents Press, 1978, pp. 92-110 (reprinted from *New Letters*).

Identity Crisis in the Tragic Novels of Isidore Okpewho

V. U. Ola

There is something diffusing about the theme of culture clash in African literature. Larson's famous argument on the situational novel is a way of grappling with this issue.[1] The emphasis on communal experience whether in joy or sorrow is one which easily militates against the personal struggle and identity of the hero in a tragic work. Despite the artistic competence of a writer like Chinua Achebe critics are still quite often unable to decide whether the tragedy of *Things Fall Apart* is that of an individual or a community; whether the reader should lament the fall of Okonkwo or that of Umuofia and its customs, or in fact whether the tragedy of one is separable from that of the other. Isidore Okpewho is one novelist who has succeeded in portraying characters whose individual identities are clearly distinct from those of their communities. At the same time the landscape of his works, their setting, their characters and the problems that confront them, as well as the language in which these experiences are expressed are very typically African and even particularly Nigerian.

For his first novel, *The Victims*[2] Okpewho explores in psychological depth a topic that most African writers have treated mostly as a mild social problem and sometimes as a semi-serious one. The family has from classical times served as the most fitting locale for a tragedy for reasons that are convincingly outlined in Aristotle's *Poetics*. The parties must necessarily be either friends, or enemies, or indifferent to one another:

> Now when enemy does it on enemy, there is nothing to move us to pity either in his doing or in his meditating the deed, except so far as the actual pain of the sufferer is concerned . . . Whenever the tragic deed is done within the family – when murder or the like is done or meditated

by brother on brother, by son on father, by mother on son, or son on mother – these are the situations the poet should seek after.[3]

The polygamous situation rife with insecurity and jealousy provides a fertile ground for the clash of identities and the violation of the delicate human ties which are implied in Aristotle's analysis. Okpewho avoids any form of sentimentalizing and exposes those natural psychological problems which are often typical of polygamous homes – the fight for the husband's favour and recognition, the anxiety over the welfare of one's children or child as in the case of Nwabunor, and sometimes the recourse to unnatural means for the elimination of the opponent. Nwabunor is a perfect heroine for such a tragedy. Her childlessness, attendant insecurity, frustration and jealousy set off a chain of events that finally engulfs the whole family. Obanua simply aggravates a situation that demanded love and understanding by taking a second wife.

The theme of *The Victims* is polygamy which Okpewho has treated as a very serious emotional and psychological problem since it touches on the fundamental question of human identity; in this case not just of the husband and his wives, but also of their children. That Obanua, the husband, is not allowed to go free testifies to the novelist's belief that the human person in any tragic work is expected to suffer in some way for having been the source of evil and for having brought untold suffering on his fellow human beings.

The book has all the ingredients of a successful tragedy in the African context – 'a not-very fruitful' marriage to an ageing wife, a husband who as a result sees himself as a failure, a wife gnawed by fear and frustration and a very tactless, unsympathetic and younger wife blessed with children. The stresses and strains and the deep psychological war which result from this state of affairs are given summary tragic treatment and expose forcefully the problems posed for the institution of polygamy in Africa today.

It is understandable that Obanua should take a second wife after his ten-year-old marriage has yielded only a son, albeit a very bright one. Nwabunor, his first wife, despite her conviction that fate is against her, sees her position as the first wife threatened. Obanua's action therefore becomes a necessary mistake that immediately sows the seeds of hatred, suspicion and despair in his household. The first irony of the work is that Ogugua, the new wife, is a woman of easy virtue whose twin daughters are the by-product of her youthful misdemeanour.

Even her own children in their own innocent way give the impression that their mother was a wayward woman who enjoyed going to parties. To lose her position and identity to such a woman was more than Nwabunor (whose name ironically means that a child is the mainstay of the home) could bear. Her problems are compounded by a recent miscarriage one year after Ogugua had a boy for Obanua. Convinced now even more that fate is against her she decides to fight her own fight. The presence of the second wife not only sharpens her frustration but gives her more courage and determination to fight for her rights. The hostility in the family is established very early in the novel:

> When Ogugua moved in later that week, she was immediately struck by the strangeness of the atmosphere she had walked into. After all the rejoicing and other manifestations of welcome (from which Nwabunor had been conspicuously absent) she proceeded, with her two children from a previous life, to move her belongings into place. Then she noticed that she was going to be alone in one room. She turned round to her husband, who was standing around and anticipating the confrontation. (p. 7)

While all these can be construed as the remote causes of this compelling tragedy the immediate cause lies in the nasty habit Ogugua's twin girls have of stealing Nwabunor's money and the provisions she sells to support herself and her son. That Ogugua counters her complaints with taunts and abuses is only a further revelation of her character. Okpewho's handling of the problem of the twins is typical of the deep psychological insight that runs through the novel. The children's behaviour stands out as the inevitable consequence of their upbringing by a reckless and wayward mother. Even when Nwabunor overhears them admit to Ogugua that they stole the missing biscuits, their mother is brazen enough to enter into a fight on a cause where she is guilty. Ogugua has no redeeming qualities as a character. Her arrogance, shameless effrontery and stinging tongue contribute as much as her opponent's jealousy to the final holocaust. But she too is anxious to establish some recognizable identity as the favoured wife of Obanua. The author obviously sees individuals caught in the polygamous situation as victims of a long-established social practice – hence the title of the book.

The hero's mother is one character in the book who is sure of her own identity and performs her role creditably in the struggle. Obanua's mother plays a very significant role in the book. Her relationship with her son is one of displacement or exchange of identities. Okpewho rejects the archetypal image of the wicked and scheming mother-in-law and presents us with a woman who devotes her whole life to the search for sanity in her son's home. Her perceptive nature comes out in her objection to her son's marriage to Ogugua. In spite of this objection she assumes the central position of adviser and judge in a home where a man has abdicated his responsibilities as husband and father. Ma Nwojide is cast in the same positive mould as Soyinka's Mrs Faseyi. She is not one of Munonye's sulking and jealous mothers-in-law; nor Konadu's scheming type. She is the symbol of sanity, courage and discipline. A large, imposing woman she likes to make her wishes clear and commands respect wherever she goes. During one of the fights between the two women she intervenes with fiery comments:

> 'Take a look around the whole neighbourhood . . . and see if you can find any two people exchanging spittle or poking at each other's eyeballs. Wretched things! Every wife in Ozala who respects herself is now about her responsibilities, trying to see what she could do for the good of her household. But when you come to my son's house you will find two vultures trying to make carrion of one another. Shameless things. I say take a look round the neighbourhood and tell me what two people you will find trying to strip each other naked for a public spectacle.' (p. 63)

She is equally strict with both women, castigating the older for her selfishness and paranoia and the younger for her boldness and over-confidence. Ma Nwojide represents a passing generation, one that accepted polygamy unquestioningly. Her poise, dignity and self-possession endear her to the reader. Nevertheless the old woman shows more sympathy for Nwabunor than for her rival. Ironically her advice to the former to go back to her parents before she loses her life leads to Nwabunor's last desperate act of poisoning Ogugua and her children. Yet it is an advice given in good faith. Ma Nwojide eventually becomes convinced that Nwabunor must have some disease which has not yet been diagnosed and advises her in her own interest to leave Obanua's house so that in case of any other serious attack she would at least have her parents to take care of her:

> 'Do you hear me? I am tired of shouting and do not wish to do that any more. Tomorrow morning pack your things and go. When you are sure you are fully recovered you can then think deeply whether or not you wish to come back here. I don't want to drive you away from your

husband's house. But I am sure you will agree that it is better to be alive than to die the death of a dog. Do you hear what I am saying? Nobody worships a master with as much as their life.' (p. 171)

Her vehemence, however, does not end with her daughters-in-law; it extends even to her son. Her appearance at her son's usual drinking house is an instance of such confrontation. As soon as she appears, the people at the bar observe a respectful silence. Even the woman of the bar stands at a distance after assessing the situation, but it is Obanua who takes the brunt of her fury:

'You vagabond! . . . You wretch! You disgrace! Did I not warn you? Did I not tell you you would regret it? Look at yourself now – do you not feel any shame for one moment? You toss your dead body here on the ground for all the world to see. Go back to your house and see what is happening there.' (pp. 172-3)

From this context the tragedy can be seen as the outcome of a prophecy foretold by Ma Nwojide, and reminds one of the classical tragedies with their ominous prophecies. For the first time in African literature the theme of polygamy has been raised to the grandeur of tragedy. In addition Okpewho has made it the fatal mistake which the culprit must pay for dearly. *The Victims* is so thoroughly infused with the feminine viewpoint that the author cannot avoid making the three men who feature in it unsavoury human beings. Obanua and his jobless friend Nwanze are irresponsible drunks while Gwam is a business exploiter involved in an illicit love affair with a married woman. But it is Obanua who is punished because his decision is responsible for the conflict in the novel; it poisons human relationships and perverts the values of a home. When Obanua goes home:

This was not because he thought that home was the logical place to go after a man was through with whatever it was that kept him outside so late. He could not reason now. More than anything else he was being pushed home by the natural instinct that an animal has for its habitat. If he could bring himself to think, he would not want to go home. But now no place of escape could well be contemplated under such giddy circumstances. (p. 53)

This feeling links Obanua with Armah's hero of *The Beautyful Ones Are Not Yet Born* who dreads his home, though for different reasons.[4]

So Obanua's character deteriorates. His marriage to Ogugua, who is notorious for her moral irresponsibility, has obviously aggravated Nwabunor's jealous suspicion, paranoia and sense of alienation in his family. This marriage creates a big problem for him but he lacks the moral strength to bring the situation under control and as conditions in his own home grow unbearable, he seeks escape through drink. As a result, he loses one job after another, runs into debt, and resigns himself to a life of self-indulgence and hopelessness. His picture after the ghastly tragedy in which his whole family is wiped out is very telling and pathetic:

> No sooner had she said that than they saw Obanua approaching from a distance. Heavily drunk and holding a tattered shirt in one hand, he was sauntering unsteadily towards his house as unintelligible notes issued from his dripping mouth. His lips looked swollen and so too his eyes. And from his shouts he appeared to be singing. (p. 200)

Okpewho's story is told with a keen eye for detail and a deep understanding of human psychology. What differentiates him from other African novelists dealing with the theme of polygamy is his absolute exclusion of the supernatural from his treatment. Nwabunor's anxieties over her son's future are the natural ones of any woman of her age with an only son in a hostile polygamous situation. Obanua's failure as husband and father is that of any ordinary, though weak, man. The bitter fight between him and Nwabunor over Ubaka's school fees is the normal outcome of all their pent-up hatred for each other. For Nwabunor, Ubaka's education is a matter of survival. Neither Nwabunor nor Ogugua is an exceptional woman like Flora Nwapa's Efuru, Idu or Amadi's Ihuoma. Both are capable of hatred and jealousy, and this makes them much more credible than some of the above-named women in African literature. One can easily identify with the tensions under which the characters live. The localized and restricted reading makes the novel's tragic impact all the more poignant. As the preface to the book says:

> The book is essentially a story of every-day small town life, ruthlessly and often poetically observed, and few African novels have utilized such graphic local colour in a way that not only preserves the flow of the story but establishes a bond between the events of the drama and the natural scenes around them.

A good example of this marriage of event and natural phenomenon is the heavy and prolonged downpour of rain that aided Nwabunor when in the dead of night she stole away and dropped poison into Ogugua's soup pot. So also on the night when Obanua loses his job as night-watchman over the church compound the tragic incident is accompanied by rain and howling winds. To add to the effect Okpewho invests the event with an otherworldly character. He describes the thieves as wearing white loincloths tied around their waists, moving in a single file down the stream in what he calls 'the funeral procession of white'. All these devices are a strong testimony to Okpewho's training in classics. Perhaps his most effective technique is the use of 'the chorus' to achieve an atmosphere of the macabre. The book begins and ends with the words of the two old sisters, neighbours of Obanua, who jointly own a little cat which is always in their company and apparently is the only other companion they have. Ubaka consoles Bomboy in order to make him stay away from the cat:

> 'I am sorry. I am sorry. I only wanted you to leave the cat. Don't you know she belongs to those two women? Papa says they are witches and fly about at night looking for people who have wronged them. If you hurt the cat they will fly in here in the middle of the night and scratch out your eyes. Do you want your eyes scratched out by witches?' (pp. 55-6)

The effect is powerful; it is weird, and heightens the darkness of the whole tragedy.

Okpewho's knowledge of human psychology and the power of blind fate to destroy the most beautiful of human relationships is illustrated by the cordial relationship that exists between Bomboy, the four-year-old son of Ogugua, and Ubaka, Nwabunor's only, and much older, son. Throughout the tragic sequence of events the two remain the symbol of affection, peace and understanding in the midst of hate and fear. Ubaka is a hero to his younger half-brother. Bomboy's attitude to him is one of respectful love. The two maintain their warm relationship despite pressures from their respective parents.

As is to be expected, Bomboy offers Ubaka part of his meal, which has already been poisoned by the latter's mother, as a farewell present. In a rigorously executed form of poetic justice Nwabunor's crime engulfs her only son. Fittingly she laments her woe alone and the book ends on this very sad note:

> She began to rave uncontrollably, her hair dishevelled and her cloth falling loose off her waist. The rain had stopped completely, and only her ululations broke the quiet expanse of the emptiness around. Beneath the sky an ash-coloured screen of cloud hung motionless like a permanent shroud, severely weakening the light of the departing sun. In the adjacent shrubbery a lone finch fluttered noiseless, without any visible mission, until it finally disappeared and was blotted out of view in the smoky distance. (p. 176)

This last scene concludes the theme of loneliness that runs through the whole book. Nwabunor has been a very lonely character. The thread of communication between her and her husband has already been broken at the beginning, for our first contact with the husband and wife is during a savage fist-fight between the two. Although her exceptional and only son Ubaka lives with her, the boy is too young to grasp fully the state of emotional pressure in which his mother exists. As for Ogugua, the second wife, her arrival in the house does not provide any form of companionship or understanding. Nwabunor shows from the start that she is not in favour of her husband marrying another wife. Ogugua senses this resentment very early in her stay and reciprocates the feeling. As the second and unwanted wife, Ogugua needs to establish her own identity in a very hostile situation; the only bond between the two wives is that of hatred.

Perhaps it is to heighten this mood of loneliness that Okpewho has made use of a 'chorus' similar in its function of commentator to the chorus in a Greek play. Right at the beginning we meet the two old women, who are called either the 'two old women', 'the first or second woman' or 'the two aged women'. Their conversation as usual centres on a cat and the squabbles in Obanua's household. It is from them that the reader finds out that the family in question exists in a state of physical and mental violence:

> Another loud cry came, a female voice, followed by the harsh sound of tumbling things. The two old women looked round at each other with quiet wonder and waited. The woman's voice wailed again loud and pained, and soon after the worried cry of a little boy followed.
> 'He must be back,' the first old woman sighed knowingly.
> 'Yes,' replied her sister, 'they are at it again,' hissing and getting ready to lie down again.
> 'Night after night. Things have certainly grown worse in the house lately.'
> Then she lay her head down, and before two winks of the eye she was already asleep. 'Which of the wives do you think that is?' asked the first woman. But there was no reply.
> 'It must be the first wife,' she said, more to herself now. 'That other sounds like the voice of her son.' Then she shook her head, mumbling, 'Poor woman. Poor woman.' (p. 2)

The old women are therefore presented as commentators on the horrible story of Obanua's alienation from his wives. Their involvement in the tragedy is all the more interesting because we are not given much information about them. We know them merely

as the two old women or the two sisters. The author makes no
attempt to identify or differentiate one from the other, since they
play mainly a symbolic role. They both carry the badge of old age,
weakness and loneliness. But the two women do understand the
problem in the family, that basic problem which the author
describes for us in these words:

> It had all the unguided bitterness and frustration that comes to a family
> when love has long since died, when the one has discovered that there
> is nothing to look forward to, particularly as she has little to offer, and
> the other wonders what use it has all been and decides that he loses
> nothing now by hating. (p. 4)

The author has deliberately created the setting of this first scene to
reflect the troubled times described in the novel. It is a rough,
stormy night, with gusts of wind howling and tearing.

The two women consistently comment on the moral of the book.
They provide the first comments and the last words of the tragedy.
Ironically these two lonely creatures in their uneventful lives
represent the qualities of sympathy and understanding the absence
of which has wrecked Obanua's family. Their presence therefore
contributes thematically to the question of identity crisis in the
book. The tragedy is complete with vivid pictures of the three
protagonists: Ogugua and her children dead through poison,
Nwabunor, a raving mad woman on the streets of her town and
Obanua a pathetic and broken man.

The identity issue is even more central in Okpewho's next novel,
The Last Duty,[5] a book set in the context of the Nigerian civil war,
this time disguised under the fictitious combatants, Simbia and
Zonda. As a novelist, Okpewho is of course not interested in the
external drama of violence that war always entails. He is interested
in the human and emotional dimensions of war – broken homes,
the fate of widows and widowers, marital infidelity, the sufferings
of orphans, even insanity and general moral decadence. In this he
re-echoes Achebe's *Girls at War*[6] and Munonye's *A Wreath for the
Maidens*.[7]

The Last Duty therefore straddles two areas of the Nigerian
literary tradition. Its war theme makes it a political novel but its
focus is on the human implications of war. But within this broad
plan Okpewho is interested in exploring the problem of each
character individually and thereby seeks to establish his separate
identity. This is why structurally the novel is a series of personal
confessional statements indicating the individual reaction of the

protagonists to the composite circumstances that confront all of them. In the words of the author:

> This essentially is the tragedy of any civil war: lofty political speeches, declarations, etc., take little notice of lives of the small people involved in the war, yet have far reaching effects on their fortunes. Why that title *The Last Duty*? Basically because the story makes the point that a man's ultimate concern, his 'last duty' is to his conscience – his deep human conviction of what he must do in accordance with dictates of his manhood or his sense of justice.[8]

The question of individual choice is therefore a central one and in a situation of insecurity, hatred, tension and widespread deprivation individual choices are bound to assume strange dimensions. In a sense Okpewho's characters are once more the 'victims' of circumstances even more disastrous than those in which the characters of his first novel find themselves. The strength of Okpewho's book lies in the thoroughness and understanding with which he portrays the inner thoughts and actions of each individual as he grapples with his own predicament. The particularized language of the characterization is a deliberate device to aid in the evolution of the full identity of each of these characters. The author uses the confessional style as that which best reveals both the conscious and unconscious responses of the speaker since the individual cannot be false to himself. It is a highly calculated style:

> Okpewho calls it 'the collective evidence technique'. It is in essence a series of personal statements indicating the individual reaction of the protagonists to the composite circumstances which they all share. Each segment thus adds a further dimension to the tale by exposing another separate point of view. When all compounded, these make the social statement. The device is a mode that recognises that the social is quite literally the compound of the individualised experiences.[9]

Toje, the villain of the piece, is preoccupied with the question of his personal identity. He is a crooked local chief and businessman who seeks to turn the circumstances of the war to his own financial advantage. His former corruption in peace is now accentuated by the realities of war. In the book there is a concentration on people, the honour and honesty with which they maintain their integrity under the ferocious pressure of war; but Toje as an opportunist scorns such virtues. In Toje's hands Aku the unfortunate wife of the jailed Oshevire suffers the same fate as Mumbi does at the hands of Karanja her former suitor. In both *A Grain of Wheat* and *The Last*

Duty two erstwhile faithful wives succumb to seduction as the result of the deprivation of war. But Mumbi ironically falls when she is closest to victory, though she is forgiven at the end. Aku in contrast undergoes a prolonged series of sexual abuse at the hands of the impotent chief who now turns the helpless woman into a human laboratory for testing his failing manhood:

> For I felt that Mukoro Oshevire stood in my way. And that again is why I have not hesitated to seek carnal pleasure with his forlorn wife now that I feel my manhood flawed, my potency questioned. For it seems only in the nature of things that everything possible should be done in the interest of a reassertion of my manhood . . . (p. 5)

As Toje meditates on his past glory in the community and frantically struggles to recover that identity he consoles himself in his splendid application of the motif of appearance versus reality:

> Every town must have a few people whose names lend respect to the community. They should be the town's foremost citizens, men of some distinction . . . A town is worth nothing if it has no names on whom its very credit hangs. I am one of those very few names that mean anything here in Urukpe. Everybody knows that – or should. (pp. 4-5)

Toje believes in power. He believes that power is happiness and that happiness lies in finding that a whole town still looks up to you even in war. He gloats over his power over Aku who helplessly obeys whenever he summons, over the respect Major Ali shows him, and over the amount of money that still comes to him:

> That's money. And I am determined that this money will bring back to me everything I appear to have temporarily lost. (p. 27)

Toje is living in a world of the past, a world of illusion, and has in reality lost all he says he appears to have lost: his manhood, his former charm, his monopoly of the rubber business and his ability to indulge in flagrant violation of justice as in the case of Oshevire. Ali constitutes a deep-seated thorn in his flesh since the major is determined to do justice to all. Toje needs constant self-reassurance:

> I am determined to use his wife to prove to myself that I still possess that power which I know lies within me. I am still Toje Onovwakpo. (p. 27)

His exploitation of Aku continues until the final violent confrontation with Odibo who has displaced Toje in Aku's favour. It is the central irony of this pathetic work that Odibo (meaning servant), who is crippled and totally dependent on Toje for his livelihood, should harbour within his deformed mass of a body the store of manhood that finally satisfies the pent-up sexual passion aroused in Aku by his master:

> Frustration had driven me to the point where I would rather live the fact than the fiction of sin. Loyalty and devotion had been strained beyond all possible endurance, and neither the mind nor the body could any longer fight the overwhelming presence of temptation. (p. 184)

In losing her former identity as the 'very jewel of a wife, matchless queen whose courage and nobility demand only equal demonstration of fortitude from me' (p. 209), Odibo discovers his full identity as a man rather than a terrified slave to Toje. Odibo celebrates:

> I have lived a false existence, a prowling shadow, bashful, timorous, without a voice without a face, without any kind of identity . . . Now all that is gone. Gone! Now I know that I am a man like any other man (p. 179)

Before his hour of victory he had lived encaged in fear and slavish caution, hiding his stump of an arm, talking very little and avoiding women. The final reversal of fortune is that Toje who appears a complete and successful man is no man at all, while Odibo the seeming weakling possesses within him all it takes to be a full man and in the final release of his passion and realization of his identity drags down a woman who for three years and more had succeeded in remaining faithful to her absent husband. Odibo's hour of victory is Toje's and Aku's hour of failure, and like Gikonyo, Oshevire dreams of coming home to a wife who on the surface is devoted but in reality has become a slut.

Oshevire is made of the stuff of which tragic heroes are made. He is the injured victim of social injustice, the betrayed husband and the unfortunate plaything of fate. Meditating on his lot he says:

> 'I still don't know what I am doing here. But I don't care. The important thing is to be able to stand up to the situation and bear it all like a man. To be able to prove to your enemies that the forces of truth and honesty are stronger than any burden they will unjustly have laid upon you. To be able to vindicate the cause of justice, and, even if they succeed in taking your life at the end, prove to them all too clearly that theirs was an idle victory, for your honesty towers tall and superior above everything, like a wild palm, tough and upright.' (pp. 32–3)

At no time does he doubt the justness of his cause in saving a little boy whose life was threatened by a bloodthirsty mob. But Oshevire is also guilty of hubris – excessive pride – which fails to take cognizance of human frailty. He therefore refuses to forgive his wife and blindly walks into the mouth of death in a desperate attempt to defend his identity as a husband and to protest against his fate. And so like Obanua in *The Victims* he commits a fatal error and leads his whole family into destruction. Even the innocent Oghenovo never comes to know the father whose identity and good name he had spent his brief life defending, for his own identity is at once bound together with that of his father.

Okpewho understood too well what the existentialists have been saying for a century – that essence precedes existence; that man ultimately makes himself what he is, and he does this by making a choice to realize whatever he considers the reason for his existence. The choice is always fraught with danger but man is condemned to choose, hence Okpewho's characters jostle against one another in a cruel world in an attempt to make a dent in this staggering reality of a universe; for in Ali's words:

> A man must do what he has to do. It may hurt a few people, but right and expediency must always be the determining factors in his decisions. (p. 15)

NOTES

1. Charles Larson, *The Emergence of African Fiction*, Bloomington, Indiana, Indiana University Press, 1971.
2. Isidore Okpewho, *The Victims*, London, Longman, 1970. Subsequent page references are to this edition and incorporated in the text. Washington, D.C., Three Continents Press, 1979.
3. Justin D. Kaplan (ed.), *The Pocket Aristotle*, New York, Pocket Books, 1960, p. 353.
4. Ayi Kwei Armah, *The Beautyful Ones Are Not Yet Born*, London, Heinemann, 1969.
5. Isidore Okpewho, *The Last Duty*, London, Longman, 1976. All further page references are to this edition and are incorporated in the text.
6. Chinua Achebe, *Girls at War*, London, Heinemann (AWS 100), 1972.
7. John Munonye, *A Wreath for the Maidens*, London, Heinemann (AWS 121), 1973.
8. Isidore Okpewho, 'The Last Duty', *African Arts*, vol. 6, no. 2, pp. 14–15.
9. ibid., p. 14.

The Revised *Arrow of God*

Bruce King

Although the preface to the second edition of Chinua Achebe's *Arrow of God* (1974) quietly mentions 'certain structural weaknesses' that Achebe has taken 'the opportunity of a new edition to remove', the revisions are extensive and are more of style and technique than 'structural'. The second edition contains perhaps two hundred revisions. While the largest number of changes are in the early chapters, there is probably no chapter in the second edition that has not been in some way modified, except chapter XV, and the later chapters of the book contain the most significant revisions. As a detailed study of the changes in the second edition would require a small monograph, it is possible here only to summarize the kinds and effects of the revisions. For this purpose I shall list the changes in chapter I and the major revisions in the remainder of the book. (In my references the chapter number is followed by the page number of the Heinemann paperback edition of 1965 and that in the revised paperback edition of 1977).

First edition	Second edition

Syntax and word order

The woman who will bear the man who will say it has not yet been born.	has not been born yet. (I, pp. 4, 3)

The more emphatic sentence is in keeping with Ezeulu's character and usual way of speaking.

May this household be healthy.	*This household may it be healthy.* (I, pp. 7, 6)

The syntax of the former sounds 'English' and the phrase echoes Christian blessings. The inverted word order of the latter is in Ezeulu's Igbo speech patterns. Italics are used in the revised edition for interior monologue, prayers, public speeches, and so on.

May our wives bear male children.	*And let our wives bear male children.* (I, pp. 7, 6)

Here and in the next quotation 'let' is less like church English and has a somewhat different meaning from 'may'. 'Let' is an exhortation; 'may' expresses a wish.

May good come to the land.	*Let it come to the land* (I, pp. 7, 6)
Sacrifice a cow and not a chicken.	*Sacrifice to you a cow, not a chicken.* (I, pp. 7, 6)

'To you' is less anthropological and general; more a prayer to a god.

Additional information: setting, character descriptions, etc.

'It kills little girls,' said Nwafo.	'It kills little girls,' said Nwafo, her brother. (I, pp, 3, 2)

The reader probably does not have the family relationships clearly in mind this early in the novel.

said Ezeulu with a smile	said Ezeulu with a smile, and Nwafo was full of happiness. (I, pp. 9, 8)

There is now more interaction between the characters.

She told her mother about it.	Then she gathered the bowls and went to tell her mother about it. (I. pp. 11, 9)

This makes the situation more concrete.

they would come out in force to defend their brother.	they will come out in force to defend their brother. Then there will be work for you. (I, pp. 13, 11)

There is more interplay between the characters and the situation is thus more dramatic.

Verbal economy

But in spite of this no one would be so rash	Nevertheless no one would be so rash. (I, pp. 4, 4)

The substitution of an emphatic for a weak idiom is more in keeping with Ezeulu's personality.

What kind of power was it if everybody knew that it would never be used?	What king of power was it if it would never be used? (I, pp. 4, 4)

This internalizes the thought.

'When a woman marries a husband she should forget how big her father's compound was' she always said. 'A woman does not carry her father's *obi* to her husband.'	the kind of woman who carried her father's compound into the house of her husband. (I, pp. 12, 10)

The former is didactic; the latter is witty and consistent with Ojiugo's mother's attitude towards Akueke.

Deletion of explanations

What I am carving for the man of Umuagu is a Mask	What I am carving for the man of Umuagu is not . . . (I, pp. 5, 5)

The first explains; the second is part of a dramatic dialogue.

turning it with the stick whenever the side nearest the fire had had enough.	rolling it over with the stick again and again. (I. pp. 4, 5)

The first explains; the second is closer to the action.

You told me not to carve them.	You told me to avoid it. (I, pp. 5, 5)

The former is explanatory; the second is part of a dramatic dialogue and is in keeping with the psychology of Edogo.

Substitutions

the proud dog who tries to put out a furnace	the proud dog who sought to put out a furnace (I, pp. 4, 4)

'Tried' is a weak, trite expression.

and would use a human pillow to rest its head	and would take a softer pillow for its head (I, pp. 8, 7)

'Take' is more correct than 'use'; the vague 'softer' is appropriate for an oracular message.

This is what we do not understand.	This is the part we do not understand. (I, pp. 14, 12)

'What' is vague and British; 'the part' is stronger and sounds Nigerian.

afraid to speak	afraid to begin (I, pp. 15, 13)
I agreed and sent you	I agreed to send you (I, pp. 16, 14)

Internalization

His mind still persisted in trying to look too closely at the nature of his power	His mind never content with shallow satisfactions crept again to the brinks of knowing. (I, pp. 4, 4)

The former sounds like the comment of an English narrator; the second, with its Nigerian usage ('brinks'), expresses the psychology of Ezeulu.

One of the rough, faceless *okposi* belonged to Nwafo. It was carved for him because of the convulsions he used to have at night. They told him to call it Namesake.	Nwafo's eyes picked out the special *okposi* which belonged to him. It had been carved for him because of the convulsions he used to have at night. They told him to call it Namesake, and he did. (I, pp. 7, 6)

In the revised version the scene is portrayed through the eyes of the characters.

Everytime he prayed for Umuaro bitterness rose into his mouth. A great division had come to the six villages and his enemies tried to put it on his head. For what reason?	Every time he prayed for Umuaro bitterness rose into his mouth, a great smouldering anger for the division which had come to the six villages and which his enemies sought to lay on his head. And for what reason? (I, pp. 7, 6)

By joining the first two sentences, the revised version gives the second sentence the effect of Ezeulu's thought.

as he returned each greeting.	and returned their greeting. (I, pp., 7)

The precision of the first edition is an outsider's comment.

looking towards Ugoye's hut	looking towards the other woman's hut (I, pp. 11, 10)

The revised version internalizes the perspective.

Accuracy

even the smallest piece of the yam	even the smallest crumbs of the yam (I, pp. 6, 5)
about as tall as a man's forearm and having two strong horns	about as tall as a man's forearm, its animal horn as long as the rest of its human body (I, pp. 6, 6)
showed him the ripe fruit on the tree which were as big as water pots	showed him the threatening ripe fruit on the tree, as big as water pots (I, pp. 13, 11)

'Threatening' brings out the meaning; 'as' is more economical and direct than 'which were'.

Improved English

shrine like a woman	shrine, like a woman (I, pp. 7, 6)

'Like' in the former incorrectly refers to 'shrine', whereas in the second edition it correctly refers to the legs described earlier in the sentence.

Translations of Igbo into English to make the text more readable

| Usa bulu Okpili | long throat (I, pp. 3, 2) |

Nigerian usage

| that the white man should come from so far to tell them the truth | that the white man whose father or mother no one knew should come to tell them the truth (I, pp. 8, 7) |

The changes in chapter I contribute towards a greater concentration on the action, on the texture of local society, and on feelings. English clichés are replaced with phrases that sound more Nigerian and are more appropriate to the characters. The language of narration and the dialogue is more in keeping with the enclosed world of the village. The narration is more internalized as if seen and felt from within the perspective of the characters. In general the sentences are more emphatic precise and dramatic (in the sense of arising from the response or interplay of the characters).

The changes in the remainder of the book reveal a similar concern with the craft of fiction, especially in the creation of character and in the use of the English language to show an active, dignified Igbo culture. In the second edition revisions sometimes give more *gravitas* to a character; for instance they make Ezeulu's speeches more emphatic and proud:

| Then it would be death to its tormentor | Then it would say to its tormentor: Here I am! (XVI, pp. 227, 184) |

The revised version adds dramatic defiance. Some revisions delete passages that explain Igbo words to foreigners:

| Akukalia nwadiani or Son of our Daughter | Akukalia *Son of our Daughter* (II, pp. 26, 22) |

Other changes clarify ambiguous phrases:

| calling her father | calling, 'father, father!' (II, pp. 26, 22) |

In general the style and language are more active, tight, less abstract, and closer to the psychology of the characters. The perspective appears more from within the characters than that of the narrator or story teller. The addition of 'nowadays' to Aneto's speech is a small touch that adds a colloquial tone to the dialogue and contributes to the supposed contrast between past and present: 'everybody you see nowadays sounds like a broken pot' (XIX, pp. 279, 224). There are also revisions that expand and make clear the feelings of the character:

bury him like an Ezidemili	bury him with the ancient and awesome ritual accorded to the priest of Idemili (IV, pp. 51, 42)

While the revisions mentioned above contribute towards a more consistently textured fictional world than that of the first edition, they are relatively minor changes in contrast to some of the major revisions that begin with chapter IV. The major revisions are mostly the deletion of the kind of anthropological material that often filled novels of cultural assertion during the independence period at the expense of narrative speed and focus. Five lines of such material are deleted in chapter IV: 'the hut which faced the forest . . . guarding the entrance' (IV, pp. 62, 51). In chapter VI, Obiageli's song (pp. 79–80, 65) is reduced from forty to five lines. It is possible that the description of Nwaka's salute (XIII, pp. 176, 143) was deleted because it was too similar to various European gestures of political loyalty ('he shot his arm forward and upward thrice in salute'), or because it is similar to a Yoruba gesture signifying 'power'. A major structural change is the treatment of Ugoye's tale of the man with two wives, which is reduced from four and a half pages to six lines (XVI, pp. 235–9, 190–1). The general effect of such deletions is to speed up and concentrate the narrative, making the story more novelistic and less an anthropological record. This is especially useful as the story moves towards its dramatic conclusion.

The use of italics in the second edition instead of single quotation marks for interior monologue, prayer and some public speeches, and for speeches that are reported by characters, both clears up various ambiguities about who is speaking and contributes to the focusing of the novel's perspective more on the psychology of the characters than on a record of communal life.

Compare the effect of:

> Will he say to the guns and the arrows and the matchets: Hold! I want to
> return quickly to my medicine-hut and stir the pot and find out what
> has gone wrong; perhaps someone in my household – a child, maybe –
> has unwittingly violated my medicine's taboo? No.

with:

> Will he say to the guns and the arrows and the matchets: Hold! *I want to
> return quickly to my medicine-hut and stir the pot and find out what
> has gone wrong; perhaps someone in my household — a child, maybe —
> has unwittingly violated my medicine's taboo?* No. (XIX, pp. 285–6,
> 228)

Several other kinds of revision should be noticed. There are
changes that contribute to the dignity of characterization, event
and diction:

| he had not asked his son to do too much | he had not asked his son for more than was justly due (XIX, pp. 271, 217) |

There are revisions that subtly contribute towards characterization
and psychology. Goodcountry's brand of Christian missionary
spirit is better conveyed:

| received this year from God. And not only yams, any crop whatsoever or livestock or money | received this year from Almighty God. And not only yams, any crop whatsoever livestock or money. Anything (XVIII, pp. 270, 216) |

Some changes significantly develop the themes and their social
background. For example, Winterbottom's reflections on the
British creation of local chiefs:

| Chief Ikedi was still corrupt and high-handed but he had become even more clever than before. . . . This among a people who never had kings before! | Chief Ikedi was still corrupt and high-handed only cleverer than ever before . . . This among a people who abominated kings! (V, pp. 70, 58) |

While, in a sense, this is an editorial insertion by Achebe, it is one
of several instances where he had revised or added to the thoughts

of Europeans to bring out their character further, as in Wright's new comment about 'in this God-forsaken place' (X, pp. 129, 104). Whereas Winterbottom in the first edition speaks of 'Defender of Faith', his scholarly side is shown in the second edition's 'Fidei Defensor' (X, pp. 133, 107). Such touches contribute towards a fuller realization of character in the second edition.

Three revisions from the final paragraph of the novel will indicate how the tone of the 1974 version has moved from an external to an internal perspective:

If this was so then Ulu had chosen a dangerous time to uphold this wisdom. In destroying his priest he had also brought disaster on himself, like the lizard in the fable.	If this was so then Ulu had chosen a dangerous time to uphold that truth for in destroying his priest he had also brought disaster on himself, like the lizard in the fable.
For a deity who chose a time such as this to destroy his priest or abandon him to his enemies was inciting people to take liberties.	For a deity who chose a moment such as this to chastise his priest or abandon him before his enemies was inciting people to take liberties.
Thereafter any yam that was harvested in the man's fields was harvested in the name of the son.	Thereafter any yam harvested in his field was harvested in the name of the son. (XIX, pp. 287, 230)

It will be obvious from the revisions that I have selected that the first *Arrow of God* is somewhat different from the revised edition. While the themes, characterization and narrative form have not changed, the second edition is better written, technically more satisfactory and focuses more on the drama of individual emotions than on reporting community life. The critic or lecturer will need to state which edition he or she is using and will need to be careful to distinguish between the effect of the two versions. The author of the first version is somewhat less secure in his craft and less consistent in his reshaping of the English language to a Nigerian context; the various explanations show the author's relationship to foreign readers. The excessive anthropological material reflects a decade when the portrayal of traditional culture was a nationalistic assertion. The author of the revised edition is a more mature craftsman who is less concerned with explaining local culture to Europeans; he has a more secure control of English and, relatively, is more interested in the drama and role of his main character within a period of cultural transition.

As Achebe was always a conscious craftsman of the novel, the difference between the two editions is a matter of emphasis. The first edition is somewhat more external and explanatory; its tempo often slows to allow a portrayal of traditional culture. It is still influenced by the methods used in *Things Fall Apart*, where there is often a double perspective shared between focus on the hero's tragic hubris and the recording of the life of a community. In the revised *Arrow of God* the greater detail, the suppression of explanation and the deletion of some anthropological material result in a more unified perspective as the events are seen more from within the vision or thought of the characters. The pace is quicker and the emphasis is somewhat more on psychology than on narration. The use of italics instead of quotation marks and the transformation of speeches into indirect reports of what characters say or feel make the novel more dramatic. Instead of being told and offered illustrations, the reader is placed more within the feelings and vision of the characters. The first edition still has many characteristics of a story; the second edition is more novelistic.

Colonial Contact and Language in Ferdinand Oyono's *Houseboy*

Leonard Kibera

> In a strange psychological process persons who are viewed by those in authority as numbers on punch ards, tend to view themselves as numbers rather than persons, un' ss they deliberately guard against it.[1]

Houseboy is a study of an almost total and unapologetic uprootedness.[2] In such cases as Achebe's Oduche (*Arrow of God*)[3] or Kane's Samba Diallo (*Ambiguous Adventure*)[4] we have young Africans who, like Toundi, are drawn to the world of whites. But they at least return to their changing communities even if, in the case of Oduche, it is to turn Ezeulu's world upside down.

When Toundi leaves home, however, he cuts himself off from African history and all that went before, never to return except in a distant, emaciated fashion. What he sees of the white world attracts him immediately, and his commitment to it is immediate and absolute when, on the day before his initiation into manhood in the African sense, he escapes to Father Gilbert. This is important if we are to understand Toundi's peculiar behaviour in the novel. For Oyono does not intend Toundi to be the child of two worlds who comes back to his people, for better or worse, after his experiences in the white world. What is intended is a study of the extent to which the African *could* sign himself into bondage under colonialism.

It is quite natural, therefore, that Toundi's very first statement as he begins his dairy should be a rejection of Africa. He begins by telling us not who he is but what 'Father Gilbert says' he is, acknowledging, therefore, that the white world has recreated him, given him a new identity and language, so this new African can now proceed into the future. How he would define himself is stated in the third paragraph of the novel as an afterthought, and with no particular pride, because his past no longer matters to him. We note how ruthlessly he has cut himself from his traditional environment:

> In the afternoon my father came. All he said to me was that I was still his son, the drop of his liquid and that he bore me no grudge . . . I put out my tongue at him . . . I was not afraid while Father Gilbert was there. Father Gilbert seemed to cast a spell over my father. *He lowered his head and went out crestfallen* (my italics). (p. 13)

It is not enough to leave traditional Africa. It must be humiliated, be seen as worthless, in order to be rejected more completely. We find that as this severing of the blood tie takes place, Father Gilbert encourages no reconciliation. It is not his business to create an atmosphere of love or understanding (he does not have the language for it as we shall see later) but rather hatred between father and son, in order to recreate the son more completely. Toundi himself never regrets this treatment of his father even when he suffers great physical and psychological pain under the whites. Indeed he realizes very early the painful irony of colonialism. He is the loved one, a 'masterpiece' of Father Gilbert's creation. Yet he is savagely punished, goes badly dressed, and notices – with that characteristic detachment that generally runs through the novel when he is looking at his own suffering and that of other Africans – that the priest is exploiting him. He takes delight in being treated 'like a pet animal' although he has observed earlier, if rather sarcastically, that 'since the white men came we have learnt other men must not be looked upon as animals'. He wishes, in fact, to be colonized.

It is interesting to note the quick rationalization of events after he and the white man dismiss the elder Toundi. In the first place there is a thin attempt to involve his mother:

> She told me I had done well to leave my father's house and that my father did not love me as a father ought to love his son. (p. 13)

His purpose here is to win the reader's sympathy. But he has already admitted to us that the primary reason he disobeyed his father was that he 'wanted to get close to the white man . . .'. For this reason what is traditionally more natural to an African mother – that is, to run away from her husband with her children – cannot be allowed to happen, although he has told us that she, too, experienced a great deal of violence in the home: 'Whenever he went for either my mother or me, it always took us a week to recover' (p. 10). The truth is that he has already been *enslaved* by the flashing of the fireflies in the white world and he must turn his back on *all* his traditional environment, which includes attacking his extended family: his uncle has scabies and he and his wife smell of bad fish, so that given this type of environment, Toundi quickly adds, 'You could begin to see the flashing light of the fireflies' (p. 12). The uncle eats all the food and Toundi reaches the mission at an opportune moment to find the more hospitable priest at dinner. Having been so conveniently used, however, Zama Toundi like her husband before her is dismissed from the story *forever*. In other words she is never remembered after this except on those occasions when our hero is in deep trouble. The contact he maintains with his sister is no threat to his decision. She is seen as living in the location not the village; she is not portrayed as traditional, and she leaves him alone. We do not even see them talking.

In the second place, there is, immediately after this dismissal of his parents, a vigorous attempt to strike out on his own, to prove the point that he is already one with the whites:

> Two days later Father Gilbert took me on his motor cycle. We spread panic through the villages by the noise we made . . . The speed intoxicated me. I was going to learn about the white men and live like them. (p. 13)

This is the alternative security he finds for himself. The trip of course represents the ritual of initiation, while the motor cycle itself is an obvious extension of those lumps of sugar that first drew him to the Catholic priest, and which had been given out contemptuously as 'corn to chickens'. But the two-week tour coming as it does at this particular time serves Toundi very well. Here is his chance to proclaim to the villagers in general, and to his father in particular, that in spite of a certain opposition a local heathen boy is already making good. Consequently, his remark that he caught himself 'thinking I was like one of the wild parrots we used to attract in the village with grains of maize' is, for him, no more than an interesting observation. Having rationalized his departure so cleverly and having convinced himself of the rightness of his decision, Toundi is now ready to trade all his feelings into the white world, striking off traditional Africa with a cold, emphatic indifference: 'My parents are dead. I have been back to the village' (p. 14). Contrast this for a moment with his reaction when Father Gilbert dies:

> The Catholic Mission is in mourning.
> But for me, it is more than mourning.
> I have died my first death . . . . (p. 20)

The problem that is to afflict Toundi from now on is that while he will not regret having cut off links with traditional Africa, he will never know exactly what it is he seeks from his new world. All that has happened is that he has been captivated by the priest's playfulness and hopes to be at the centre of Father Gilbert's favours in future. This is all he means when he says 'I was going to learn about the city and white men and live like them' (p. 13). Oyono has clearly not chosen an African character with substantial ambitions in life. Throughout the novel Toundi's only real wish is to be treated kindly. And his only real achievement in this world of whites is that he does learn French. Nowhere is it mentioned, for example, that he is making a conscious effort to rise above his status as a servant. Even his French becomes an end in itself, a basically useless acquisition which is used, not to open up new horizons for himself, but to serve the whites better. In fact the only time we are aware of his knowledge of French is when he judges that spoken by other Africans. He does not even write his diary in it. That 'The dog of the King is King of dogs' is, then, quite enough for him since, as Engamba might say in *The Old Man and the Medal,* 'Isn't the friend of the chief something of a chief himself?'[5] And although he seems to us on the surface to be the one African who *sees* most into the dehumanizing nature of colonialism, although his eye as a house servant is in many places at the same time keenly observing the whites 'inside' and the Africans outside, and although he considers himself more intelligent than people like Baklu, Toundi emerges in fact as a strangely myopic character. He refuses to appreciate that even that very humble relationship he wishes to establish with the whites has already started on a misunderstanding of the colonizer's purpose. This misunderstanding is best examined by us through a study of the nature of black–white contact in the novel, and how the two races, to use E. M Forster's phrase, go about the business of 'only connect'.[6]

Toundi wishes to learn French from Father Gilbert so that he can understand the white world and his place in it better. But Father Gilbert sells illusions; he does not buy them. It has never been the intention of Prospero to connect on a human level with Caliban,[7] so that the priest (who is ironically in Africa on the pretext of making the word clear in what is to his brand of Christianity the heart of darkness) has, long before teaching Toundi French, actually put a much higher price on gibberish as his means of contact:

> He knew a few words of Ndjem but his pronunciation was so bad that the way he said them, they all had obscene meanings. This amused everybody and his success was assured. (pp. 9–10)

Oyono is probably angry here at the rather complacent way in which Africans could sometimes play easy victims in this deadly game. Notice when we are told that the priest 'went from hut to hut trying to make converts to the new religion' the implication is that every African from child to adult thought him no more than a joke, thereby generally falling for his trick. And the author could be angry too that under colonialism we have often underestimated the power of language. When the whites introduce their language they also introduce a definite colonial ideology. What appears above to be gibberish, Oyono is telling us, is in fact very well calculated colonial jargon that actually works for the colonizer. Father Gilbert's continuing mission is to establish France in Africa using divisive language as his means. He is not interested in a human dialogue because what he is advancing is itself not human. As the Brazilian educator Paulo Freire has observed:

> dialogue cannot occur between those who want to name the world and those who do not wish this naming – between those who deny other men the right to speak their word and those whose right to speak has been denied them. Those who have been denied their primordial right to speak their word must first reclaim this right and prevent the continuation of this dehumanizing aggression.[8]

But in this the Africans are seen by Oyono as passive and uninterested in working out their own language to counter the priest. And we realize that his incoherent chatter carries, in fact, a very clear message of violence; he succeeds in dividing the Africans, leaving behind an almost fatal misunderstanding between two African families who previously had no such quarrel. And we see also how in the church he establishes before his death:

> The faithful are supervised by catechists ready to pounce at the least sign of inattention. These servants of God march up and down the central aisle that divides the men from the women, carrying sticks. (p. 34)

Peace and brotherhood are not part of Father Gilber's mission; they cannot, therefore, be part of his language.

Given this type of tutor, it is not surprising that as soon as Toundi masters his alphabet well enough to write, his first act is not to tell us how he is discovering positive possibilities for himself, but to complain that he is being taught subservience, and that violence has become his most important experience. Or, to put it another way, what inspires the diary in the first place is not so much Father Gilbert's commendation of Toundi's ability to 'read and write fluently', but the fact that 'In Father Gilbert's diary I found the kick he gave me . . . I found my bottom burning all over again' (p. 9). This is consistent with Father Gilbert's vision; this the African does not see. For what Father Gilbert really intends to teach Toundi is *patience* under colonialism. And Toundi must continually prove that he has the patience to go on being patient:

> I serve up to three or four Masses every day. The skin on my knees is now as hard as crocodile skin. When I kneel down I seem to be kneeling on cushions. (p. 14)

But because there is no one to tell him whether he is doing the right thing or not (he is merely rewarded with violence when he fails to please) his life is marked by a certain dilemma which is Christian in character: How best to praise the Lord? This is why he writes. He must empty out his bitter experiences. More than this, he attempts to laugh out these experiences in his diary as the only way he can ease the pain in a world where the whites offer no guidance and the Africans cannot advise him meaningfully, firstly because they too are sufferers, but also because he would not listen to those he thinks are intellectually inferior to him; which is why he never takes their advice. In other words, his only real alternative is to talk to himself in the diary, and a diary is, of course, essentially a monologue. His language, then, becomes that of a pilgrim who is equipped with little more than naïve faith in the future. He can only trust to his medal of St Christopher, his patron saint of travels in a difficult world. The medal is of course all he inherits, along with his tattered clothes, when Father Gilbert dies. But even here there is a basic deception. The saintliness of Christopher is largely mythical and illusory; it has never been proved.

For the purpose of the novel, of course, Father Gilbert must die or at the very least disappear from Toundi's life, much like a character in a folk tale who is dispensed with after seeing the hero through a crucial stage. Historically, Oyono knows that Christianity often came to Africa as a way of introducing the more ruthless realities of imperialism, and this is what is happening in his novel. From now on he aims to study colonialism in the raw, in the shape of the Commandant. When Gilbert dies and Toundi says 'I have died my first death . . .' (notice the unfinished sentence), his reaction means more to the reader than he is able to tell us. Gilbert's death is in fact Toundi's opportunity to begin to mature outside the cloistered vision of pseudo-Christian ideals and to see the world through his own eyes. In due course Father Gilbert's dubious influence recedes more and more and his teachings, when tested on the solid landscape of colonialism, become more and more open to doubt and scepticism. Finally, Christianity in its colonial context is to be seen as sick:

> Visit from Obebe the catechist.
> A tedious little old man. He still suffers from the gonorrhoea he has had since before the war. (p. 116)

Toundi is faced then with the Commandant who is more down to earth. Free of Christian pretensions, the Commandant's language is characterized by a hard realism ('he asked me point-blank if I were a thief') which Toundi's disorganized Christian jargon cannot match. It is not that the Commandant objects to Toundi's Christianity. Like his wife who asks, 'You are a Christian, aren't you?' he knows that Christianity teaches the colonial subject to accept his station in life, not to question it. He catches Toundi precisely at that time of night when the soul is least sure of itself and we immediately have a cloak-and-dagger game with language where the question of who is to be Master has to be settled on the spot. The Commandant does not speak with the voice of a human being but rather that of the colonial system he represents. The human question of how the other feels or whether Toundi is happy to come to work for the Commandant is, therefore, done away with. The very first comment is to ask the African to prove that he is not a thief, not just because the servant is often expected to steal, but because the colonial subject has to be humiliated into psychological servitude along with the physical one. And he must continue to accept the dilemma of his situation:

> From the sitting-room his sharp voice came demanding a beer. As I ran to serve him my cap rolled across the floor to his feet. In a flash I saw his eyes grow as small as a cat's eyes in the sun . . . I was turning to go to the refrigerator when he pointed to the cap at his foot. I was nearly dead with fear. (p. 23)

The symbol of servitude falls off and the Commandant will of course take it as a rebellious act. But what should Toundi do first — go for the beer or pick up his cap? It makes no difference. The fact is that the Commandant *means* to kick him in the pants sooner or later (the kick is even more painful than that of Father Gilbert) and thereafter as often as possible.

Toundi's response to this dilemma is to be complicated by the fact that Christianity has taught him to feel pity for himself as an African. He aims to escape his blackness. He is convinced that because he knows French and works for the Commandant he already has an enviable special relationship with the whites. But what he says of the Commandant later in the novel applies to himself exactly: 'He has no memory and no imagination' (p. 102). He never grows out of his sentimentality, and he never learns meaningfully from experience. When, for example, M. Janopoulos sets his dog on the Africans, we find Toundi raised physically and symbolically 'to the top of the huge mango tree'. The irony is that the Commandant fails to recognize the one African who assumes that special individuality. But instead of seizing upon that experience to reassess his own attitude, Toundi reacts only with blind emotion. 'How could he recognise me?' he says, 'All Africans look the same to them'. If the other Africans in the book are not particularly admirable, they are to an extent at least commonsensical. After Toundi patronizingly introduces the laundryman to us, the latter immediately gives us what would have been his own practical answer; all whites look the same to him:

> I asked him what he thought of Madame.
> 'Like all the white women round here,' he said.
> 'But the prettiest,' I insisted.
> 'You know,' he said, shrugging his shoulders, 'I don't know how you tell whether a white woman is pretty or not.' (pp. 59–60)

His feelings having been rejected by the Commandant, Toundi's alternative is not to identify with other Africans, but to begin to feel for the Commandant's wife. He begins to wonder, even before she arrives, if she will prove 'kind-hearted underneath' towards him like the Commandant although so far we have found no such evidence of his humanity. In great sexual excitement, he breaks into an irrational moment of lofty poetry on her arrival (p. 47). And we realize now that he had refused to respond to Sophie not merely because he was afraid of the engineer, but because black as a colour had lost its attraction to him. We also realize that the black girl at the communion whom he had begun to feel for was so swiftly dismissed from his mind ('She is stupid') probably because her blackness would have tied him down; that what he would really have liked to continue to do was to stroke 'the white girls under the chin with the paten'; that even a woman of Kalisia's sexuality ('A real girl of the soil') cannot touch him.

Madame, like the Commandant, puts Toundi in a dilemma, and his dilemma now extends to feelings. Which one should he feel – her sexuality, or the fear that his life might be 'mingling with hers' ominously in a way dangerous to himself? She provides an answer soon when, standing directly opposite him, she, too, fails to recognize him.

Toundi gets warnings from other Africans, the most important being that from Kalisia whose very appearance is a clear hint that he is being replaced. Her advice is not self-serving. Hers is the voice of experience, the last opportunity Toundi has of getting away. But such advice is really unnecessary for he himself actually knows what is happening. He begins to realize the chilliness of his contact with the white world as he increasingly takes his position 'quietly by the refrigerator' (p. 67, also pp. 72, 85 and 97); he recognizes that he should get rid of his 'ridiculous sentimentality'; he begins to feel his affinity with other Africans as he watches M. Moreau torture two prisoners, sensing that this could happen to him too; indeed he begins to sense his own death:

Shut the door, Saint Peter,
Shut the door and hang up your keys. (p. 80)

But he never has the courage to get away precisely because his psychological attachment to white aesthetics is already too great. Indeed the more we read the diary, the more we realize that it is not about Toundi's development but about his mental regression. He now wishes to remain to show only that they can break all else but not his body. The Commandant deliberately steps on Toundi but he does not cry out; when arrested he seeks to show off his physical endurance. The reader begins to lose patience. But here too (note that the broken style of his diary is part of his final breaking up) they win:

Water-party.
Water, sweat. Whip, blood.
Up the slope, killing. All in.
I cried. (p. 117)

He has now fully felt ('All in') the total physical and psychological impact of colonialism's brutality. And even then it is,
ironically, only when death actually stares him in the face that he
has the sense to break this umbilical cord. The appearance of the
last white man Toundi sees – Moreau on the last page of the book –
is of course the appearance of death. We have already been told that
Moreau is the one who sends prisoners to the 'Blackman's Grave'
where they 'spend a few days painfully dying'. We know that he
has a personal interest in Toundi's death; he holds him responsible
for the gossip regarding him and the Commandant's wife.

Given Toundi's fatalistic attitude in life, we must say, then, that
his question as he dies, 'What are we? What are we blackmen who
are called French?' is in the end futile, neither arising out of, nor
leading to, any significant awareness. Coming from someone who
has endeavoured to live more intelligently and *questioningly*, it
would have been a moving question; coming from Toundi it is
simply a statement of self-pity.

On this level Oyono is consistent. His characters are not like some
black characters who struggle with a consciousness that life *could*
be lived better; rather, they are defeatist even when on the surface,
as in the case of Kalisia, they seem to be winning over colonialism.
Kalisia in fact lives by her wits from moment to moment; she is like
Defoe's Moll Flanders without the latter's sense of the future.[9] And
precisely because the author's vision is not one that allows for the
possibility of the African mastering his colonial situation or even
confronting the colonialist, we find that all his black characters use
language explicitly or implicitly to accept colonialism. See in what
manner the schoolchildren are being groomed to be the new
generation of enlightened Africans:

> They huddled together like chickens who have sighted the shadow of a
> vulture. The instructor gave them the note, then beat out the time. The
> children sang, without any pauses, in a language which was not their
> own or French but the strange gibberish which village people suppose
> is French and Frenchmen suppose is the vernacular. When they had
> finished everybody clapped. (p. 40)

It might seem here that the Commandant and his entourage have
come in style merely as a formality, to keep up appearances. Indeed
the whole area has been cleaned up for the occasion. But the
Commandant must have proof wherever he goes that everybody
from Chief Akoma right down to the schoolboys is obeying colonial

orders. It is for the act of obedience under colonialism, the act of indicating already that they are growing up in appropriate fear of colonial authority, that the children have to be rewarded with an ovation. The meaning of what they sing is irrelevant. Akoma for his part plays the game of pretending he understands French. But there is honesty not pretence in his language when we are told that he can only nod 'Yes, yes', like a hen. As a character in this novel he cannot say no to the colonizer. We find also that Mengueme who is chief of the Yanyans 'understands and speaks French but always pretends not to'. His game is of no consequence. The important thing to the colonialist is that Mengueme 'puts on his chief's uniform when he comes to visit the Commandant...'. As a defeatist African whose two sons and a brother were killed in a white man's war, he can only say that life 'is like the chameleon, changing colour all the time', by which he means he has suffered enough to know that he must never fight his colonial situation now or in the future. He is hardly like Achebe's Ezeulu who seeks to adjust his tempo to the changing 'dance' in order to find out how best he can continue serving his people. We know then that were Mengueme to speak back in French, he too could only nod 'Yes, yes'. That he takes off his uniform 'as soon as he is out of the European town' may be a clear expression of a certain psychological discomfort, but it is hardly a firm gesture of protest. He is simply shifting in his seat to readjust the angle of the pin in his buttock, not standing up to be seen as uncomfortable by the colonizer. It is not that the Africans are completely ignorant of what is happening. Indeed shortly after the schoolboys receive that applause, the attendant in a remarkably concise aside hits at the reality:

> 'This is the house of my second wife,' said the attendant with a broad smile. 'The stream and the wells are on the other side of the courtyard. The lavatory you can smell from here.' (p. 41)

Exactly. Colonialism stinks. But let us not say it in the hearing of the colonizer lest our remark be interpreted as indicating a desire to improve our 'position in life'.

Other black characters have their game with language too and the main strength of the diary method here is that Toundi is often able in a few fleeting observations to comment on the most striking colonial incidents without necessarily being called upon to relate these incidents specifically to his story. Having chosen the diary form, he need not in fact have a particular story to tell; the diary is its own story and will automatically comment on his own life directly or indirectly so that all he need do is record, day by day, as faithfully as possible, the most memorable events. That they are all living under colonialism will itself provide the general motif in one way or another. But eventually we find that what have been most memorable to him as he observes other Africans are basically those events that seem to tie their predicament to his, although consciously he refuses to identify himself with them. For example, we find that Sophie's very first comment in the novel is a complaint. Living in a world where normal values have been turned upside down, and lacking both the will to resist and a firm moral sense herself, her ambition rivets upon being a successful thief. Today she has skipped a move in her game of hide-and-seek with the agricultural engineer in which she hopes to break even by rifling his pockets. She is a sort of Kalisia in apprenticeship, the aim of the training being to learn the art of manoeuvring about on a day-to-day basis in the world of colonialism, never to confront colonialism itself. She could never, for instance, answer Gullet back; she can deal with him only when he is asleep (p. 26). Her long-standing solution to difficulties is, therefore, to *escape* and become a refugee from what should rightly be her own country. But perhaps the most tragic observation is the situation of Ondoua. Indeed by watching *meaningfully* the tragic lot of Ondoua the drummer, Toundi could have learnt a basic lesson on racism: that no matter what he tries to be in the white world, colonialism has its own definition of his humanity and would be happy if the affected 'Monsieur Toundi' would stop considering himself anything more than an automaton.

The agricultural engineer has dragged Ondoua from his village and has enslaved him to 'a huge alarm clock which he carries about with him everywhere'. Ondoua sounds the hour on time, so that the lives of other slaving Africans working the land like Friday for Robinson Crusoe to harvest fruitfully are governed also by this mechanical regularity.[10] His personality as a feeling and thinking human being has ceased to exist. Toundi is able to observe (merely as a curiosity since Toundi is capable of sympathy only when he himself begins to get into trouble in the second exercise book) that Ondoua has 'No particular age. No wife. Only his enormous clock' (p. 30).

Let us pause to note here the colonizer's ideal picture of his subject: the Third World man in bondage, reduced to a mere appliance, a piece of mechanics to be wound at the pleasure of the colonizer; *while the Third World man does nothing about it.* For

Ondoua's *real* tragedy is of his own making. He uses language not to free himself, to attempt to establish a rebellious personality even, but to cultivate a desperate and fatalistic acceptance of his lot. Each time he beats the hour on his drum he sings to abuse the whites in his local language, assuming that since they cannot understand him, he is making a meaningful protest. The irony is that his message is precisely what they would like to hear. It anticipates Madame's comment exactly: faced with colonialism, 'There is nothing you can do . . . In the plantation songs of black Americans during slavery, there was at least a rebellious sense of the future, even if in most cases this was contrived within the Christian sense of hope. But by repeating this message to the labourers with such regularity Ondoua is in fact unwittingly urging them to a greater helplessness and slavery. Like the sentry who calls 'down a vernacular curse on all white men', Ondoua knows that his primary obligations are to the white man, and these must be fulfilled. He drinks to escape this painful realization.

All this indicates a limited satirical approach which seeks to show that no African is capable of reacting intelligently. Oyono gives us an excellent bird's-eye view of a great deal of movement on the ground, but one that suggests that like Meka the African will continue to exist solidly within the limits of 'a whitewash circle',[11] always obeying the whites' commands exactly as if he has been programmed. Sophie must sleep with the agricultural engineer when he wants her; the cook must cook, Baklu must wash underwear, the sentry must watch – all on time. And it seems that for Oyono too, 'nothing can be done about it'. They are free to complain in between if they wish. But even Kalisia, who has some of the mentality of the roving gypsy and who storms in at the end of the novel with such self-confidence, will either have to follow a strict colonial schedule, or be on the move again. There is not a *single* African here who is capable of making even a positive comment, let alone retaliate. One retaliates in this novel by spitting, off-stage, into the colonizer's drink. And if we can indeed take this another step, we note how even Toundi's father (who was certainly no coward and who was ready to take on Tinati's father on the spot) incredibly remained mute on a crucial matter of his son, retreating under the superior silence of the priest as if a whole African culture had been programmed to accept without resistance that moment of arrival of the white man who would achieve his wishes at a glance. We are reminded of Achebe's Umuofia where a fearless people who have always stood proud suddenly go weak in the knees.[12] A certain immaturity in the African is assumed by Oyono; not only is the African unable to confront the politics of the twentieth century, he could never learn how to.

Equally important is the fact that Oyono feels that every African thinks colonialism is a trivial matter. We are given to understand, for example, that the deeper Toundi gets into trouble, the more amusing he finds his colonial situation, remaining quick-witted to the end and, except for that brief moment when he breaks down, continuing to write very clearly, no matter what the pain. On the day he is arrested and after being beaten unconscious, he feels 'a terrible urge to laugh', actually teases Gullet, spends 'the day playing cards', and generally finds his captors not at all disagreeable. And instead of showing consistent concern for her brother, Toundi's sister is herself heard to say, 'Don't let Gullet eat my bananas'. We are asked to believe that she can say this at a moment like this when Toundi is covered with bloodstains and that the crowd outside – which already knows Toundi is in trouble – bursts into laughter.[13] The point is that Oyono himself does not seem to approach this tragic moment with seriousness; he has hinted at that joke before (p. 24); he thought it was a very good one, and so he must seize upon this moment to tell it more precisely. This is the trouble with Oyono's satire. Once he starts to be amused at those on the receiving end of injustice, he finds it difficult to stop and begins to contrive situations to accommodate his largely one-sided satirical vision.

Also, periods of rest or social contact are never used by Oyono's Africans to reflect on their situation but to joke about colonialism. Thus outside the European club the Africans childishly 'hang about . . . to . . . watch the whites enjoying themselves' and willingly have the dog set on them. When Akoma 'King of rings, King of wives' comes to welcome the Commandant he seizes the occasion to stage a childish circus in which he is followed by 'his train; three wives, a porter to carry his chair and the umbrella, a xylophone player and two bodyguards'. Given the mentality of colonial chiefs this may be realistic. But when Sophie who has been deeply insulted by the engineer is left with Toundi, she uses the moment not to reassess her life under colonialism, which has turned her into a prostitute, but to make jocular advances to Toundi, as an attempt to achieve both a momentary sexual identification with blacks, and a temporary light-hearted relief from the engineer. And when the Commandant's wife appears at the market, the African men joke admiringly about her not because she is beautiful as a woman but because she is a beautiful *white* woman.

Later, Toundi tells us, these men hold a discussion. Its sole aim is to glorify, even sanctify, as a group the tantalizing beauty of white womanhood about which each one of them already accepts – after seeing Madame – that there can be no debate. That Mekongo the elder was crippled in a war that was hardly of his own making does not seem to matter, nor would the question why he is today not living like them if his 'comrades were white men, real white men' (pp. 57–8). In *Things Fall Apart* we find that the traditional idea of the elder is mocked. Wisdom under colonialism consists of accepting one's fate. After Okonkwo dies and Obierika the elder says 'That man was one of the greatest men in Umuofia. You drove him to kill himself; and now he will be buried like a dog . . .'[14] we are told that he could not say any more, and the reader is grateful for that. We do not need his wisdom. Having now accepted to be colonized all that Obierika can hold on to is a piece of culture. It is much like Toundi's assumption that because the Commandant has yet to lose his foreskin, Toundi is culturally superior although it will not stop him from being colonized. Okonkwo may or may not have committed an escapist act. For Obierika – whose society never hesitated to fight other black men and has itself in a sense now committed suicide by refusing to fight for the very survival of its economic, political and cultural institutions – is hardly fit to comment on Okonkwo's greatness, let alone bury him in any manner at all. In Oyono, this wisdom is satirized even further. There is, for one, the cook's self-flattering 'voice of wisdom'. We find him advising Toundi on how to survive. Yet he himself cannot realize what his ultimate fate under colonialism must be. Like Evina in *The Old Man and the Medal* who 'had been cook to the priests and had retired to Doum after he had lost his last tooth in the service of the white man', his last days must similarly be spent 'warming himself in the sun and waiting calmly for death.'[15]

We note rather painfully, then, that the gathering to discuss the virtues of white womanhood is not merely one of young men, but an inspired conference of elders who should know better. Mekongo considers himself the wisest elder in the group. There are those of course who, like Mengueme the sycophantic chameleon, are, to borrow from Toundi, already 'wise without travelling'. In the case of Mekongo, his wisdom lies in having lost his leg *without regret*. It is almost as if it is being suggested that to have taken advantage of that foreign conflict to sleep with white women is to have more

than made up for the loss of a mere limb, so that in losing his leg he
is now seen as having taken a very wise step:

> Our ancestors said, 'Truth lies beyond the mountains. You must travel
> to find it.' I have travelled . . . I have slept with white women . . . I can
> answer your question. (p. 57)

This social moment of self-abuse which lasts late into the night
('We have never sat up so late') ends on a fatuous note in which
Mekongo is congratulated by those who are themselves wise
without travelling: 'You were lucky to go to the war.'

Similarly, when the Commandant's wife is suspected of sleeping
with the prison director, an urgent meeting is held in which the
Africans must 'figure out whether it had happened or not'. 'You are
the laundryman,' says the sentry who has in the past been
colonized by Germans also and who, therefore, must consider
himself doubly wise, 'you can have a look at the sheets'. In this vein
also we find them discussing contraceptives 'all afternoon'.

This lack of seriousness is all-embracing. And this is exactly why
they are able to accept Toundi's death so casually, as Toundi
himself seems to do. Given the fact that prisoners of Toundi's type
spend their time dying with no hope of being freed, the first three
pages of the chapter entitled 'Second night at the police camp'
represents, in fact, a funeral procession. The Africans come in one
by one to pay their last respects, ending with dubious last rites by
Obebe the catechist. No real anger is expressed by the visitors at the
unfairness of colonialism, not even by Toundi's sister; only
acceptance, tears and laughter:

> I felt pleased to think that neither the Commandant nor M. Moreau nor
> Sophie's lover . . . nor any other European in Dangan could have stood
> up to it like we did. (p. 115)

The whites for their part are seen by Oyono as reacting more
pragmatically to their colonial situation. They may make jokes
about the colonized but they will never joke about colonialism
itself. Like the Africans who are shown in the one dimension of
fatuousness and immaturity, they too are not shown in a
particularly favourable light. They are seen in very conventional
clichés of Europeans sacrificing themselves in the tropics: the
heartlessness of colonial administrators (the Commandant,
Moreau); the loose moral code (Gullet, Moreau, Madame); the
complaints about the weather ('rain, heat, no hairdresser . . . how
one perspires!' says Mme Salvain. 'How hot it gets!' says Madame);

the unhealthy climate ('I have had fever in the night,' says Gullet 'gravely' after a simple change of environment); the easy bourgeois boredom out of having nothing worthwhile to do (Madame); and the general vacuousness of the colonial female who has nothing to show except pretentious knowledge of her own culture (as when one of the 'pair of sacks' known as the Mesdemoiselles Dubois attempts to talk seriously on music). But regardless of how they are drawn by the author, their strength is that individually and collectively they achieve the general goals of colonialism. They at least are able to act in a *definite* direction.

As a group we find that they might occasionally quarrel among themselves but on crucial colonial matters they must speak the same language. For example, in the interest of French imperialism, the tug of war between M. Fernand and the schoolmaster in the Commandant's Residence must end as a mere academic game; in fact we find M. Salvain argued into silence. M. Salvain is a liberal educationist whose real character emerges earlier in the book when he invites the Commandant to come and inspect his school. He believes, if we may paraphrase his platitudes, that without his educational 'experiment' the African is 'an idle and irresponsible lout whose major vocation in life is sex' (pp. 32–2). The end purpose of the discussion at the Residence is to reaffirm in clear language that 'the African is a child or a fool'. This attitude is very important to them collectively – holds them together – and it is only when there is no more debate on the issue that we see 'The Americans had forgotten everyone else and were now talking in their own language'. Similarly, there is no indication that the love triangle has created lasting hatred between the Commandant and the prison director. We see how quickly the Commandant and his wife make up, as if he has been more hurt by the breach of protocol ('the natives had to know all about it before I did',) than by his wife's behaviour (which he is used to from past experience). Their feelings for France and her imperial aspirations must come first.

As individuals, they act the same way. Father Gilbert for one is here precisely because of the freedom Africa gives his lax personality and it is suggested that he could never obtain this freedom in Europe. His precious symbol is that motor cycle, not the Bible. One of the reasons he wants Toundi is that the motor cycle is difficult to start and someone, preferably black, must push it, since no amount of swearing on the part of a white priest will do. This is particularly crucial on Thursday which is this priest's most important day of the week. On Sunday he obeys the call of duty; on

Thursday he follows his own free instinct, which is to race about with the valid excuse that he is going to collect the mail. And it is not at all surprising that he should die in his favourite sport, where our last image of him is the spectre of a demonic witch:

> This morning, the motor cycle was more difficult than ever to get started . . . I was bathed in sweat from pushing him. He was cursing and swearing and calling the motor cycle names. I had never sen him so on edge. At last after one or two sudden starts and then a thunderous noise he burst away and I caught a glimpse of him through the dust, his body bent slightly forward disappearing at speed like a thing bewitched . . . (p. 17)

But by the time Gilbert dies and is of course buried 'in the corner of the cemetery reserved for Europeans', he has achieved a vital and concrete goal; firmly establishing a colonial church whose proud trademark is racism, where 'The Europeans receive communion separately' sitting on 'armchairs covered with velvet cushions', while the Africans sit *behind* on tree trunks. The latter must stay for the sermon that consists of a pre-meditated brand of vulgarity and wild insults which are the special pride of Father Vandamayer. As a person he is in Africa because he is a sadist and sexual pervert. And here, of course, he also can get away with it. But the point is that by his grace too, and in the memory of Father Gilbert, this eccentric colonial cult can only continue to thrive, and so will colonialism itself. Oyono's whites in this novel will always be the achievers; the Africans never will be.

NOTES

1. Bruno Bettelheim, *The Informed Heart*, a study of the Jews in a Nazi camp, New York, Avon Books, 1971, p. 61.
2. Ferdinand Oyono, *Houseboy*, trans. John Reed, London, Heinemann, reset 1975. All page references are to this edition.
3. Chinua Achebe, *Arrow of God*, London, Heinemann (AWS 16), reprint 1975; New York, Doubleday, 1969.
4. Cheikh Hamidou Kane, *Ambiguous Adventure*, trans. Katherine Woods, London, Heinemann (AWS 119), 1972.
5. Ferdinand Oyono, *The Old Man and the Medal*, London, Heinemann (AWS 39), 1967, p. 39.
6. E. M. Forster, *A Passage to India*, Harmondsworth, Penguin, 1936; New York, Harcourt Brace, 1949.

7. Shakespeare, *The Tempest*. Caliban and his 'vile race' are robbed of their island by Prospero. The only thing left Caliban is language to express his bitter anger and even that is taught him by Prospero's daughter. See Act 1, Scene 2 : 'You taught me language, and my profit on't/Is, I know how to curse.'

8. Paulo Freire, *Pedagogy of the Oppressed*, New York, The Seabury Press, 1968, p. 76.

9. Daniel Defoe, *Moll Flanders*, London, Dent, 1930, first published 1722.

10. In Daniel Defoe's study of economic man, *Robinson Crusoe*, published in 1719, Crusoe completely destroys the former identity of his servant in order to teach him more completely the benefits of European civilization. This primarily means, as M. E. Novak observes in *Defoe and the Nature of Man*, Oxford, Oxford University Press, 1963, p. 37), teaching Friday 'to farm and to accomplish all the tasks which Crusoe had formerly performed for himself', thus leaving Crusoe free to think and to philosophize on life itself.

11. Oyono, op. cit., p. 85.

12. Chinua Achebe, *Things Fall Apart*, London, Heinemann (AWS 1), reset 1976; New York, Fawcett, 1978.

13. *Houseboy*, p. 106 "What's happened?" shouted my countrymen . . .'.

14. Achebe, op cit., p. 147.

15. Oyono, op. cit., p. 18.

F. Odun Balogun

Ideology: Commitment to a Point

Kole Omotoso is a unique phenomenon in contemporary African literature. His uniqueness goes beyond the sense in which every writer, as a possessor of certain peculiar thematic and stylistic characteristics, is unique. His uniqueness derives from the fact that he represents a completely new development in African literature. Unlike the vast majority of our writers, Omotoso does not write about, nor for, the elite classes of our society. In fact, he once said: 'Even if I tried, I couldn't write about the elite.'[1] He concerns himself instead with the common people, and among the common people he singles out the 'dejected, rejected and neglected'.[2] Invariably his characters consist of people for whom suffering has 'become so much routine that they no longer seem to realise that there could be any happiness'.[3] Omotoso, in fact, vividly reminds us of the Dostoevsky of *Poor Folk*, *The Insulted and the Injured*, *The Double*, *Dream of a Ridiculous Man*, *Notes From Underground* and the creator of such characters as the Marmeladovs and Raskolnikov in *Crime and Punishment*. Omotoso also recalls the Dickens of *Oliver Twist*, *David Copperfield*, *A Tale of Two Cities*, *Hard Times*, *Great Expectations* and other works where this English writer depicts exploited and neglected orphans and poor and deprived people.

However, Omotoso's uniqueness does not reside solely in his writing about the 'wretched of the earth'. Other African writers such as Cyprian Ekwensi, Sembene Ousmane and Ngugi wa Thiong'o – to name a prominent few – have done and are still doing the same thing. The difference is that Omotoso has adopted a completely new method of dealing with the problems attendant on writing literature with a mass appeal. He is, for instance, far more ideologically committed than a writer like Ekwensi who is not particularly concerned with strategies for effecting the socio-political reorganization of our society. On the other hand, however, Omotoso is not as committed as someone like Ngugi wa Thiong'o who has embraced the revolutionary Marxist option. Omotoso is not like Ousmane either. The latter has lost faith in the efficacy of the verbal art as a medium of social change and has consequently moved from writing to making films. He believes that the cinema is more immediate and more effective as an instrument of creating social awareness and achieving revolutionary social change. Omotoso, on the other hand, still has faith in the verbal art although he also employs the dramatic medium by writing and producing plays.[4] Dramaturgy is the twin brother of cinematography. What Omotoso does is to devise different ways of making the novel form as immediate and as effective as the cinema, perhaps the most popular of the forms of artistic expression. The means by which he achieves this is the subject of the third part of this article.

It is difficult to pin a precise ideological tag on Omotoso. From his pronouncements it is obvious that he resents elitist writers with their precious concern for bourgeois ideals. He pitches his camp uncompromisingly on the side of the exploited masses:

> Both Chester Himes and Sam Greenlee used the popular genre of the crime story and the thriller to call attention to the situation of the Black American in the American society. I have attempted to do this on two levels – to call attention to our position vis-à-vis the powers within the structure of the Western World that would keep us slaves for ever and within Nigeria to pour venom on our own home-grown tyrants and abetters of our foreign oppressors.[5]

> One of my aims is to be able to awaken the conscience of those who have been able to make it, to the realisation that we can only enjoy what we have made if those who have not made it enjoy being what they are, that is, that the rich men only enjoy their riches, if the poor enjoy poverty.[6]

He is even more emphatic in the following quotation:

> My basic commitment is to writing as a way of life, and also to a specific social ideology: that is, the richer should become poorer, and the poorer richer in a process of levelling up and that except a society like ours accepts that then it is just doomed.[7]

In spite of this Omotoso categorically rejects the role of an activist-writer and even thinks that 'somebody like Chris Okigbo died for nothing'.[8] He would not consider himself a teacher either because he believes that 'it is very presumptuous of a writer to think that he can teach anybody anything'.[9] In fact, he declares: 'But I'm very pessimistic. Wole says there exists a recurrent circle of human stupidity. I quite agree.'[10] And Omotoso actually demonstrates this belief in his play, *The Curse*, where a once exploited and misused servant ends up becoming a highly exploitative and cruel master. Finally, Omotoso does not seem to entertain the hope that literature can act as a positive agent of change in the context of Nigerian society: 'I don't see our society as poised for a change, social change. So whatever you write doesn't touch off anything.'[11]

During a personal discussion with Omotoso in June 1980 the writer confessed that he writes simply because he wants to be a witness to our lives. If anything good results from his witness account, he will be gratified. At the same time if nothing positive happens as a result of his writings, he will not feel aggrieved; in any case, he finds writing a highly therapeutic experience. This, he explains, is a good thing in itself.

Thus it is clear that while Omotoso prefers to highlight the wretched conditions of the poor in our midst, he will not go so far as to champion their cause as a political activist nor does he expect any good to result from his witnessing to their wretchedness. There is a poem by Don Lee which Omotoso loves to quote. This poem probably holds the clue to Omotoso's rather pessimistic view of the efficacy of literature as an instrument of positive social change:

> i ain't seen no poems stop a .38
> i ain't seen no stanzas break a honkie's head
> i ain't seen no metaphors stop a tank
> i ain't seen no words kill
> & if the word was mightier than the sword
> Pushkin wouldn't be fertilizing russian soil/

thus far Omotoso and Don Lee's hero are in agreement. However, they soon part company. Unlike Omotoso, Don Lee's hero believes that the inefficacy of art as an agent of social change dictates the need for a revolutionary option:

> & until my similes can protect me from a night stick
> i guess i'll keep my razor
> & buy me some more bullets[12]

Omotoso has a fundamental ideological reason for rejecting the political activist option as the following quotation shows:

... Literature must not be subservient to any form of political organisation – democratic, progressive, dictatorial, tyrannical or military. Once Literature becomes the voice of a particular political organisation it loses its ability to portray the typical. Moreover there is no perfect political system. Literature as the collective conscience of the community must continue to advance the frontiers of freedom for humanity . . .

In the process of Literature being also concerned with human welfare it finds itself side by side with progressive and revolutionary elements. This is logical given the aspect of Literature's relationship with society and the Revolutionary's concern for change in society. But Literature does not and cannot afford to consider its war won at the end of the successful prosecution of the revolutionary struggle, this is merely one battle in the process of its being of service to human welfare. Literature finds invariably that those with whom it has fought for revolutionary change are forced, in the process of the consolidation of political organisation, to betray those specific causes for which Literature joined the struggle.[13]

It would appear from this that Omotoso is not, in fact, fundamentally opposed to the idea of literature joining the struggle for revolutionary change. Thus his decision not to be an activist must be seen as a personal choice. One therefore wonders why he denies others, Christopher Okigbo for instance, the right to opt for the alternative choice. Omotoso's concern seems to be that literature might be swallowed up, in fact destroyed, once it identifies itself with a particular political organization. He does not believe that such a risk is worth taking since, after all, no organization can establish a perfect political system. This raises the question of the nature of the cooperation Omotoso expects of a literature 'which is concerned with human welfare' with 'progressive revolutionary elements' – a cooperation that Omotoso believes is natural and logical.

Since in Omotoso's view it is not compulsory for a writer to be an activist, the only other way for him to serve the cause of revolutionary social change is by giving moral support to progressive revolutionary elements in terms of the ideas expressed in his work. This probably implies awakening social consciousness in his readers, criticizing societal ills, highlighting the situation of the wretched, insulted, injured, dejected, neglected and rejected and also satirizing exploiters, oppressors and tyrants – all of which actions would help to undermine an inhumane system thereby paving the way for positive change. This is exactly what Omotoso does in his works, and if he remains dissatisfied and sounds pessimistic notes, it is precisely because significant positive change has not yet occurred in Africa in spite of the intensely critical and satirical tone of African literature. This, however, does not confirm the view that literature is ineffectual as an agent of change. Evidence abounds elsewhere to prove that the word can indeed at times be mightier than the sword. Politicians like Lenin, Plekhanov and Trotsky, for instance, would never have succeeded in bringing about the Russian Revolution without the groundwork done by populist Russian writers such as Saltykov-Shchedrin, Nekrasov, Ostrovsky, Goncharov, the early Dostoevsky and others. What the populist writers began was continued and intensified by writers of the Revolutionary Democrats' camp such as Belinsky, Dobrolybov and Shernishevsky. And the eventual success of the Revolution owed a lot to the contribution of activist writers like Gorky and Mayakovsky. It needs to be noted, however, that a hundred years lay between the humanist populist writer, Saltykov-Shchedrin, and the Marxist activist, Mayakovsky. What emerges from all this is not that literature is incapable of causing social changes, but that it takes considerable time for such changes to materialize. In any case, it seems we cannot take Omotoso's pessimism too seriously. Deep down in him there must reside some hope that in the long run his writing, even as the records of a witness, will prove useful. If this were not the case he would have given up writing altogether. For a person with his social concern, writing is not undertaken merely for fame or for material rewards as would be the case with a writer with bourgeois ideals.

In expressing the view that literature is always betrayed by the politicians together with whom it has fought for the revolution, Omotoso is no doubt referring to the Russian experience. His claim that there can be no perfect political system re-echoes the opinion that there can be no 'final revolution' – an ideal expressed by the so-called 'fellow travellers' of the Russian Revolution. A belief in a 'final revolution' implies a belief in the possibility of a perfect political system. A character in a novel by one of the 'fellow travellers' states the case against a 'final revolution' in this manner:

> 'It's unthinkable! Absurd! Don't you realize that what you're planning is a revolution?'
> 'Yes, revolution! Why is this absurd?'
> 'It is absurd because there can be no revolution. Because . . . our revolution was the final one. And there can be no others. Everyone knows this . . .'

'My dear – you are a mathematician. More – you are a philosopher, a
mathematical philosopher. Well, then: name me the final number.'
'What do you mean? . . . I don't understand: What final number?'
'Well, the final, the ultimate, the largest.'
'But that's preposterous! If the number of numbers is infinite, how can
there be a final number?'
'Then how can there be a final revolution? There is no final one;
revolutions are infinite. The final one is for children: children are
frightened by infinity, and it's important that children sleep peacefully
at night . . .'[14]

Like the 'fellow travellers', Omotoso believes that literature can
safeguard its freedom and work for the continual renewal of man
through infinite revolutions only by steering clear of active
political commitment. This naturally would sound false and
idealistic to a writer who believes in political involvement. Such a
writer would think that the only logical step for a writer who
implicitly or explicitly believes in the efficacy of literature as an
agent of social change is total commitment, the more so if such a
writer also believes that a literature concerned with human welfare
is a natural ally of progressive revolutionary elements. Not to take
this logical step would, in the opinion of a poltically committed
writer, amount to taking half measures, a case of partial commitment. But partial or total commitment is a matter of personal choice
and Omotoso is perfectly entitled to whichever he prefers. Besides,
we must not forget that there are those who argue that literature has
no business with any degree of commitment; literature, they say, is
its own purpose and exists only for itself.

Theme: *The Wretched of the Earth*

The ambiguity that characterizes Omotoso's ideology is altogether
absent from his themes. His writing is dominated by a serious
concern for the vast majority of our population who live under
wretched conditions. Omotoso feels a great disquiet about this
unjust situation and has therefore dedicated himself to the task of
exposing the scandal of a society where a few live in what he
describes as a 'wretched opulence'[15] while the majority know only
want, deprivation and suffering. Those who suffer most, as shown
in Omotoso's fiction, are the helpless innocent children of the poor.
They never experience parental or societal tenderness and care.
Instead they are treated callously like the orphans in Dickens'
novels. A typical example is Isaac, a youth who appears in both

Omotoso's second novel, *The Combat*, and his short story entitled 'Isaac'. Isaac was born out of wedlock and left with his grandparents in a provincial town, Akure:

> Moni's child never had a chance. Between the two aging grand-parents, Moni's mother and father, the child didn't have a chance. As far as they were concerned, the child was merely an extension of their ageing limbs. He would run errands for them. He would go to the market for them. He would do everything for them, and in return they would do nothing for him. He could die, for all they cared. But as long as he lived, he was an extension of their feeble limbs. (*The Combat*, p. 72)

It is not surprising therefore that Isaac takes to the streets most of the time in order to escape his insensitive grandparents and to hunt for food. In the end he is run over and killed by a car. Significantly, the short story identifies the car as a Mercedes Benz Sports belonging to a wealthy young man.

The fate of almost all the children in Omotoso's works is uniformly tragic. Another child is run over in *To Borrow A Wandering Leaf* and we are given the significant detail that his death is caused by the motorcade of a touring head of state. In *The Edifice* a four-year-old boy is drowned in a well by his grandparents because he is a half-caste. Duro, a little girl, is burnt alive in 'Firelash', while Patrick, an infant boy, is sacrificed to make an ineffectual medicine that was to have ensured wealth for the murderer. This happens in a story appropriately entitled, 'The Victim'. Although the schoolboy, Lasisi, escapes death in the story 'Miracles Take a Little Longer', the boy suffers a whole year lying in a hospital receiving treatment for total paralysis. In 'The Gamblers' we meet Kunle, another schoolboy, who is grief-stricken because he might be expelled from school for not paying his fees. As if this were not enough misfortune, the only money he has is tricked out of him by gamblers with whom he is travelling. Unable to pay his fare at the end of the journey, the driver strips him naked and takes away his school shirt.

Against this grim background of unmitigated misery and tragedy daily experienced by the children of the poor, Omotoso paints the contrasting picture of love, tenderness and care constantly lavished on the children of the rich. Dr Mrs Flor Siwaju, the wife of Dr Siwaju, the chief character in *Sacrifice*, for instance, recalls:

> One evening recently I went for a walk. . . . But that evening, the harmattan returned with a vengeance and I needed to wear a sweater to keep the thin sharp cold fingers of harmattan away from my

body. . . . As I walked I saw a little boy far in front of me, . . . It became my objective to overtake him and talk to him. . . . He had never been to school because his brother said that he must be a drum maker. But he would have liked to go to school because of the uniform. The question is, what kind of love was expressed in sending such a young child to that distance and telling him to come, no matter what time, that same evening, walking? What chance has he got against our child? Yet both of them are growing up in the same country and would be faced with the same problems, the same demands. Should such inequalities be permitted? (*Sacrifice*, pp. 45–7)

The question posed by Dr Mrs Siwaju is the question Omotoso wishes his society to answer and this is why he has depicted the tragic fates of his children–protagonists.

Women come after children in Omotoso's pathetic gallery of the wretched of the earth. The ruthlessness displayed by men in their treatment of women is paralleled only by the callousness with which the society treats children. Dele for instance brings Daisy, his white wife, from Britain and heartlessly abandons her in Lagos, totally unmindful of 'all the social spite' she had endured on his account while they were still in the racist British metropolis, London. This novel, *The Edifice*, closes with Daisy heartbroken and wretched. The fate of Omolara, the heroine of *The Scales*, is even more pathetic. Chief Daniran, an impotent pervert, who makes millions of naira by crippling people and thereafter enlisting them in his begging enterprise, quickly arranges the death of Omolara, his 'wife', the moment he suspects she is about to reveal his secret. She is run over by the agents of Chief Daniran who continues to live in superfluous luxury while his crippled army of beggars live in want, misery and disease, often dying of wounds inflicted in Chief Daniran's special laboratory for crippling prospective beggars. Chief Daniran represents the millions of people who thrive on the misery they deliberately cause men and women. Unfortunately, women are those who most easily fall prey to men such as Chief Daniran.

If children are helpless victims of society, some women prove capable of taking revenge on a society that has brutalized them. Moni and Mary, the female protagonists of *The Combat* and *Sacrifice* respectively, are examples of such women. Each had been seduced as a young girl and later abandoned with child; and each had eventually become a prostitute. Moni prospers and becomes Dee Madam, a woman with money and personality who can therefore afford to choose her man. Although not as prosperous as

Dee Madam, Mary is equally successful. She trains her son to become a medical doctor and takes pleasure in giving venereal diseases to her customers. She passionately hates men, and destroying her clients with disease is her way of taking revenge on the men who had destroyed her life.

Omotoso further stresses the great injustice directed against women by men and society in general by depicting women as generous beings who deserve sympathy, respect and love:

> Women were made to sacrifice. They are the ones who are always ready to forget the past, and face the future. They are the ones who are capable of forgetting the past in the hope of a great future. And when that dream turns ashen, then they start anew, hoping, dreaming of another future. They alone have any historical perspective to life. (*Sacrifice*, p. 66)

Omotoso also shows concern for the plight of minorities. Even the unlikable Dele, the chief protagonist of *The Edifice*, is treated with great sympathy. Omotoso's sympathy for him emanates from the fact that Dele represents African students in Britain who suffer as an oppressed minority in a hostile foreign environment. But when Dele returns home and starts behaving uncharitably towards his British wife, Daisy, who is now a member of a minority in Nigeria, Omotoso loses sympathy for Dele and starts depicting him with devastating irony and criticism.

Omotoso also displays the same sympathy towards the people of the village whom he portrays as the underdogs of city-dwellers. Young girls, for instance, who leave their village or provincial town for the city invariably suffer the fate of the heroines of Ekwensi's stories. Moni becomes a prostitute after arriving in Lagos from a provincial town, Akure. The scenes on the streets of backward Aiyede and the villages surrounding it (*To Borrow A Wandering Leaf*), as well as the scenes at the forgotten Akure (*Sacrifice*, *Miracles*), compel sympathy when compared with the scenes on the streets of the comparatively opulent Ibadan (*The Scales*) and Lagos (*The Edifice*, *The Combat*, *Fella's Choice*), not to mention the beauty of Hotel de La Mare in Abidjan (*Fella's Choice*) and the beauty of London (*The Edifice*, *Fella's Choice*). The people in the villages are constantly subjected to oppression and exploitation at the hands of petty tyrants such as the Bale and the Prince at Aiyede. In fact, the difference between the few village rich – as represented by the Bale and the Prince – on the one hand, and the poor villagers who are in the majority on the other hand, is so great that one character is forced into these revolutionary reflections:

> The situation in the village was deteriorating. There were far too few
> people who had everything. Sooner or later the many who had nothing
> would realize that the few who had everything held on to it because
> those who had nothing did nothing. The day they realized that property
> was not sacrosanct, that the earth belongs to all and that its fruits
> should be used to feed all her children, then living in the village would
> be different. For that day I had to prepare.
>
> *(To Borrow A Wandering Leaf,* p. 111)

Finally, Africa is often depicted in Omotoso's novels as the
underdog of Europe, the purpose being to awaken our consciousness as Africans and to stir the conscience of those who for
centuries have exploited us economically. A typical example is
The Combat where foreign powers, using their embassies, wade
into a purely local and brotherly quarrel and help to intensify the
conflict until the matter grows completely beyond imaginable
proportions and ends in disaster and tragedy. The case of *Fella's
Choice* is even more scandalous. Here a fanatical group of white
racists is planning to either wipe out black men from the surface of
the earth or else reduce Africans to mere docile animals who will
always do whatever their white masters bid them. And almost
everywhere in his works Omotoso recalls the African past of
slavery, colonization and exploitation at the hands of Europeans.
In fact, Omotoso makes us conscious of the fact that our African
past is still very much with us and that like Dr Siwaju in *Sacrifice*
we have a massive problem on our hands deciding how to cope
with this disgraceful past. The suggestion in the novel is that if we
are not careful, we will mess things up like Dr Siwaju, and create
greater misery and tragedy for ourselves.

In fact, a considerable amount of space is devoted in Omotoso's
novels to the debate as to how the problems of Africa can be solved.
This debate is often rather uncomfortably direct and pointed but
that is perhaps because Omotoso wants to stress its importance. In
The Edifice, for instance, African students in London are
constantly debating the ways to achieve the salvation of Africa.
Unfortunately, however, as soon as these students return home to
Africa they conveniently forget their idealistic debates and
become, instead, political opportunists constantly seeking ways to
exploit their less fortunate brothers. This is the sad fate of Dele, the
major character of this novel.

But it is perhaps in *The Scales* that Omotoso most thoroughly and consistently discusses the means of bringing salvation to Africa. Here the question goes beyond mere academic debate to the level of practical action. The option of abandoning idealism and making common cause with the exploiters of Africa is first considered by the hero, Barri Jogunde, but it is immediately dismissed. Barri is a hero who combines in his person both the idealism of Ofeyi and the ruthless Machiavellianism of Demakin — two major characters in Soyinka's *Season of Anomy*. Like Ofeyi, Barri tries to work within the system but he is painfully disillusioned:

> He was not angry with those who had beaten him to this living death. He was not angry with them as individuals. He was only sorry for himself that he had hoped to work inside the system, to fight from within. He smiled ruefully. To work from within. To join them hadn't sounded as foul as it would have if this aim of fighting from within, this hope of being able to effect change from inside the house, this pious expectation, if all these laudable aims hadn't been part of his attitude at that time. But what aims? What hope! What pity! What naivety!!! It couldn't work. You only made it worse. made it worse for the one who would change things. You couldn't complain of the foundation of a house as being weak, improperly laid, badly put together and then watch the walls being built on that foundation. You permit the roof to be placed. Then you move with them into the house telling everyone that you were going into the house to put it right. What ego-centric stupidity! What self-centred emptiness! What a lie of a life, a life of lies! Why not simply earn your keep and spare everybody the tedium of excuses?

> (*The Scales*, pp. 73–4)

After this, Barri decides on the violent revolutionary option in the spirit of Demakin. His reason for choosing this option is that he knows that people like Daniran 'are the first to condemn the use of pain, cruelty and violence to change what they have erected on the pillars of pain, cruelty and violence'. Besides he is now convinced that 'the only way to tame a wild horse is by mounting him' (p. 96). But even though, like Demakin, Barri resolves on selective elimination of obnoxious exploiters like Chief Daniran, he, unlike Demakin, will not act alone. Barri thus rejects the individualist approach and goes out to form a socialist commune of 'gentlemen of courage and conviction' whom he lectures in a language reminiscent of Armah's *Two Thousand Seasons*:

'We, Gentlemen of Courage and Conviction, we are the vanguard of a new way of life; we are the spearheads of a renewed system of thinking which sees man as man. Man whose skin must never be broken in the necessary search for food, clothing and shelter. Man, as the person to be accumulated and preserved not manipulated and expended in the wish to acquire things. The connecting link between profit-making and human misery is greed. Greed says 'I must have. All beings in my way must go. Details are anyone's guess.' Know therefore, Gentlemen of Courage and Conviction, that you are the front line of a turning point in our history. We despised and neglected our ways because we were made to feel that the British way, the American way, all marked Profit Way was the only way, the Universal way. We knew nothing of other alternatives, valid altruistic ways from Ancient Amerindian ways to the ways of ancient China, India and Egypt. Now that alternatives dawn on us, are we not encouraged to dust our ways, patch it here and there from modern experience and walk our way?

'Gentlemen of Courage and Conviction, we as instrument may fail. That is not unusual. The Knife edge may get blunted, but the cause of cutting down weeds must go on. We are mere instruments in the cause of preserving humanity, our way, the same way. If we fail, others will go on and succeed. Let us go!'

(*The Scales*, pp. 97–8)

It is also significant that Barri's communalistic soldiers defeat Chief Daniran's army of mercenaries because the latter were engaged in enjoyment, feasting and drinking on the eve of battle just as the defeated Arab army of occupation were in *Two Thousand Seasons*.

Barri's experimentation with revolutionary communalism – another idea borrowed from *Two Thousand Seasons* – succeeds but, unfortunately, the author represents this even as being only an experiment and not something permanent. Thus, at the end of the novel the reader is still left with the vital question: Where do we go from here?

Perhaps the direction is that suggested in the story 'Miracles Take A Little Longer'. This solution requires patience, determination, resourcefulness and the ability to synthesize the best aspects of two worlds:

You, for instance, are a Nigerian son of a native doctor qualified in British medicine. Could you not combine both to produce something to cure paralysis?

(*Miracles*, p. 87)

The doctor in question accepts this challenge and after a year of persistent effort accompanied by many failures, he finally discovers such a cure. This is a miracle. Is Omotoso suggesting that we must perform such a miracle to save Africa from her cultural, economic and political paralysis? We do not know, but what we do know is that Omotoso is ruthless in castigating all those who caused this paralysis in the past and those others who are consolidating the disease today. As is evident from the case of Chief Daniran in *The Scales*, Omotoso simultaneously does two things in his fiction: he enlists the reader's sympathy for the wretched victims in our midst at the same time as he provokes the reader's wrath against those who cause agony and suffering for others. In his satire against negative traits in individuals and in society, hardly anyone is spared the painful sting of his irony. Omotoso attacks the stupid head of state who honours a visiting foreign dignitory by 'ordering that a black figure pissing in the streets with a parabola of water coming from his fly should be put in the middle stripe of our national flag' (*Sacrifice*, p. 94), the petty Prince and Bale of Aiyede who notoriously exploit their wretched subjects (*To Borrow A Wandering Leaf*), the foreign imperialists, the 'home-made exploiters' (*The Edifice*, p. 114), the politicians 'who had fought for independence and now think that the country is theirs as an inheritance from the colonial overlord' (*Fella's Choice*, p. 81), the 'University contractor – lecturers who do not know how to contain their local success stories' (*Sacrifice*, p. 122), foreign embassies, churches – both of which fan the quarrel of two brothers so completely out of proportion that tragedy ensues (*The Combat*) – the elites with their 'wretched opulence' in the midst of want (*Sacrifice*, p. 12), the poor commoners when they deserve castigation, civilians, men in uniform,[16] Africans as individuals and as a people (note, for instance, Dr Kofi Mensah's indictment of the African personality in *Fella's Choice*), absurd social customs such as public mournings turned into public displays, social ills such as corruption and exploitation, public corporations such as NEPA (*The Combat*, p. 94) and professional bodies such as the press.[17] Nothing, absolutely nothing that contributes to make Africa backward and underdeveloped and helps to increase the number of the 'neglected, dejected and rejected' in our midst is spared the poison of Omotoso's corroding satire.

Style: Complexity in Simplicity

Omotoso's approach to the genre of the novel is highly innovative in the context of African literature. Most African novelists write about, and more importantly for, the elites. Consequently their works hardly interest the masses even on the rare occasions when they are written about the masses. Omotoso believes that the novel can be as interesting to the masses as the cinema which they generally patronize, if the novelist makes his themes more relevant and his style more accessible to the common man. Our discussion so far has revealed that Omotoso's themes are highly pertinent to the everyday reality of the common man. As we proceed it will also become evident that Omotoso conscientiously seeks to make his style comprehensible to his select audience, the masses. He outlines what it takes to do this:

> Simplicity of language and of technique is one of the most important characteristics of any literature whose appeal must be to the masses of the people. Other characteristics are that such a literature must be brief and that it must be cheap.[18]

It is precisely because Omotoso wanted to cater for the reading taste of his select audience that he branched out into the sub-genre of crime novels and spy stories which are avidly devoured by the common man in Africa. If this type of fiction is considered rubbish, Omotoso's answer is that 'it is ultimately better for us to consume our own rubbish than to hanker after foreign rubbish'.[19]

If there is any one single word that adequately defines Omotoso's style of writing, that word is simplicity. This simplicity is primarily reflected in the way he has further reduced the size of the novel. African novels are generally short but Omotoso's are exceptionally brief, ranging from between 88 to 155 pages. His novels would have been more properly defined as novellas but for the fact that thematically and stylistically they are more comprehensive in scope. Unlike the novella, which presents only some limited aspects of life, Omotoso's novels depict life in its totality. His fiction succeeds in combining comprehensibility in thematic scope, characterization and point of view with slimness in volume because the second hallmark of his style is economy. The economy of Omotoso's style is similar to that which characterizes the narrative technique of the short story, a genre that specializes in isolating individual moments in life. Omotoso includes nothing superfluous in his narrative and he is brief almost to a fault. Omotoso would, no doubt, agree with Taban lo Liyong who writes:

A Story doesn't have to have many characters in it. In this one, for example, we have two people, and we feel they are enough. One is he, the visitor from the country, and the other is him, the object of the visit. The subject, I may add, is the visit of he to town.

As we feel that what he ate for breakfast that morning has no relevance whatsoever on the visit, nor the colour of the sky while he passed through the countryside, nor how sharp his nose is, nor how blue his eyes – in fact, since we feel that these extraneous things other writers use for fleshing up scanty stories are not constitutional ingredients of the story, we shall cut them out – for the readers' benefit. We understand our readers are busy people, rushing from one phase of life to another.[20]

The following extensive passage from *To Borrow A Wandering Leaf* is in several respects characteristic of Omotoso's narrative style. Consequently it will be examined closely with a view to pointing out those qualities that the passage shares in common with other works by Omotoso:

Throughout the village, dust powdered everything, turning the green to dust-desiccated dryness. Throughout the village.

Simide, wife of Chief Atoba, has a buka here. I ate there in those days of market days and weaver birds. Now I saw her bent over a small pot boiling okro. I strolled over and offered greetings. She answered as if I was a visitor of twenty years duration used to seeing me everyday, not a man unseen for over a year. Lack of cheer and I felt she hadn't seen me. Her okro was white. In front of her were two bottles, almost empty; one of palm oil and the other of salt. She picked up the salt bottle and addressed the pot of soup.

'Okro soup, okro bubbling soup listen to me. Salt is plenty in the world, and salt I bring to you. Accept and taste salt in my mouth.'

Three times she touched the small pot of soup with the bottle of salt. She put the bottle of salt away and picked up that of palm oil.

'Okro soup, drawing okro soup hearken to me. Oil is plenty, we swim in it. Oil I bring to you. Freshen us with the memory of oil and nourish us.' She thrice touched the boiling pot with the bottle of palm oil. Then she called her daughter:

'Bunmi, take these bottles into the house.'

'You have put oil and salt in the soup, Mama?'

'I have put them. Keep your mouth shut and take the bottles away.'

She brought down the pot and put another one on the fire. She cut up three plantains and boiled them. Bunmi, fourteen, pounded the plantain and I refused to eat when I was invited. Was that the day I arrived? Or was it another day? Of gaiety and noise, oily-oil mouth, noise of munching and the sucking of marrows? When did I arrive? (pp. 39–40).

The first thing that claims attention in this passage is its characteristic linguistic simplicity. The language is easily comprehensible to those who have not gone beyond the School Certificate level. Local words easily recognizable by the common man, such as 'buka', 'okro', 'plantain', 'palm oil', 'market days' predominate in the vocal outcry. As is usual with Omotoso, the activity described here is familiar to his audience – in this case, the traditional process of cooking soup. If we realized that the incident encapsulated here in a page could stand on its own as a complete short story, we would be able to appreciate fully the economy of Omotoso's style. Although in Omotoso's characteristic manner the passage is full of individual realistic details, we notice at the same time that nothing is superfluous. In fact, a lot has been left out, and readers are expected to use their imagination to supply the omission. Often, when unnecessary details are excluded, the resulting sentence is telegraphic and grammatically incomplete as in 'Lack of cheer and I felt she hadn't seen me . . . Was that the day I arrived? Or was it another day? Of gaiety and noise, oily-oil mouth, noise of munching and the sucking of marrows? When did I arrive?'

Here too, we notice the usual fast tempo of Omotoso's narration which is achieved with a succession of short simple sentences or with brief dramatic dialogues that are memorable for their terseness and masculinity of tone. It is this masculinity of tone, this sparseness of detail and, above all, this strong control over the emotions, that have saved Omotoso's novels from sentimentality. The story of this abjectly poor woman, pathetic as it is, does not move us to tears; instead it provokes our anger against the injustice of society, the more so since in the same village the Bale, the Prince and other members of the village elite live in affluence – an affluence achieved through exploitation of the poorer members.

Noteworthy also in the last paragraph of the above quotation is the repetition of words, phrases and sentences of similar syntactical structures, a device Omotoso is fond of employing in order to achieve linguistic simplicity and some degree of poetic cadence. On many occasions Omotoso's prose attains the beauty of poetry through the use of folkloric elements, for example when the old woman speaks in a manner that recalls the incantatory tone of traditional prayer:

'Okro soup, okro bubbling soup listen to me. Salt is plenty in the world, and salt I bring to you. Accept and taste salt in my mouth.'

'Okro soup, drawing okro soup hearken to me. Oil is plenty, we swim in it. Oil I bring to you. Freshen us with the memory of oil and nourish us.'

Generally, Omotoso loves to incorporate folkloric elements into his narration. His pages teem with proverbs, riddles, puzzles, puns and sentences cast in the mode of folk speech. Here are some examples:

This time you have climbed the tree beyond its leaves and you have yourself to blame.

(*The Scales*, p. 60)

If the blacksmith does not die, might he not yet fashion another knife, better than the one that was lost?

(*The Edifice*, p. 118)

Let Jilo return the vessel after he has collected his shipload.[21]

(*To Borrow A Wandering Leaf*, p. 146)

Passages where folkloric elements such as these occur acquire additional beauty and their aesthetic satisfaction is further heightened by sentences that reveal Omotoso's humorous and original, if ironic, mind:

I wished for an ivory tower, I found towering foolery.

'What are you working on now?'
'On my two legs, that's what I am walking on!'

(*To Borrow A Wandering Leaf*, pp. 6–7, 9)

In the new era of city boom and village doom the wealth of a household was enveloped in a letter from a son in the city. ('The End of Johnbool', pp. 51–2)

But such tarred memories this road had were bumps in its centre now.

(*The Scales*, p. 10)

The cracked lips of the village river.

Lightning and thunder slashed the sky into shreds of blackness.

(*Sacrifice*, pp. 83, 109)

'I usually trailed the motorcades, follow the rush of leadership hurrying through the people, over the people, by the people, for the people, and felt myself part of it.'

(*To Borrow A Wandering Leaf*, p. 11)

This was his sandwich – first page bread, second page akara, and third page bread; or simply akara in hard-back.

(*The Combat*, p. 4)

A more subtle and not so easily definable quality of the story about the old woman and her okro soup is the relationship between reality, on the one hand, and fantasy, on the other. Cooking soup – particularly okro soup – is a simple, mundane, realistic exercise. Yet in the passage this activity is imperceptibly transformed into a spiritual experience, steeped in mystery, prayer, magic and esoteric communication with higher, other worldly powers. Suddenly we are no longer dealing with an ordinary okro soup but with a spiritual essence commanding supernatural forces:

Okro soup, okro bubbling soup listen to me. Salt is plenty in the world, and salt I bring you. Accept and taste salt in my mouth.'

'Okro soup, drawing okro soup hearken to me . . .'

Without warning reality is replaced with fantasy. This is what happens on a grander scale in *The Combat*, where the transition from reality to fantasy is so elusive that the reader is surprised when he finally discovers that as the novel progresses, reality steadily recedes further and further. On the other hand, with every successive minute more and more fantastically improbable things happen. What is most significant is that all these improbable incidents are actually reported as if they were probable. The short story 'The Protest of the Dead' is Omotoso's latest experiment in this style. Here reality is not allowed to intrude even for a moment because the improbable begins to happen right from the start.

This type of narrative technique, defined as 'Marvellous Realism' by Omotoso,[22] is not new in African literature, having been immortalized by Tutuola, who himself appropriated the device from folklore, where it is still very much alive today. There is, however, a greater subtlety in the way Omotoso handles the device.

Like Achebe, Omotoso is fond of inserting brief digressive narratives into the main story of his novel. In Achebe these narratives are usually anecdotes that serve as comic relief, whereas in Omotoso the stories are usually heavily burdened with tragic undertones. The story about the old woman and her okro soup is an example. In the same vein is the depressing anecdote about a prime minister who after publicly urinating in the streets and in the presence of a visiting foreign delegation seeks to immortalize his indecency by ordering that 'a black figure pissing in the streets with a parabola of water coming from his fly should be put in the middle stripe of our national flag' (*Sacrifice*, p. 94).

In the bid to make his novels simple, clear and accessible to his chosen non-elite audience, Omotoso often uses a simple plot structure; his stories are largely narrated from a straightforward first-person point of view. The type of tragedy his novels examine is modern tragedy which the common man can more readily understand because he experiences it in his daily life. Unrelieved wretchedness is something the poor man can identify with whereas the portrayal of the tragic flaws of heroic characters in works tailored to the demands of classical tragedy will not make sense to him. Even when presenting his tragic stories, Omotoso takes care to ensure that the ordinary reader understands everything by proceeding in a methodical manner, showing how trivial events in life gradually acquire tragic proportions.[23] A simple quarrel between two good friends, for instance, soon develops into a combat involving foreign powers (*The Combat*).

The principle of characterization in Omotoso's works is typicality. This is because Omotoso believes in a 'collective rather than individual working out of our salvation'.[24] Consequently, he portrays characters who subsume in their persons the qualities of many, of a group, rather than esoteric individuals lost in personal psychologies. The typical represents the majority, and in our society the majority are the poor, the dejected, neglected and rejected. Therefore Omotoso devotes his time to presenting characters who stand for the different categories among this wretched majority. Isaac, for instance, typifies the unfortunate children of the poor; Mary, the women forced into prostitution; Dele, African students abroad; and so on. Even in his detective novels (*Fella's Choice* and *The Scales*) Omotoso, who is a pioneer in this genre of fiction in Africa, departs from the stock character, the superman, typical in this type of writing. Instead of a James Bond performing superhuman feats, Omotoso depicts Fella and Barri – two ordinary human beings with human frailties who nearly lose their lives preventing crimes but for the timely intervention of their comrades. Without his army, Barri could never have defeated Chief Daniran; and Fella succeeds in destroying the agents of BOSS (International) only because of the cooperation of Joko, the boatman and others. Unlike traditional detective novels, which stress personal heroism and individualism, Omotoso's detective novels stress unity and collective effort in achieving a common goal. This is their moral.

As in folk tale, a genre that is more familiar to the masses than to the elites, Omotoso's stories always have a moral. This message is usually undisguised, simple and easily identifiable, although it is not usually spelled out as is normally done in folk tales.

Western publishers might, understandably, be reluctant to publish works with strong anti-capitalist ideologies such as characterize the novels of Omotoso. In any case, these publishers' readers are sure to classify his works as mere socialist propaganda. Moreover, books published abroad usually cost much more than the common man can comfortably afford. These are some of the considerations that made Omotoso turn to indigenous publishers who have produced all but the first two of his novels. Omotoso, in fact, had to subsidize some of his locally published works so that they would be cheap enough for the common man to afford. One of the advantages that have accrued to him from publishing locally is that he has been able to write to the taste of his audience. This, among other things, has led to the proliferation in Omotoso's works of untranslated Yoruba words and songs and a wide use of Yoruba speech patterns as reflected in proverbs, puzzles, puns, riddles and in the names of his characters. Foreigners now find it more taxing to understand his works while conversely his African audience finds itself more at home with them.

Thanks to their economy, simplicity of language and technique and low cost, any literate worker who so desires can buy, read and understand the novels of Omotoso. However, it will be naïve to expect that such a worker will comprehend their meaning fully. The reason for this is that beneath their surface simplicity, Omotoso's works usually conceal great complexity. Only a sophisticated reader, for instance, can fully appreciate those of his works written in the style of 'Marvellous Realism'. The ordinary reader will follow only the surface story. At times this style is so subtle that even a sophisticated critic can miss the point, as revealed in Cheryl M. L. Dash's comment on *The Combat*: 'there are loose ends ... And the snowballing of events is out of all proportion to the original incident which is supposed to have started it all'.[25] Apparently, Cheryl Dash had read the novel as if it were a 'realistic' work. In any case, she is so biased against works with obvious moral and unpalatable ideologies that it would have been a marvel if she had seen anything good in Omotoso's novels.

A literature that operates on the level of fantasy, as does 'Marvellous Realism', is usually highly symbolic. There is a complex network of symbolic meanings attached to characters, events and things even in the simplest of Omotoso's novels and stories. Mary, the heroine of *Sacrifice*, for instance, is not only the past and the shame of her son, Dr Siwaju, but also a symbolic representation of Africa's shameful past of slavery and colonialism. Her prostitution earned the money that trained Siwaju as a medical doctor. In the same way, slavery and colonialism, which her prostitution represents, made Africa what it is today. Can Dr Siwaju forget by whom and how he was trained? Can he forget this shameful past? Or should he try to whitewash its ugliness? Can we as Africans ignore the ugly reality of our recent past or even romanticize it? These are the questions posed through the medium of symbols in *Sacrifice*. It is doubtful if any ordinary worker will understand the novel at this level.

Omotoso uses the first person narrator in both a simple and complex way. In his novels the first person narrator tells his story in a clear, straightforward, understandable manner, and is therefore simple. Complications develop, however, because the first person narrator often changes. The first half of *The Edifice*, for instance, is narrated by Dele in the first person, while the second half is narrated by Daisy, also using the first person. This device becomes even more complex in *Sacrifice*, where the first person pronoun, 'I', stands first for Mary, then for her son, Dr Siwaju, and later for Flor, the wife of Dr Siwaju. As this 'I' constantly keeps shifting between these characters, one is at times at a loss to identify who exactly is speaking at a given moment. The situation is made even more complex by the constant use of flashbacks to illuminate the same events in the past using different first person points of view. In fact, the story often begins to make sense only if we relate the confused form of narration to the confused state of mind of the three characters who cannot resolve the problem confronting them. In other words, Omotoso has very subtly made his form reflect his subject matter. Only the sophisticated reader can grasp this aspect of the novel.

In fact, Omotoso's most successful works are those in which outward simplicity and inner complexity are artfully balanced. This is why *The Combat* and *Sacrifice* are the most aesthetically rewarding of his works. It is for the same reason that Omotoso's latest novel, *To Borrow A Wandering Leaf*, is the least successful. Here the shifting narration is not well handled and there is confusion in identity. Are Rekia and Rekhia the same character? Similarly, are Uluro Laniya and Aina Laniya one and the same person? The different parts of the novel are also not well integrated. Why is it that on page 147 we hear that a marriage already celebrated on page 95 is going to take place? And as is usual with most of Omotoso's novels, there are many typographical errors and even cases of clumsy, ambiguous sentences.[26]

The greatest defect of *To Borrow A Wandering Leaf*, however, is that it fails to justify the expectations it raises at the beginning. The panoramic presentation of events and characters, the grave and at times philosophical tone associated with individuals such as Akowe and Kobina, the use of the form of the quest novel which invites a mythological interpretation – all of these raise the hope of a serious content to be revealed during the unusual trek. This hope is, however, frustrated. The subject matter turns out to be much more trivial than expected. Furthermore, instead of combining surface clarity with inner complexity as is usual in Omotoso's novels, this one dispenses with the former and assiduously cultivates the latter. It appears as if the author is consciously attempting to make the work difficult and, consequently, juxtaposes events in a random fashion in order to achieve ambiguity, obscurity and difficulty of comprehension. Is this the sign of things to come? Is Omotoso changing his audience and his aesthetic? Only future works by him will tell.

Up to now Omotoso's works have not been receiving the critical attention they deserve. This, however, is not surprising: it always takes some time before we get used to something new, the more so if this new thing challenges our cherished attitudes. Omotoso is challenging the aesthetic canons of a literature written by the elites for the elites. He is substituting instead the revolutionary aesthetic of a populist literature. We are understandably scandalized, but it is to be hoped that we soon recover from our shock and settle down to a serious, objective and critical examination of this new literature.

It follows from the above analysis that to give a correct assessment of Omotoso's achievements as a novelist, the critic must overcome personal biases and take account of Omotoso's aesthetic as a writer of a mass-oriented literature. Peter Nazareth understands this necessity and hence his analysis of Omotoso's works is objective, penetrating, perceptive and therefore useful.[27]

NOTES

1. Kole Omotoso being interviewed by John Agetua sometime between July 1973 and August 1974; see John Agetua (ed.), *Interviews with Six Nigerian Writers*, Benin City, Bendel Newspapers Corporation, p. 14. Date of publication is not stated.
2. ibid.
3. Kole Omotoso, 'Miracles Take a Little Longer', *Miracles and Other Stories*, Ibadan, Onibonoje Publishers, 1978, rev. edn, p. 93.
4. Omotoso has written three plays: *Pitched Against the Gods* (1969), which has not been published but has been performed several times and has won a prize; *The Curse*, which was published by New Horn Press, Ibadan, 1975; and *Shadows in the Horizon* which was published personally by the author at Ile-Ife in 1977.
5. Kole Omotoso, 'Crime Novels and Spy Stories', an unpublished article, p. 1.
6. Agetua, op. cit., p. 14.
7. ibid., p. 16.
8. ibid.
9. ibid., p. 12.
10. ibid., p. 15.
11. ibid.
12. Don Lee, 'Sketches from a Black-Nappy-Headed Poet' in R. Barksdale and K. Kinnamon (eds), *Black Writers of America: A Comprehensive Anthology*, New York, Macmillan, 1972, p. 809. This poem serves as epigraph to Omotoso's unpublished article, 'The Ritual Dream of Art'. Omotoso also declaimed it during a public lecture in February 1980, in Benin City as guest speaker of the English and Literature Students' Association of the University of Benin.
13. Kole Omotoso, 'Producing Literature for the Masses in a Developing Nation: The Nigerian Experience', a paper presented at the Independent Papua New Guinea Writers' Conference, 1–4 July 1976, pp. 1–2.
14. Evgeny Zamyatin, *We*, trans. Mirra Ginsburg, New York, Bantam, 1972, p. 174. This question is discussed in great detail in Leon Trotsky's book, *Literature and Revolution*, trans. Rose Strunsky, Ann Arbor, The University of Michigan Press, 1971, pp. 256, and in Zamyatin's book of essays, *A Soviet Heretic*, trans. Mirra Ginsburg, Chicago, University of Chicago Press, 1970, pp. 322.
15. Kole Omotoso, *Sacrifice*, Ibadan, Onibonoje, 1978 rev. edn, p. 12, first published in 1974. Altogether Omotoso has written six novels. The other five are: *The Edifice*, London, Heinemann (AWS 102), 1971; *The Combat*, London, Heinemann (AWS 122), 1972; *Fella's Choice*, Benin,

Ethiope Publishing Corporation, 1974; *The Scales*, Ibadan, Onibonoje, 1976; and *To Borrow A Wandering Leaf*, Akure, Fagbamigbe, 1978. He has also published a collection of short stories under the title, *Miracles*, Ibadan, Onibonoje, 1973, revised 1978. Quotations will be indicated in parenthesis in the body of the essay where possible; and in the cases of *Sacrifice* and *Miracles* citations are from the 1978 revised editions.

16. See Omotoso's story 'The End of Johnbool', *Top Life*, May 1979, pp. 28–9 and 50–1.

17. See Omotoso's story 'The Protest of the Dead', to appear in *Positive Review*, no. 4.

18. Omotoso, 'Producing Literature for the Masses', op cit., p. 7.

19. Omotoso, 'Crime Novels and Spy Stories', op. cit., p. 5.

20. Taban lo Liyong, 'He and Him', *Fixions*, London, Heinemann (AWS 69), 1978, p. 32.

21. 'The Vessel' is actually a woman illegally impregnated by her physician and 'the shipload' is the expected child.

22. Kole Omotoso, *The Form of the African Novel*, Akure, Fagbamigbe, 1979, pp. 24 and 68–70.

23. I had the opportunity in 1978 of supervising the research of Isaac Ufomata, who wrote his final year essay on Omotoso under the title, 'How the Trivial Becomes the Tragic: A Study of Kole Omotoso's Novels'. A copy of this twenty-page essay is in the library of the University of Benin, Benin City, Nigeria.

24. Omotoso, 'Crime Novels and Spy Stories', op. cit., p. 1.

25. Cheryl M. L. Dash, 'Introduction to the Prose Fiction of Kole Omotoso', *World Literature Written in English*, vol. 16, no. 1, April 1977, p. 50.

26. It is true that Omotoso's novels published abroad are technically superior to those published locally. It is, however, false to suggest, as Dash has done, that serious mistakes relating to structure and language are peculiar to the locally published works. *The Edifice* and *The Combat*, the two novels published abroad, disprove this theory. The conversation on p. 5 of *The Edifice* is incorrectly and confusedly arranged with the parts interchanged between the speakers. There is contradiction in logic in the second sentence on p. 7: 'Although it was still September, the end of September in fact, the weather was already becoming unbearable for me.' That it is in fact the end of September is the more reason the weather should be colder. There is a word omitted in the first line of the third paragraph on p. 47 of *The Combat*: 'When she had [?] out of her car . . . .' In the second paragraph on p. 68 of the same novel there is an irrelevant digression poorly integrated into the rest of the story. These few examples suffice to disprove the misrepresentation.

27. See Peter Nazareth, *The Third World Writer: His Social Responsibility*, Nairobi, Kenya Literature Bureau, 1978, pp. 71–86.

Narrative Method in the Novels of Ngugi

Florence Stratton

Ngugi has published four novels to date: *Weep Not, Child* (1964), *The River Between* (1965), *A Grain of Wheat* (1967) and *Petals of Blood* (1977).[1] The purpose of this discussion is to present a detailed analysis of Ngugi's narrative method in these novels, to chart its change and development, and to determine the characteristic features of his narrative style. The well-known fact that, although *Weep Not, Child* was published a year earlier than *The River Between*, the latter was written first, will be significant at some points in the discussion.

Ngugi's basic point of view in all four novels is that of the third person. However, in all four novels there is at least one other narrator, an unnamed narrator who is inside the events, referred to by Larson as 'the lyrical centre' or 'collective consciousness'.[2] In *The River Between* and *Weep Not, Child* the voice of this narrator is marked by the presence of the pronoun 'you', for example:

> A river flowed through the valley of life. If there had been no bush and no forest covering the slopes, you could have seen the river when you stood on top of either Kameno or Makuyu. Now you had to come down. (*RB*, p. 1)[3]

This same convention is used in the first third of *A Grain of Wheat* (see, for example, pages 16 and 63), after which it is dropped and replaced by a different marker, a 'we', sometimes in combination with 'you', which is also used throughout *Petals of Blood*:

> Many people from Thabai attended the meeting because, as you'll remember, we had only just been allowed to hold political meetings. (*GOW*, p. 57)

We used to crowd his little shop and look curiously at his stumped leg and his miserable face and listen to his stream of curses at Joseph. Soon we were glad that at long last we had a place from which we could get salt and pepper. But we were rather alarmed at his donkey because it ate too much grass and drank too much water. (*POB*, p. 8)

Both conventions have the general effects, as Larson suggests, of underscoring the communal nature of the experience and injecting the reader into the heart of the matter.[4] However, they differ significantly and one of the questions we should attempt to answer is why Ngugi drops the 'you' of the earlier novels and adopts 'we'.

The 'you' of the earlier writing is the indefinite or generic 'you' meaning 'people in general'. It is only personal by style, not as a result of inherent meaning, and thus, although it has the effect of involving the reader in the events, the bond between speaker and reader is comparatively weak. Also, although its use denotes a speaker who is inside the events, it does not refer to the participants in the speech event itself. In other words, there is no first person narrator, but rather a consciousness through which the experiences of the people are filtered.

The 'we' and 'you' of the later work are, of course, personal pronouns referring to participants in a speech event. 'We' refers to the speaker and others who have had a similar experience, while the reader, whether or not 'you' is present, is the addressee. By this means, not only is a conversational situation created through which the reader as addressee is made to experience a greater sense of personal involvement than when the generic 'you' is employed, but all the advantages of the first person method of narration are also gained. *A Grain of Wheat* is flawed in a minor way by the unaccountable switch in pronouns part way through, but by exchanging the generic 'you' for the personal pronouns, Ngugi has acquired a much more effective device for his purposes.

The distribution of these markers of an internal narrator also influences their effectiveness and indicates Ngugi's increasing craftsmanship. A consistent pattern emerges only in *Petals of Blood*, while steps towards establishing one can be discerned in the earlier novels. Either of these markers, if used frequently, would create a stylistic awkwardness. Thus a distribution which maximizes their effectiveness is desirable. In *The River Between* the generic 'you' is employed randomly throughout the chapters and the novel as a whole, whereas it occurs only in the first third of both *Weep Not, Child* and *A Grain of Wheat*. The first occurrence of 'we' in *A Grain of Wheat* appears between the last two occurrences of the generic 'you' following which there is a gap of fifty pages after which 'we' is used regularly and always at the beginning of chapters or subsections. In *Petals of Blood* 'we' occurs throughout chapter 2 which functions as the opening of the first section of the novel, 'Walking', and chapter 11 which opens part 4; and at the beginning of chapters 4 and 9 as well as that of several subsections. In addition, the device is used only in the first and final quarters of the novel, not occurring at all between pages 89 and 240.

The effect of this patterned distribution in *Petals of Blood* is that a psychological framework is created which gives the reader the impression that he is listening directly to the voice of a participant more often than is the case, and at the same time avoids the awkwardness of using 'we' frequently.

Petals of Blood has another first person narrator, Munira, through whose prison notes some of the story is presented. Most readers, I believe, are left with the impression that a great deal of the story has been presented through these notes. In fact only twenty-three to twenty-four pages have been presented in this manner. To create this effect, Ngugi once again begins and concludes parts, chapters and subsections with Munira's notes; inserts occasional excerpts from the notes (for example, pp. 226–7) and refers to what in fact has been presented in the third person as if it had been contained in the notes. For example, 'Munira leaned over the table to see what the officer was pointing at, what it was that he had picked out of all the things that Munira had scribbled' (p. 295).

As Robson notes, considerably more use of time-shifts is made in *Petals of Blood* than in *A Grain of Wheat*.[5] One of the functions of Munira's prison notes is to give a formal structure to some of the shifts. Also, although suspense is created in both *A Grain of Wheat* and *Petals of Blood*, in the latter Ngugi actually experiments with the trappings of the detective novel of which Munira's prison notes, made in response to Inspector Godfrey's probings, form a part. A more general effect of this narrative device is that, as Munira attempts to put the events of the past twelve years into perspective for himself, they are put into perspective for the reader.

Why was Munira chosen to play this role of storyteller rather than one of the other characters who, with a few adjustments, could have filled it? The central point about Munira is that unlike the other characters he is by choice and with only a few exceptions an uninvolved, uncommitted observer of life, in addition to which his view of everything but his own personal dilemmas is clear-sighted

– qualities that are neatly symbolized early in the novel by his reaction to the golf course scene (p. 12). He has thus been carefully moulded to perform the function in Booth's terms of narrator as observer.[6] He is also basically conservative. The result is that the reader feels that he has been given, not only a first-hand view of the situation, but also an objective and possibly a conservative one; and as this view corresponds with other points of view, in particular those of the author as narrator which is discussed below and of Karega the trade unionist, it is difficult to reject them as extremist or radical as some readers might be tempted to do.

Both Palmer[7] and Robson see Munira as the hero or central figure of *Petals of Blood* and, judging the characterization unsatisfactory, find a major flaw in the novel. Although I do not agree with their assessment of Munira's character, the point at issue here is his position in the novel. Is he the hero or central character? The only evidence I can find on which this view of Munira might be based is that he is employed as a first person narrator. This does not on its own make a character central or a hero. The effects achieved by placing Munira in this role are very important ones, particularly given the political nature of the novel, but when his role as a character is compared to that of Abdulla, Wanja and Karega, it is clear that we know them all equally well and that they are all equally central to the events. In addition, Abdulla, Wanja and Karega at various points in the novel narrate their own experiences in the first person, as will be discussed next. Like *A Grain of Wheat*, *Petals of Blood* has, not one central character, but four.

In both these novels, too, the main characters at various points take on the role of first person narrators as they tell other characters their past experiences in the form of long, first person recollections. For example, there is Mumbi's recollection of the Emergency which she tells to Mugo, and Wanja's of her seduction which she tells to Abdulla and Munira. As he has done with 'we' and Munira's narration, Ngugi also often creates a first person framework with these recollections by opening and concluding them in the first person and employing the third person in the central portion, thus gaining the advantages of both points of view while creating a first person effect throughout. Gikonyo's narration of his experiences to Mugo illustrates this (pp. 64–106).

The effects of these recollections in terms of the shifting chronology they help to create have been discussed by Palmer, Cook and Robson.[8] As with the use of 'we' and other devices to be discussed below, they also underscore the communal nature of the experience of suffering and betrayal in *A Grain of Wheat* and of exploitation in *Petals of Blood*. However, in the much more politically committed *Petals of Blood*, the multi-faceted point of view afforded by these first person recollections in conjunction with Munira's prison notes is much more crucial to the success of the novel as it provides the necessary illusion of objectivity.

In addition to the voices of speakers who are inside the events, the voice of the author as narrator is heard very distinctly in all of the novels except *Weep Not, Child* where it is less evident. One of the reasons for this is that in *Weep Not, Child* much of what happens is presented from the point of view of the child, Njoroge, as several critics have noted.[9] However, on comparing *Weep Not, Child* with Ngugi's first novel, *The River Between*, another reason for the reader's greater awareness of the authorial voice becomes evident. This can be exemplified by looking at the ways in which in these novels Ngugi introduces the names of his main characters and one of their parents:

> The boy's name was Waiyaki, the only son of Chege.
>
> (RB, p. 6)

> Nyokabi called him. She was a small, black woman, with a bold but grave face. One could tell by her eyes full of life and warmth that she had once been beautiful. But time and bad conditions do not favour beauty. All the same, Nyokabi had retained her full smile – a smile that lit up her dark face.
> 'Would you like to go to school?'
> 'O, mother!' Njoroge gasped.
>
> (WNC, p. 3)

The first quotation above is clumsy because information that is usually presented dramatically in a context in which other information is also conveyed (as in the second example where the education theme is introduced) is told to the reader. Although in *The River Between* Ngugi employs dramatic devices which become characteristic of his style, as will be discussed later, much less of the material is dramatized and much more is told to the reader in such a way that the reader is made more aware of the author's voice than is justified. It would seem that at the time of writing his first novel, Ngugi had not entirely mastered dramatic presentation. This is one reason among others, such as unintegrated sociological material and melodramatic elements, why *The River Between* is a less accomplished novel than the later ones.

The distinctive voice of the author in *A Grain of Wheat* and *Petals of Blood* is of a different sort than in *The River Between* as the examples below indicate:

> Then, as now, Thabai Ridge sloped gently from the high ground on the west into a small plain on which Rung'ei Trading Centre stood.
>
> (*GOW*, p. 62)

> The Trans-Africa road linking Nairobi and Ilmorog to the many cities of our continent is justly one of the most famous highways in all the African lands, past and present. It is symbolic tribute, although an unintended one, to those who witnessing the dreaded ravages of crime and treachery and greed which passed for civilisation, witnessing too the resistance waged and carried out with cracked hands and bleeding hearts, voiced visionary dreams amidst sneers and suspicions and accusations of madness or of seeking pathways to immortality and the eternal self-glory of tyrants.
>
> (*POB*, p. 262)

In both cases, the authorial intrusion is not inadvertent, as in *The River Between*, but deliberate. However, there is a good deal of difference between the functions of the authorial intrusions in *A Grain of Wheat* and *Petals of Blood*. In *A Grain of Wheat* they function to provide perspective, often an historical one, the author's feelings not being involved; whereas in *Petals of Blood* their function is to convey directly the author's feelings.

That Ngugi has moved towards more direct authorial commentary can hardly be seen as surprising given his view of the role of the African writer. For example, as early as 1969 he wrote:

> It is not enough for the African artist, standing aloof, to view society and highlight its weaknesses. He must try to go beyond this, to seek out the sources, the causes and the trends. Today the revolutionary struggle which has already destroyed the traditional power-map drawn up by the colonialist nations, is sweeping through Africa . . . The artist in his writing is not exempted from the struggle. By diving into the sources, he can give moral direction and vision to a struggle which, though suffering temporary reaction, is continuous and is changing the face of the twentieth century.[10]

One might predict that when Ngugi's fifth novel, *Devil on the Cross*, is published, authorial comments of the type found in *Petals of Blood* will be equally prevalent.

However, the use of direct authorial commentary in *Petals of Blood* has aroused adverse criticism. For example, Robson comments:

Conveying information is a legitimate part of a novelist's role, but in *Petals of Blood* Ngugi goes beyond what is acceptable in fiction; he is giving us polemic.[11]

For a number of reasons this reader does not find the authorial intrusions objectionable. First, there is a generic justification for the use of this narrative method. *Petals of Blood* is an epic, and direct authorial commentary is an integral part of the epic style. Secondly, the tone of the comments, which is generally ironic and often satiric, has a distancing effect. Thirdly, the comments are balanced by a number of other points of view as discussed above and by other narrative techniques discussed below.

There are signs that Ngugi anticipated this adverse reaction to the authorial intrusions in *Petals of Blood* and thus sought a means of distancing himself from them. In every direct authorial intrusion, the speaker refers to himself as 'we'. What this suggests is that Ngugi has attempted to disguise his voice as that of the collective consciousness. However, this ploy leads to confusion and incongruities. The voice of the 'real' collective consciousness belongs to an Ilmorog peasant who could not possibly express what is presented in such excerpts. Two first person narrators using 'we' to refer to themselves is rather awkward and, in the case of the well-read speaker, either pompous or pointless given the Ilmorog setting. In addition, the reader has the confusing and distracting task of constantly attempting to readjust his view of a speaker he thought he had already identified. Thus the problem with the authorial intrusions for this reader is not with the fact that there are intrusions, but rather with the means Ngugi has employed to identify the speaker. A third person presentation would, I believe, have been much more satisfactory.

The discussion thus far might suggest that there is much 'telling' and little 'showing' in Ngugi's novels. Although the balance is a little one-sided in *The River Between*, in the three later novels a balance is struck between what is related and what is represented directly in dramatic presentations and in the presentation of the thoughts of a character. The rest of this discussion will focus on the characteristic features of Ngugi's handling of these two techniques.

What is noticeable about the dialogue in all the Ngugi's novels is that it is more direct, more dramatic, than is usual in novels. Several times in *Weep Not, Child* and occasionally in *A Grain of Wheat* and *Petals of Blood* Ngugi is at his most experimental, presenting exchanges in a form usually found only in the scripts of plays:

Teacher   What am I doing?
Njoroge   (thinly) You are standing up.
Teacher   (slightly cross) What are *you* doing?
Njoroge   (clears his throat, voice thinner still) You are standing up.
Teacher   No, no! (to the class) Come on. What are *you*, *you* doing?

(*WNC*, pp. 44–5)

The bulk of the dialogue, however, rather than being presented in a play-script form, resembles the stage presentation of a play, the characters, usually two but sometimes three, simply presenting their lines in turn with little or no interpretation provided by the third person narrator. It is to Ngugi's credit that the reader, despite the lack of visual presentation afforded by a play and with little or no help from a third person narrator who in novels usually provides much more interpretative aid in the form of periodically naming speakers and suggesting tone, feels confident that he recognizes not only the voice of the speaker but the tone of the remarks as well:

'You remember the incident I told you about yesterday?'
'The dog?'
'No, no–The-the-my story.'
'Yes.'
'You remember I told you about the houseboy.'
'Yes.'
'He was never caught.'
'Yes, I believe you told me so.'
'I am frightened. I don't know what to do.'
'Why, what's happened?'
'Because–because, I saw him again–'
'When?'
'Yesterday.'

(*GOW*, p. 143)

In both cases vitality and immediacy are achieved, the reader being given the impression that he has direct access to the scene. With the stage-presentation type of dialogue, the reader is in fact given the impression that he is eavesdropping on a conversation.

It should also be noted that Ngugi not only presents exchanges between individual characters, but also ones in which at least one of the speakers is 'generalized', is 'the people', this being yet another means Ngugi uses to indicate the communal nature of the experience:

'Perhaps it is the white man's learning!' they said.

'No! Do you remember him as a boy?'

'Yes – always queer – and full of quiet courage.'

'It is the line he descends from. Don't you remember his father?'

'Yes. He was–'

(RB, p. 70)

Ngugi also employs direct speech in a number of circumstances in which reported speech might be considered more the novelistic norm. These include recollections by a character of an earlier conversation, the summary of a conversation, the presentation of a group or crowd reaction, what individuals usually say, and inner feelings, as the examples below indicate:

'But Karanja told them to leave me alone, and told them to move ahead, he would follow.

' "Why didn't you let them kill me?" I burst out.

' "Please, Mumbi."

' "Don't you call me Mumbi, Mumbi."

'I was angry and I did not want to remind him of the gift of food.'

(GOW, p. 129)

Few words passed between them. But when Chege stopped near a certain tree or bush, Waiyaki knew that his father had something to explain.

'The bark of that tree is good for a fresh wound.'

'The roots of this plant are good. When your stomach bites you, you boil them in water. Drink the liquid.'

And sometimes it would be a warning against that tree, 'whose fruit is full of poison.'

(RB, p. 14)

But they saw that he always came back, and they said amongst themselves: 'This one will stay.'

(POB, pp. 16–17)

Bad boys walked slowly after school for if they reached home early they would be asked to help in the evening chores. When they reached home they said, 'Teacher Lucia (or Isaac) kept us late.'

(WNC, p. 15)

For she too yearned for him and wanted him to be near her all the time. She cried: 'Waiyaki, you are mine. Come back to me.' But he did not come.

(RB, p. 134)

The general effects here, too, are vitality and immediacy. However, the presentation of recollected dialogue in direct speech as in the first passage above is particularly critical to the success of *A Grain of Wheat* and *Petals of Blood* in which much of the narrative is in the form of reminiscences. What they provide are scenic demonstrations in the midst of narration which might have become tedious without them.

Regarding the presentation of the thoughts of characters, Palmer states that in *A Grain of Wheat* 'Ngugi frequently makes use of techniques we have come to associate with stream-of consciousness or interior monologue'.[12] In fact interior monologues are common in all four novels, for example:

> Waiyaki often found himself trying to puzzle out the meaning of the old prophecy. Did Chege really think Waiyaki would be that saviour? Was he to drive out the white man? Was that the salvation? And what would a saviour do with the band of men who, along with Joshua, stuck so rigidly to the new faith?
>
> (*RB*, p. 80)

As with the dialogue, Ngugi does not restrict his interior monologues to individual characters but also presents the inner thoughts and feelings of the people:

> Most still clung to the vision of the Teacher they knew; the teacher whom they trusted, in whom they believed, a man they could always follow, anywhere. How could they believe that he would betray them? How could they believe this story about his marrying an uncircumcised girl, a daughter of Joshua, the enemy of the people? Waiyaki had awakened them to new visions, new desires, new aspirations. He had restored to them their dignity as a tribe and he had given them the white man's education when the missionaries had wanted to deny them that wisdom. Waiyaki had been too clever for them. He had taken the oath of loyalty to the purity of the tribe. That had been an example to all. Could he then go against the oath, could he?
>
> (*RB*, p. 143)

As the above examples show, in most cases Ngugi presents these monologues in the third person and the past tense of narration. However, on a few occasions in *Weep Not, Child*, he briefly experiments, it would seem, with using the first person and the present tense in the monologues:

> Then he wondered. Had she been to a magic worker? Or else how could she have divined his child's unspoken wish, his undivulged dream?

And here I am, with nothing but a piece of calico on my body and soon I
shall have a shirt and shorts for the first time. (Ngugi's italics) (pp. 3–4)

The interior monologues in *A Grain of Wheat* and *Petals of Blood*
have much greater depth, provide a much more complex view of
the workings of the characters' minds. Also, although Ngugi often
presents these monologues in the third person, he makes more
frequent use of the first person:

> But she sat in the same position as if she had not heard his question.
> What pained her was not so much the man's lies, not so much Njuguna's
> attitude, not even Karega's question, but what Njuguna had said about
> Joseph dying. She would be responsible for the death of another who
> did not even belong to her. She looked back to the origin of the journey.
> Maybe she was to blame. If she had not suggested, indeed insisted on
> their coming into this place where others had opted for a continuation
> of the journey . . . if . . . so many ifs and they all weighed heavily on
> her. What was she to do? Give it to a man she hated, and hardly six
> months since she had vowed to herself? If she didn't . . . and Joseph
> died . . . and Nyakinyua and the others . . . in the cold . . . hun-
> gry . . . thirsty . . . the drought in Ilmorog . . . failed mission . . . no
> rescue . . . more deaths . . . what shall I do? What shall I do?
>
> (*POB*, p. 156)

With such passages, the reader, who initially views the character
from the outside, is given the impression in the course of the
passage that layer after layer of the character's conscious and then
subconscious mind is being peeled away and that he is being taken
closer and closer to the essential 'I'.

However, even when only the third person is used in the
monologues, the reader is left with the impression that he has been
given an intimate view of the inner thoughts of the characters.
Apart from using truncated phrases and dashes as in the passage
above Ngugi achieves this effect by using those subsystems of
language that realize what Halliday calls the interpersonal
function of language.[13] This function, which, as the name implies,
allows a speaker to express his feelings and attitudes and his role in
the speech situation, is realized in English through two subsystems, modality and mood.

Modality embraces the modal verbs ('must', 'may', 'should' and
so on); attitudinal disjuncts expressing possibility, such as
'perhaps'; and non-factive conditionals. All of these occur with
great regularity in the monologues:

They ought to have listened to him. The white man should never have set foot in Siriana. (*RB*, p. 58)

The man and woman must have been blessed to walk in the new kingdom with Murungu. (*WNC*, pp. 24–5)

Perhaps life was a contradiction. (*RB*, p. 64)

Maybe he had better come tomorrow. (*GOW*, p. 27)

But was there a time when she maybe could have helped it? (*POB*, p. 336)

If it failed then he would lose a job and that would keep him away from the lands of his ancestors. (*WNC*, p. 52)

If she did not like the clumsy offering, she ought to do the carpenter's work herself or ask Karega to help her. (*GOW*, p. 71)

The unmarked form of the English mood system is the positive indicative declarative. It is Ngugi's use of the marked forms, in particular questions, imperatives and exclamations, that allow him to suggest that an individual's innermost feelings are being expressed. Questions play a particularly important role as some of the above passages demonstrate. In some cases whole monologues consist of nothing but questions and most monologues contain at least one. However, imperatives and exclamations also play a role as the examples below indicate:

To know that he was actually learning! (*WNC*, p. 34)

How he had yearned for the woman! (*GOW*, p. 182)

Look at the sinners moving deeper and deeper into the dirty mud of sin. (*RB*, p. 32)

Let it be . . . Let it be. (*POB*, p. 340)

As all of the examples given in this discussion of monologues indicate, not only do the structures employed create the effect of intimacy, many of them also convey doubt and uncertainty. In an interview in 1964 Ngugi made the following comment on Conrad:

With Conrad, I'm impressed by the way he questions things like action, the morality of action, for instance . . . This kind of questioning has impressed me a lot because with Conrad I have felt I have come into contact with another whose questioning to me is much more important than the answers which he gives.[14]

One of the ways in which Ngugi incorporates this same kind of questioning into his own work is through the use of the structures discussed above. Through many of these the characters question and express doubt about their actions and those of others and thus the dilemmas which they all face are highlighted and, particularly in the two later novels, positive ways of behaving in the kind of world Ngugi depicts are suggested.

In addition to conclusions already drawn, several points emerge from this study, all of which might be given further weight if a discussion of such elements as Ngugi's use of traditional material and the exploded time scheme of the later novels had not been considered beyond its scope. However, certain trends are obvious. First, it can be seen from the novels that Ngugi experiments with the resources of the novel form. This is illustrated by his use in all of the novels of narrators representing the voice of the people and of devices more often associated with drama, and in the two later novels of a multiplicity of points of view. Furthermore, the fact that Ngugi's development has been in the direction of greater complexity and depth can be seen from the multiple points of view and the interior monologues of the later works. In addition, it might be noted that in a variety of ways Ngugi attempts to maximize the effectiveness of the narrative techniques he uses. Examples of this include the usually dramatic nature of the dialogue and his distribution of material narrated in the first person.

Finally, the emphasis that Ngugi has placed on the collective nature of the experience presented .in the novels cannot be overlooked. The experiences of the individual characters are not only representative, but the reader is given direct access to the thoughts and feelings of the people through an unnamed internal narrator who is one of them (their private thoughts and feelings being expressed by interior monologues) and dialogues in which they are the participants. Through making the people a character in his novels, Ngugi not only achieves a very strong statement of theme, but, particularly in the later novels, appeals to the reader so effectively that the reader eventually feels that the voice of the people embraces his own.

NOTES

1. Ngugi wa Thion'o, *Weep Not, Child*, London, Heinemann (AWS 7), 1974; *The River Between*, London, Heinemann (AWS 17), 1975; *A Grain of Wheat*, London, Heinemann (AWS 36), 1975; *Petals of Blood*, London, Heinemann (AWS 188), 1977; New York, E. P. Dutton, 1978. All further page references are to these editions.

2. Charles Larson, *The Emergence of African Fiction*, London, Macmillan, 1978, p. 22; Bloomington, Indiana University Press, 1971.
3. After excerpts the novels will be identified as follows: *RB* — *The River Between; WNC* — *Weep Not, Child; GOW* — *A Grain of Wheat; POB Petals of Blood*.
4. ibid., pp. 124–5.
5. C. B. Robson, *Ngugi wa Thiong'o*, London, Macmillan, 1979, p. 93; New York, St. Martin's.
6. Wayne Booth, *The Rhetoric of Fiction*, Chicago, University of Chicago Press, 1961, p. 153.
7. Eustace Palmer, *The Growth of the African Novel*, London, Heinemann, 1979, p. 305; Robson, op. cit., p. 99.
8. Eustace Palmer, *An Introduction to the African Novel*, London, Heinemann, 1972; David Cook, *African Literature: A Critical View*, London, Longman, 1977; Robson, op. cit.
9. See for example Palmer, *An Introduction to the African Novel*, and Larson, op. cit.
10. Ngugi wa Thiong'o, 'Satire in Nigeria', *Protest and Conflict in African Literature*, Cosmo Pieterse and Donald Munro (eds.), London, Heinemann, 1969, p. 69; New York, Africana, 1969.
11. Robson, op. cit., p. 101.
12. Palmer, *An Introduction to the African Novel*, p. 47.
13. M. A. K. Halliday, *Explorations in the Functions of Language*, London, Edward Arnold, 1973, p. 66; New York, Elsevier, 1977.
14. Ngugi wa Thiong'o in C. Pieterse and D. Duerden (eds.), *African Writers Talking*, New York, Africana, 1972.

Heroism in *A Grain of Wheat*

Eileen Julien

There can be little question that Kihika, the rebel in Ngugi wa
Thiongo's *A Grain of Wheat*, is a hero. With respect to Mugo,
however, opinion may be divided. Mugo is a traitor who finally
admits his treason. To be sure, Mugo's peers, the people of Thabai,
are deeply puzzled by the sense of his acts. Yet Ngugi's choice of
narrative form can direct the reader's interpretation, for the novel
proposes an expansion of the concept of heroism to include not
only the magnanimous gestures of an exceptional man but also
ironic self-discovery by the average man.

Mugo knows all too painfully the impossibility in his own life of
the 'old' heroism embodied by the legendary Kihika. Noble,
passionate, single-minded, caring little for his own material
existence, Kihika dominates the pre-independence world of
Thabai. He is articulate and speaks out forcefully against the
British who have robbed the Kenyan people of their lands and
freedom. It is his vision and daring that reflect the mood of the
times and announce the impending crisis. Kihika's personal heroes
are mythic figures, Gandhi and Christ, who have changed the
history of mankind and who are immortalized in legend. He thus
envisions for himself, too, an idealized role as leader:

> Unknown to those around him, Kihika's heart hardened toward 'these
> people', long before he had ever encountered a white face. Soldiers
> came back from the war and told stories of what they had seen in Burma,
> Egypt, Palestine and India; wasn't Mahatma Gandhi, the saint, leading
> the Indian people against British rule? Kihika fed on these stories: his
> imagination and daily observation told him the rest; from early on, he
> had visions of himself, a saint, leading the Gikuyu people to freedom
> and power.[1]

It is the struggle against the British, the Emergency and Mau Mau
that create for Kihika the occasion to realize his ideals for both

himself and his people. By lashing out at the enemy of his people, Kihika proves himself to be a man of 'great deeds and noble qualities'. He eventually becomes a martyr for Kenyan freedom. His bravery and death earn him the admiration of his fellows, and he becomes an inspiration for them as did Gandhi and Christ for him. Kihika is clearly a hero in the eyes of both the people of Thabai and in those of the implied reader; it is through battle and the sword that Kihika's dreams come to fruition.

Just as Kihika dominates the prelude to the novel's action (pre-independence), Mugo dominates the action itself, which starts when freedom has been won and independence is to begin. Before independence, Mugo, an orphan, lives with a cruel aunt. Unlike Kihika, he is lonely, introspective and taciturn. Yet he, too, aspires to be part of the community. Mugo feels rootless when his aunt dies:

> Whom could he now call a relation? He wanted somebody, anybody, who would use the claims of kinship to do him ill or good. Either one or the other as long as he was not left alone, an outsider.
>
> He turned to the soil. He would labour, sweat, and through success and wealth force society to recognize him. (p. 9)

Mugo's dreams of becoming prosperous and respected are shattered when Kihika comes to him and tries to pull him into the tide of violent political events. Panicked by the prospect of losing his life to one side or the other, Mugo betrays Kihika to the British – an act that the text clearly shows to be a moral failure. Yet the text also contrasts this ugly act of weakness with Mugo's many virtues. Despite his fear, Mugo is a man of courage and generous instincts which both the village and the implied reader recognize. He reaches out to the old woman who has lost her son. He defends a pregnant girl from the brutality of the homeguards, and in prison he never bends under the torture of his captors. Nonetheless it is the burden of guilt that weighs on him now – the knowledge of his weakness and treachery in the face of the village's deep admiration for his supposed heroism. When the novel begins, Uhuru is but a few days away, and Mugo is now faced with a new challenge: the Party has asked that he, a hero of the Kenyan struggle, lead the Uhuru ceremonies in Thabai. Mugo must now come to terms with himself. The only honourable course is to admit to himself his own imperfection and frailty and to confess the responsibility for Kihika's death before the village.

The challenges laid before Kihika and Mugo differ in several respects. Kihika's enemy is the British, a plain and external threat; his strategy is physical combat in which he risks his life. In contrast, Mugo's enemy is his own fears and desires; his is an internal, mental struggle in which he may lose both his life and his fragile honour. Kihika's objectives are clear and straightforward – the expulsion of the British – but Mugo's are less obvious and the rewards less certain, for there will be no tangible laurels when Mugo, true to himself at last, admits his crime.

Yet, there is an important similarity between these two struggles. Although Mugo's declaration takes place in the non-glorious world of everyday life, it, like Kihika's defiance, requires immense courage. The narrator himself likens Mugo's final effort to that of a warrior:

> His heart pounded against him, he felt sweat in his hands, as he walked through the huge crowd. His hands shook, his legs were not firm on the ground. In his mind, everything was clear and final. He would stand there and publicly own the crime. He held on to his vision. Nothing, not even the shouting and the songs and the praises would deflect him from this purpose. It was the clarity of his vision which gave him courage as he stood before the microphone and the sudden silence. (p. 204)

The other characters may grope for the meaning of Mugo's startling revelation and of his contradictory deeds, but this passage leaves the implied reader with a strong sense of Mugo's heroism.

If Kihika's heroism is achieved through brave deeds in physical combat, Mugo's is attained through the seemingly unlikely medium of language – the public forum through which we discover ourselves. From his youth, Kihika is gifted with words and the power to move his listeners – Mumbi, his friends, or compatriots – with his beliefs and visions. In contrast, Mugo rarely speaks at all. The narrator stresses Mugo's shy silence by stating early on in the novel that Mugo had given 'only one real speech' in his life, during a public meeting in which the returning detainees were presented to the people. 'His voice, colourless, rusty, startled him. He spoke in a dry monotone, tired, almost as if telling of scenes he did not want to remember' (p. 58). As Mugo describes the nightmare of the prison camp and brings back to consciousness the memory of what has happened, he faces the truth of his experience. For a brief moment he achieves a kind of purity and truly awakens from his numbed existence. Suddenly he finds that he is no longer talking of things as they were but rather things as he would have liked them to be, of the dream of home and love so dear to him who had none. Realizing the lie, he stops abruptly, leaving the audience suspended. This speech before the people of Thabai is the first occasion on which Mugo begins to articulate and thus to recognize the sense of his life. It is a bitter truth, one that he wishes to embellish and from which he finally turns away. The second and final such moment occurs on Uhuru day when Mugo admits his part in Kihika's death: 'As soon as the first words were out, Mugo felt light. A load of many years was lifted from his shoulders. He was free, sure, confident' (p. 204).

Language is the means of self-knowledge, a new heroism represented by Mugo. Indeed all the characters in the novel who move towards self-discovery do so through the act of talking. Little action in fact takes place in the story. From the moment Mugo is introduced until the race on Uhuru day, the story consists primarily of encounters in which the principal activity is an exchange of words. The leaders of the Party come to invite Mugo to speak; Gikonyo then confides in him; Mumbi, too, unburdens her heart to him, and so on. Yet the form which these words take is not dynamic dialogue so much as the voice of a character (sometimes rendered by the narrator) reconstructing aloud his or her past. By the same token, the only main characters in the novel who never ease their troubled consciences and who continue to lead unfulfilling lives are those who have no meaningful communication: Margery and John Thompson and Karanja. In *A Grain of Wheat* silence is accompanied by introspection, inertia and self-centredness which impede the integration of the individual into the whole. Speech implies sharing, energy and other-directedness which offer a path to personal fulfilment within the social context. Words are the new 'deeds' that enable Mugo and the others to unravel the sense of their experiences and heroically look at themselves for what they are. Language is the tool, *par excellence*, for the sounding of oneself; it is with Mugo that heroism shifts from bold deeds to truthful words.

Now if both Kihika and Mugo can be viewed as heroes, they are quite different with respect to depth of character. Given both his ideals and his achievements, Kihika can be likened to heroes typical of romance or epic. Such figures are, Northrop Frye tells us in *An Anatomy of Criticism*, 'superior in *degree* to other men' and sometimes to their environment as well.[2] Like other warrior heroes in literature (for example Beowulf, Roland, Shaka, Sundiata), Kihika is elevated above his companions and comrades. Of course, since *A Grain of Wheat* is highly mimetic and projects a replica of actuality, Kihika has no marvellous attributes, magic and super-natural powers, as these and other such heroes do. Ngugi makes the superiority of Kihika's intellect and the intensity of his commit-ment quite believable. Yet Kihika remains, even in the realistic mode, an exceptional individual. His home is the forest which represents in many older narratives a world apart from 'reality', in which time is of a different rhythm and nature is enchanted and volatile. This sylvan setting and the physical distance itself that separates Kihika from the village reinforce the distinction between him and his people. Furthermore, in the fashion of tragic heroes of romance and epic, his death marks 'the passing of time, of the old order changing and yielding to a new one'.[3] Kihika's demise helps usher in the dawn of Kenyan independence.

Like the heroes of older narrative forms then, Kihika loses in resemblance to the reader what he gains in glory. His death locks him into the purity of his youthful idealism, a purity that makes him more appropriate to a narrative universe of absolute heroes and villains. Because Kihika is exceptional, he wanders in the shadows of the novel where, illuminated by little light, he has little depth. He is a static, 'flat' character who is not seen in the context of the workaday world. Kihika does not grow or change, two fundamental requirements for mimetic novels such as this one. His perfection makes him seem inappropriate for the novel. These remarks, however, are not a negative judgement of Ngugi's art but refer merely to the workings of the narrative. Kihika is integral to the sense of *A Grain of Wheat*. His virtue and portrayal distance him from the reader and thereby contribute to the more moving effect of Mugo's victory.

In *The Nature of Narrative* Robert Scholes offers a description of a hero common in the days of Aristotle. Scholes' remarks, though they were not made with reference to realistic characters, help pinpoint Kihika's role in Ngugi's novel and explain Mugo's hostile reaction to Kihika's idealism:

> Together with the obsessed, the perverted, the weak, and the foolish, the hero is a mere passive product of his heredity and environment. Like the other types, however, the hero still refuses to admit that he has no control, no hand in the shaping of his own character and his circumstances. But in his case the pretense makes him insufferable in the eyes of the others. Unlike them, he bears no burden of guilt, of shame, or despair. To the unthinking, his quick wit, his beautiful body, his physical courage, and his poise still merit praise, as though he

made them himself. He is unsympathetic to the dark, inarticulate, passionate underside of human nature, for he does not experience it himself and he cannot believe that it is ever beyond one's ability to control.[4]

Kihika sees himself as the arbiter of his own and his people's destiny, but Mugo is suspicious of Kihika's sense of control. Mugo feels that Kihika is a 'mere passive product' whose freedom to choose is not of his own making but rests on Kihika's having had the love and support of a family. Mugo hates Kihika because the latter, having all those things that everyone (especially Mugo) desires and having done nothing (in Mugo's eyes) to earn them, squanders them all for illusory notions of grandeur and freedom.

Mindless of the fact that his fervour and heroism seem 'make-believe' and beyond the grasp of the average man, Kihika comes to Mugo. On that occasion Kihika admits that he himself knows fear, but Mugo is hardly persuaded; Kihika's ability to put that fear aside still seems superhuman. Kihika appears to have little awareness of the magnitude of imperfection in human life. This ignorance of human nature, his insensitivity to Mugo's fragile dreams and his presumption of Mugo's collaboration make Kihika still more intolerable to Mugo.

Also, while Kihika is hardly the 'mere passive product' that Mugo believes him to be, Kihika's righteousness and strength are nonetheless enigmatic. The novel presents a number of events from Kihika's youth which reveal a growing commitment to Kenyan freedom, but there is no sense of a struggle on Kihika's part in making this commitment. The implied reader cannot share that process. It is as though Kihika's identity and goals have always been what they are; he has always known what truth and justice demanded: 'Unknown to those around him, Kihika's heart hardened toward "these people", *long before he had ever encountered* a white face' (p. 73, my emphasis). Because Kihika's loftiness and portrayal remove him from the heart of the narrative, *A Grain of Wheat* is, above all, Mugo's story; it is his struggle that wins the empathy of the reader.

Unlike Kihika, Mugo is a flawed and intensely reflective individual, and he is for that reason a more interesting and weighty character. Frye tells us that the protagonist of the mimetic novel is 'isolated by a weakness which appeals to our sympathy because it is on our own level of experience'.[5] In Frye's view such a novel is, at its best, 'the study of the isolated mind, the story of how someone recognizably like ourselves is broken by a conflict between the inner and outer world, between imaginative reality and the sort of reality which is established by social consensus'.[6] It is the resolution of this conflict and the individual's coming into an awareness of himself that the novel presents.

Mugo is a character who, in his complexity, resembles the reader. He wants desperately to be integrated into the whole but is isolated by his crime and guilt; he is searching for a way to give meaning to his life. In Mugo we find the great tension that makes A Grain of Wheat a compelling story: Mugo is a character 'with enough crudeness for ... hamartia [imperfection] but enough sensitivity for ultimate discovery and self-understanding'.[7] Mugo is human in both the most glorious sense and in the most pathetic sense, such that his admission of his human nature is a victory – not for absolute virtue but for humility. This is a victory within the grasp of all the people of Thabai. Mugo's example is not lost, for Gikonyo, at least, sees its significance:

'He was a brave man, inside ... He stood before much honour, praises were heaped on him. He would have become a chief. Tell me another person who would have exposed his soul for all the eyes to peck at ... Remember that few people in that meeting are fit to lift a stone against that man. Not unless I–we–too–in turn open our hearts naked for the world to look at.' (p. 202)

Mugo's act calls upon the people of Thabai to look at themselves honestly as he has done and to accept the unvarnished truth that 'pure' heroism is but an ideal. Real people are rarely so pure, or their antagonists simple. Ironically, Mugo comes to accept a burden he had earlier refused:

No sooner had he finished speaking than the silence around, the lightness within, and the sudden freedom pressed heavy on him ... He was conscious of himself, of every step he made, of the images that rushed and whirled through his mind with only one constant thread: so he was responsible for whatever he had done in the past, for whatever he would do in the future. The consciousness frightened him. (p. 204)

It is an existential consciousness that fills Mugo, one that Kihika had possessed – intuitively, virtually without struggle – long before him. Thus Mugo's journey of self-discovery leads him to embrace both the existential burden of acting (with its inevitable responsibility for those acts) and the disturbing but honest view of human nature as a complex mixture of strength and weakness.

Through its juxtaposition of Kihika and Mugo then, A Grain of Wheat moves from an 'epic' to a 'novelistic' notion of heroism, from bold, stirring deeds to a quiet, unsettling awareness of self. The text furthermore shifts its focus from the external threat to well-being, such as infamous colonial powers, to the more frightening internal menace of weaknesses, fears and doubts. Thus we find that the struggle for Kenyan independence in *A Grain of Wheat* produces an 'epic' hero whereas the everyday world of success and failure produces a hero appropriate to the novel. The implication is not that noble actions are no longer needed – we have but to consider Mugo's good instincts and bravery and his final acceptance of the consequences of his acts to know that the value of noble actions is not being challenged. Rather, the novel emphasizes that it is unquestionably valiant and indispensable to see oneself honestly. This theme looks toward the future rather than the past and is expressed most succinctly in Wangari's admonition to her son Gikonyo:

> 'Let us now see what profit it will bring you, to go on poisoning your mind with these things when you *should have accepted* and sought how best to *build your life*. But you, like a foolish child, have never wanted to *know what happened* . . . You are a man now. Read your own heart, and know yourself.' (pp. 153–4, my emphasis)

Wangari's words subtly recall the novel's emphasis on language as a tool of self-discovery ('Read your own heart'). The old woman equates manhood with self-knowledge, honesty and the determination to carry on. Therein lies the novel's blueprint for heroism. Dwelling on past disappointments is of no value. One must start anew with humble acceptance of what is past.

So it is that Mugo's actions (rather than Kihika's) set the example for those around him. Characters such as Mumbi, Kariuki, Githua (and, of course, Kihika) have a romantic longing for the simple and elegant act of bravery (frequently associated with war or dangerous adventures). Githua, for example, claims that his leg was wounded during the struggle against the British, though it was in fact lost in a lorry accident:

> 'It makes his life more interesting to himself [another character explains]. He invents a meaning for his life, you see. Don't we all do that? And to die fighting for freedom sounds more heroic than to die by accident' (p. 133).

Mumbi, too, seeks the fulfilment that comes from virtue and self-sacrifice:

> Her dark eyes had a dreamy look that longed for something the village

could not give. She lay in the sun and ardently yearned for a life in which love and heroism, suffering, and martyrdom were possible. She was young. She had fed on stories in which Gikuyu women braved the terrors of the forest to save people, of beautiful girls given to the gods as sacrifice before the rains.

But the workaday world and the motivation of human beings in less extraordinary circumstances defy those clear criteria and unequivocal categories of heroism. Mugo's examples affirms that heroism is no longer the province of gods and demi-gods but is possible for any and all. It is no longer a specific deed but an *approach* to life and self. Life – with its not so clear choices, its relativity in morality and truth, its ambiguity – rarely produces pure heroes. Rather, one's goal should be *to live* heroically: to seek the truth about oneself, to face one's choices honestly, and to bear the responsibility for one's deeds.

Since the first years of independence in particular, many African novels have depicted the arduous task of re-assessment and coming to grips with the stubborn fact of human limitation. A great number have given in to a crushing sense of hopelessness. They document a crisis but do not transform it.

Readers may decry such fiction because it fails to meet its potential, that is, to render its 'singular and indispensable insight into the poetic, dramatic, or mythological dimensions and possibilities of the human situation'.[8] Because Ngugi ambitiously obeys an aesthetic impulse to search for heroism in new and complex settings, *A Grain of Wheat* is, on the contrary, a mimetic novel that does not yield to a glum naturalism. Ngugi's fiction is more powerful, his sober vision more haunting because he never abandons this prerogative of narrative to seek in one stroke both truth and beauty.

NOTES

1. Ngugi wa Thiong'o (James Ngugi), *A Grain of Wheat*, London, Heinemann (AWS 36), 1967, reset 1975, p. 73. All subsequent citations are taken from reset 1975 edition.
2. Northrop Frye, *An Anatomy of Criticism*, Princeton, Princeton University Press, 1957, p. 33.
3. ibid., pp. 36–7.

4. Robert Scholes and Robert Kellogg, *The Nature of Narrative*, New York, Oxford University Press, 1966, p. 152.
5. Frye, op. cit., p. 38.
6. ibid., p. 39.
7. Scholes, op. cit., p. 261.
8. Albert Murray, *The Hero and the Blues*, Columbia, University of Missouri Press, 1973, p. 14.

Mirror of Reality: The Novels of Meja Mwangi

Elizabeth Knight

In East Africa, it is now possible to speak of a second generation of writers in English. Meja Mwangi belongs to this group, but he still retains links with the older school. He has followed the trend set by Lennard Kibera in 1970 with *Voices in the Dark*[1] in that he too, is concerned in his novels, *Kill Me Quick, Going Down River Road* and *The Bushtrackers*,[2] with the modern, urban environment. However, his earlier works, *Taste of Death* and *Carcase for Hounds*,[3] show him clinging to his historical roots.

Meja Mwangi was born and grew up in Nanyuki, an area of intense military activity during the Mau Mau emergency and still an important army base. He was born in 1948 and would have been too young to have understood the causes of the fighting, but he lived out his childhood and adolescence at the fiercest time of the struggle in an atmosphere of fear and suspicion.

Taste of Death and *Carcase for Hounds* are part of a long line of books focusing on the emergency. David Rubadiri has written that 'basically it is politics which has excited the creative spirit in East Africa'[4] and the growth of nationalism, together with the coming of independence, led to publication of political works, firstly of a non-fictional nature. Books of this period include J. M. Kariuki's account of his experiences in detention entitled *Mau Mau Detainee*, and Rosberg's analysis of the same period – *The Myth of Mau Mau*. Later came Itote's *Mau Mau General* in which the author, General China, details the realities of the struggle in the forest, his experiences in detention and subsequent disillusionment after independence. Fictional representations of the struggle began with Ngugi wa Thiong'o's *Weep Not, Child* and *A Grain of Wheat*. In

1967 came Wachira's *Ordeal in the Forest*; Kibera and Kahiga's short stories, *Potent Ash*, appeared in 1968; *Daughter of Mumbi* by Waciuma the following year; and *A Tail in the Mouth* by Mangua in 1972. Watene's play, *My Son for my Freedom*, came out in 1973; Ngugi's *Secret Lives* in 1975; and the two plays on Dedan Kimathi – Watene's *Dedan Kimathi* and Ngugi and Micere Mugo's *Trial of Dedan Kimathi* – in 1974 and 1976 respectively. Further non-fiction accounts have continued to appear.

Writing in 1971, Bernth Lindfors was still able to state that 'the favourite subject of new Kenyan novelists is still the Mau Mau revolt'.[6] Meja Mwangi exorcized his particular Mau Mau ghost with the two novels *Carcase for Hounds* and *Taste of Death*. The latter traces the history of Kariuki, a soldier who fought in the Second World War, and who joined the freedom fighters because of the bullying tactics of the homeguard in his village. He takes part in the daring rescue from prison of the leader, several ambushes, is captured by the British, tortured, sentenced to death, then escapes to remain in the forest with two companions until independence. His story is interlaced with details of British attempts to destroy the freedom fighters by psychological and military means. Inspector Cowdrey plays a leading rôle in the former activities. He is the chief interrogator of Mau Mau suspects and is fanatical in his search for the leader whose capture he sees as crucial in defeating the Mau Mau. The demented Cowdrey leaves Kenya at independence, his wife having been brutally murdered and his career and dreams shattered. *Carcase for Hounds* is more confined in both time and space covered. It concentrates on a few days in the lives of General Haraka and his gang, and D. C. Kingsley and his men who are out to capture them. Caught between the two are the frightened and confused villagers of Pinewood and Acacia Ranch.

In both novels, Meja Mwangi concentrates attention on the freedom fighters, or 'forest fighters' as he consistently and with studied neutrality calls them. Unlike previous novels, his work also depicts in some detail the whites and civilians, giving a more complete picture of the struggle than, say, Ngugi and Kibera who concentrate more on the civilians, or Wachira who is concerned almost exclusively with the leading freedom fighter. Part of Meja Mwangi's uniqueness lies in this wholeness of vision, a characteristic that can be seen developing from the earlier *Taste of Death* to *Carcase for Hounds*. The former covers a long period of time – from the early 1950s to independence in 1963 – and has a large cast of characters but there is little depth of characterization or subtlety of plot. In part this can be explained by the audience. The book is a secondary school reader and, naturally, keeping the readers excited and involved overrides other artistic considerations. Characters tend to fall into stereotyped modes of behaviour. Kariuki is the stock freedom-fighter hero. He leads daring rescues, is a crack shot and does not break down despite terrible torture. Lieutenant Davis is the disciplined army officer who maintains a stiff upper lip throughout and gets through a Mau Mau ambush alive because of his reliance on strict military discipline. Cowdrey is the inherently racist white, caught up in the emergency in an attempt to preserve his privileged life-style.

While this tendency to stereotype may be expected of a young writer, there is some evidence of the more mature style that is to burgeon in *Carcase for Hounds*. There are little touches that add some life to the characterization. Lieutenant Davis' driver is an interesting example. British soldiers, if they are portrayed at all in fiction of this period, are either the leading officers masterminding operations and interrogations, or young privates raping and murdering villagers. Meja Mwangi adds some individuality and credibility to his portrayals. In contrast to the calm Lieutenant Davis, the anonymous driver is scared stiff at the nearness of death, intent only on escape and contemptuous of his superior's orders: 'To hell with your orders. I am not going to sit here and be blown to hell because of your lunatic orders' (p. 85). Similar details of personality and social relationships appear, sparingly, in other portraits.

The occasional details of character are not matched by similarly detailed depictions of the physical environment. This marks a sharp distinction between the two works for such particulars are part of the narrative fabric of *Carcase for Hounds*. The narrative structure is the same in both works. Although basically chronological, the stories are not simple linear narrations from one person's point of view but are built up from the viewpoints of several characters. The ambush sequence in *Taste of Death*, for instance, is shown as it is planned and executed by the general and his men, and also as it is experienced by the victims, the British army convoy. The narrative in *Taste of Death* relies heavily on thoughts, statements and descriptions of actions. Attitudes tend to be stated rather than evinced and the verbalization of feelings, while making for great clarity, leaves little to the reader's imagination. This feature would again seem to be tied up with the projected audience. In this early work, the few descriptions of the natural environment are brief in the extreme. Wounded and on the run, Kariuki reaches a cave in the western hills:

> The cave he was looking for was on the western side of the hill. The hill was covered with red light, the valley behind it was in twilight. It took him only a short time to find the cave. Near its mouth was a wide glade which made any undetected approach impossible. A nearby spring softly vomited its water into a basin which widened out into a stream and wound its way down the hill to the west. (p. 122)

Meja Mwangi is economical in his use of words here, perhaps too economical, for the picture he conveys is not vivid. His description is rather a function of the plot, as the cave and its situation are mentioned only in relation to Kariuki's flight. The only words superfluous to this function are 'red' and 'vomited'. These reflect Kariuki's own plight; his physical and mental sickness, his distaste for the fighting.

This mirroring of a character's state of mind in the description of the surroundings may not be as yet a conscious technique on Mwangi's part, but it is one that he develops in the later emergency novel, *Carcase for Hounds*. Unlike *Taste of Death*, the plot here is fairly minimal. The emergency has ceased to be an adventure story permeated by the occasional, self-conscious justification for the fighting, and has become instead a documentary, the details of which achieve the clarity of a photographic record, at times. There is, for instance, a parallel description to that quoted earlier from *Taste of Death*. In this later novel, General Haraka has escaped, wounded, from a confrontation with the homeguard following oath-taking meetings at Pinewood village. The gang are holed up in a cave:

> The approach to the hideout was completely unnoticeable from even as close as the giant fig-tree five yards away. The Liki river was about three hundred yards away to the north and its overflowing roar was muffled by the jungle before it reached the hideout. Now it was only audible as a continuous soothing hum in the background. The bewitched river too was changing like everything else. In the old days one could have found a crossing-point at the worst of the season. Now the monster had eaten away at the bank and washed away all the crossing logs. (p. 96)

The short staccato-like pattern of sentences is the same as in the earlier book and remains a distinctive feature of Meja Mwangi's mature prose style. Here though, in contrast to the earlier work, the descriptive detailing is tight and the picture drawn clearly. A vague landscape has been replaced by the more detailed map of a man whose continued existence depends on accurate knowledge of the terrain. This description also helps to explain the paradoxical 'softly vomited' of the previous book. This contradiction in terms seems to be due to slack writing, for in *Carcase for Hounds* the two ideas coalesce with the explanation that the violent action of the river is muted by the dense forest before it reaches the listener's ear. In this passage, Meja Mwangi develops the techniques initiated in *Taste of Death* of making the physical environment echo a character's mental state. The numbness that is coming over the fatally wounded general finds a mirror in the 'muffled' and 'soothing' sound of the river, but it is soon replaced by the welling-up of anxieties as the river swells and bursts its banks. The river is referred to as a 'monster' and 'bewitched', terms that are to recur later in reference to the general himself.

The hostile, menacing natural surroundings play an important role in *Carcase for Hounds*. The rivers, in particular, are seen gradually to rise from being fordable at the start, to becoming raging torrents which hem in the freedom fighters at the end. Many scenes are prefaced by outlines of the landscape, flora and fauna. This technique is used by Okot p'Bitek in *Song of a Prisoner* but there it is symbolic; Meja Mwangi's descriptions are naturalistic. The oath-taking of villagers at Pinewood is preceded by the following representative passage:

> The night was dark and cold. The leaves and the bush were wet with dew. All round them the night life went on as though the intruders did not exist. Night-birds called, hyrax screamed and crickets clicked just as they had done the night before, and the night before that, and just as they would do the following night and for ever after. (p. 55)

Nature is the permanent backdrop to Meja Mwangi's horrific depiction of the war. It both mirrors and intensifies the feelings of the actors but, unlike them, it endures. The lives of Haraka and his lieutenant, Kimamo, are seen as transient in comparison with the great river Liki, the rainbird whose call permeates the raid on Timau Police Post (pp. 34–5) and the hyena's laugh which closes the novel.

The condensation of the emergency into a few days enables the author to dwell on such incidental material but it also means that the novel lacks perspective. *Taste of Death* covers nearly the entire period of the emergency and, in that it shows a triumphant conclusion to the struggle with the coming of independence, it is a positive, nationalist work. The main character, Kariuki, retains his belief in the cause throughout. Such idealism is absent from *Carcase for Hounds*. Written in a naturalistic manner, there is no authorial voice to pass judgement on characters or to put them into some sort of historical perspective. In this the novel is part of the body of modernist literature that Lukács criticized when he commented: 'lack of objectivity in the description of the outer world finds its complement in the reduction of reality to a nightmare.'[7] Certainly there is no distancing or objectivity in the harrowing depiction of the circumstances of the freedom fighters around Mount Kenya, but is this then a falsification of reality? A comparison with eye-witness accounts by General China and Njama[8] vindicates Mwangi's portrayal.

Carcase for Hounds deals with a well-defined period in the struggle for independence after the collapse of the centrally organized movement. It covers the period of spontaneous uprisings against British oppression after 'Operation Anvil' and the compulsory villagization. The oaths that General Haraka administers are not to build up a political movement but are defensive. He uses the oath to keep the villagers of Pinewood and Acacia loyal to him so that they do not betray the gang to the security forces. Haraka, without the guidance of his predecessor who had had some contact with the Nairobi organization, only contemplates vaguely the ideas of the movement, so for him the struggle has become simply one of survival. Cut off from the villagers, the gang has to be largely self-sufficient by setting traps, sending out food-gatherers, and raiding conveys and police posts for ammunition. Haraka gets a pathetic four bullets from all that remains of his intelligence network, the frightened cook, Weru. Haraka's men have only one contact with another group. These are fleeing to Meru and peace from the Aberdares, reporting the fight as having been lost in the south, with various generals dead or surrendered.

The increased British military presence depicted by Mwangi, together with the herding of peasants into 'protected' villages of the Pinewood type, left the freedom fighters isolated and dependant on their individual leaders for their continued existence as a unit. Once Haraka is wounded, this one unifying force is gone:

> The magnet that had drawn them back to the cave and kept them in the gang had rotted away in the general's side. They no longer had that

feeling for the cause. Now that there was no general there was no cause at all. Thus they owed nobody any loyalty, no perseverance, no nothing. (p. 123)

Military defeat was inevitable given the ebbing of morale and the overwhelming odds. Meja Mwangi perfectly captures the inexorability of the defeat at this stage. He shows the freedom fighters, trapped in a cave with little ammunition and no food, being bombarded by trained, professional soldiers with sophisticated military equipment, and he follows the tone of the introductory quotation from *Julius Caesar*:

> Let's kill him boldly but not wrathfully.
> Let's carve him as a dish fit for the gods.
> Not hew him as a carcase fit for hounds.

He depicts the brutal actualities of the struggle and not the ideology.

Mwangi adopts a similar attitude in his two novels about Nairobi life, *Kill Me Quick* and *Going Down River Road*. He portrays what he sees in detail with the minimum of authorial intrusion. This is a somewhat unfashionable approach as far as the East African literary scene is concerned, for there the constant cry is for literature to be obviously committed. But Mwangi's very choice of subject-matter – oppressed workers and peasants – is evidence of a certain social commitment. *Kill Me Quick* tells the story of Meja and Maina, two street urchins attracted to Nairobi from the poverty of the countryside. Unable to find jobs, they turn to crime after a brief spell as agricultural labourers. *Going Down River Road* portrays the lives of unskilled and semi-skilled workers on a building site in Nairobi. In these novels, Mwangi follows the trend noted by Arthur Gakwandi: 'Recent novels are tending to portray the African present as an autonomous experience, without dwelling on the conflicting elements of culture within it.'[9]

In both novels, the urban drift is depicted as being due to the poverty of the rural areas, together with the superficial attractiveness – the 'gleam' to use Armah's word – of city life. At one point in *Kill Me Quick*, Meja and Maina, tired of scrounging food from dustbins, accept the offer of work on a European farm. They receive a tinful of maize meal, a pint of skimmed milk a day, and work from six until six. They live in an insect-infested dilapidated hut 'crowded together to save land for the more important wheat and maize fields' (p. 16). Space is at a premium to make modern farming economically sound, and land consolidation and the buying up of peasant holdings by big landowners makes agricultural land scarce; the frequent government calls for the unemployed to return to the land sound very hollow. Maina's family plot is not big enough to support him as well as his parents (p. 27).

On his return home from hospital, Meja is faced by his sister:

> The rays of the setting sun fell on a tiny twelve-year-old girl standing in front of him. She was dressed in a dirty old calico sheet knotted over one shoulder and fastened with a pin below the armpit. The knot was shiny with grime and her collarbone was white beneath her skin. Her head was closely shaven and hard. Her eyes peered at him from the depths of the sockets and a long thread-like neck held the head high above the chest. The only thing that showed that the little creature was a girl were the two pimples of breasts that stuck out of her thin chest and showed vaguely under the sheet she wore. Meja watched the pathetic little figure that was his sister and his stomach ached. (p. 92)

In this close, unemotional, detailed description, so typical of Meja Mwangi's style, is summed up the reality of rural life for many in Kenya. It was to escape such abject poverty that Meja headed for the town. On the first occasion he was full of hope that he would better himself and his family, but the second escape is from the same futile hope that his father had perpetuated in his sister. Of this urban drift Raymond Williams has written:

> A displaced and formerly rural population is moving and drifting towards the centres of a money economy with is directed by interests very far from their own. The last image of the city, in the ex-colonial and neo-colonial world, is the political capital or the trading port surrounded by the shanty-towns, the barriadas, which often grow at incredible speed.[10]

This is the social movement that Mwangi is depicting in *Kill Me Quick*, and it is in just such shanties that Meja and Maina are living when they take to gang life. Just as Haraka's defeat was inevitable, so too is their descent into a life of crime which Mwangi depicts with meticulous detail.

Maina almost stumbles into crime when Razor, a gang leader, appears to recognize him. As Meja has disappeared, Maina is ready to accept the companionship that such a life has to offer. Meja, too, ends up in a gang. After a spell in hospital and the second return from home, he goes to work in a quarry just outside Nairobi. Mwangi is, incidentally, one of the few East African writers to concern himself with manual workers and to record their lives so carefully. He shows the hard, physical labour of the quarry that turns the workers into grotesque muscle-men. Eventually they work themselves out of a job and, unable to find alternative employment, form a gang. Both characters meet up again in cell nine and life becomes a round of crime and punishment until Maina breaks away to go home. There, unable to find his ageing parents, cold, hungry and penniless he murders a couple who refuse him shelter. Later, in the familiar prison cell, Meja reflects that none of them were criminals by nature, but were driven into crime by city life and the despair generated by unemployment which seemed to breed a kind of anarchic violence.

When he first met Razor, Maina had thought he was entering the big time but he was soon disillusioned:

> His picture of a well-organized gang and a peaceful hideout went right out of focus. All he could see was a lot of desperately poor people trying their best to hold on to the only thing they had in the world, Life. (p. 52)

There is little difference between the conditions of these characters and those of the workers in *Going Down River Road*. In this novel, Meja Mwangi neatly contrasts the façade of development with the reality of stagnation, and even retrogression, in the living standards of the majority of the population. The novel is set on the construction site of Development House. As the building proceeds, the author presents the reader with telling vignettes of the many workers on the site and their associates. Among these characters are the drug-crazed foreman Yussaf, trapped in the money-making machine of his uncle; and Ocholla, frequently drunk, a womanizer who has left his two wives to live in a cardboard shack and who is always down to his last cigarette. Then there is Kanji Bhai, a complaining, malnourished, skilled craftsman who is excluded from the workers' parliament and labelled an Indian. Ben is the protagonist. He was dishonourably discharged from the army for being involved in criminal activities, fired from a job in an insurance office when this was discovered, then eventually found a job on the site as an unskilled labourer. As the work progresses, he enveigles his way into the foreman's good books by supplying him with *bhang* (marijuana) and *chang'aa* (local gin). He moves from a slum off River Road to his prostitute girlfriend's house. Wini got the house by sleeping with the landlord and when she deserts him Ben is unceremoniously evicted, moving into the cardboard shack with Ocholla. The city council periodically burn down the shacks.

As the building gets higher, Mwangi reveals the other side of development – the racial tensions, separation of families, pressures that lead to dependence on illicit and legal drink, drugs and prostitutes. He reveals real poverty, even among those who are lucky enough to have jobs, and discloses the exploitative nature of private and council landlords. By way of a final irony, he shows the next job after the completion of Development House to be a tourist hotel (p. 193). It is as though the first priority in the country's development is the foreigner – the tourist. Indeed, wih rather heavy-handed symbolism the workers' eating-houses are razed to the ground to make way for the hotel. Development, it seems, is a matter of outward show.

Ben is typical of the modern isolated figures of African fiction. Of such characters David Cook has commented:

> The key figures in African novels and plays are typically at variance with their societies, however closely wedded to them they may be in certain respects ... In the challenge that these protagonists offer to group behaviour, they are unrepresentative. While the issues they raise may be those unavoidably facing their societies, they themselves become atypical. It is normal to be a unit in the close-knit social pattern; so that to break the set design is abnormal.[11]

The individualist hero is not then a spokesman for society, but rather an outsider. Such is Ben. He is an anti-hero. His background is unknown, he appears to have no family ties, he is an outsider at work; he becomes an outsider at home after Wini leaves him and when Ocholla's family arrives. He is politically uncommitted – he wonders who the 'they' are that Machore and the workers' parliament are always referring to (p. 55) – and he devotes his life to the pursuit of his own modest happiness. Ocholla and Ben have a close relationship but it is a hard and unsentimental one. Ocholla 'will look Ben in the eye when they are drinking and laughing but not when they are serious. It is not in him to show concern' (p. 97) and when Ben seeks accommodation for himself and Wini's child in Ocholla's shack he is almost going beyond the bounds of friendship. Meja Mwangi's urban characters are again and again seen as trapped within themselves.

Even from such a brief outline of these urban novels, Meja

Mwangi's concern with modern social, economic and political ills is apparent. The conditions of the workers and the unemployed are not simply background material, they are the substance of his narrative. No other writer in East Africa has so feelingly and accurately depicted the real life of Nairobi's inhabitants, the transient workers, the down-and-outs and the underworld behind the gleaming, modern façade. His latest work is a venture into popular fiction, but even here his serious concern for the ordinary Nairobi citizen comes through.

The Bushtrackers, based on a screenplay by Gary Streiker, centres on two game-rangers who become involved with a Mafia-organized team of poachers and protection racketeers. It is a fast-moving thriller that is topical, full of suspense and violence. As such it works very well, making Meja Mwangi one of the very few East African writers who can write successfully for the English-reading popular market. As with his first novel, the plot takes precedence but Meja Mwangi's distinctive prose style still shines through in descriptive passages such as the following:

> Nairobi, a lively city of scurrying feet and roaring cars by day, a city of strangers and ladies of darkness by night, a retiring old hag, loverless and unlovable. Just as she belongs to no one, no one belongs to her. When asked where their homes are, Nairobi dwellers would mention some obscure little villages up in the Highlands, as yet too tiny to be discernible on any map. They come here to work, make money, have a good time and get back to the obscurity of the distant hills and plateaus. To many, Nairobi is just an opening; everyone glad to use her, sing praises to her beauty, her conveniences, while loudly denying owing her any loyalty. (p. 148)

The factual observations about attitudes to Nairobi are accurate while the comparison to an old whore, though not original, is cleverly developed and nicely suggestive of the hard, unsentimental urban mentality.

Having exorcized his Mau Mau ghost in the first two novels, Meja Mwangi now seems well set on the road to becoming Kenya's leading, modern novelist in English. He writes equally well for both the popular and the more serious market, and his subject-matter to date has been of such obvious and immediate relevance as to attract rapidly growing numbers of young readers. He is much admired by fellow writers, including Ngugi wa Thiong'o, and with his distinctive prose style he is easily the most outstanding writer in English in Kenya today.

NOTES

1. L. Kibera, *Voices in the Dark*, Nairobi, East African Publishing House, 1970.
2. Meja Mwangi, *Kill Me Quick*, London, Heinemann (AWS 143), 1973. Meja Mwangi, *Going Down River Road*, London, Heinemann (AWS 176), 1976. Meja Mwangi, *The Bushtrackers*, Nairobi, Longman Kenya Ltd., 1979.
3. Meja Mwangi, *Taste of Death*, Nairobi, East African Publishing House, 1975. Meja Mwangi, *Carcase for Hounds*, London, Heinemann (AWS 145), 1974.
4. D. Rubadiri, 'The Development of Writing in East Africa' in *Perspectives on African Literature*, ed. C. Heywood, London, Heinemann, 1971, p. 150, New York, Africana, 1971.
5. J. M. Kariuki, *Mau Mau Detainee*, London, OUP, 1963. C. G. Rosberg and J. Nottingham, *The Myth of Mau Mau*, New York, Praeger, 1966. W. Itote, *Mau Mau General*, Nairobi, East African Publishing House, 1967. Ngugi wa Thiong'o, *Weep Not, Child*, London, Heinemann (AWS 7), 1964. Ngugi wa Thiong'o, *A Grain of Wheat*, London, Heinemann (AWS 36), 1968. G. Wachira, *Ordeal in the Forest*, Nairobi, East African Publishing House, 1968. L. Kibera and S. Kahiga, *Potent Ash*, Nairobi, East African Publishing House, 1968. C. Waciuma, *Daughter of Mumbi*, Nairobi, East African Publishing House, 1969. C. Mangua, *A Tail in the Mouth*, Nairobi, East African Publishing House, 1972. K. Watene, *My Son for my Freedom*, Nairobi, East African Publishing House, 1973. Ngugi wa Thiong'o, *Secret Lives*, London, Heinemann (AWS 150), 1975. K. Watene, *Dedan Kimathi*, Nairobi, Transafrica Publishers, 1974. Ngugi wa Thiong'o and Micere Mugo, *The Trial of Dedan Kimathi*, London, Heinemann (AWS 191), 1976. B. Kaggia, *Roots of Freedom*, Nairobi, East African Publishing House, 1975.
6. B. Lindfors, 'New Trends in West and East African Fiction', *Review of National Literatures*, II, 2, 1971, p. 32.
7. G. Lukács, 'The Ideology of Modernism' in *The Meaning of Contemporary Realism*, translated John and Necke Mander, London, Merlin Press, 1963, p. 31. Atlantic Heights, NJ, Humanities Press.
8. D. Barnett, *Mau Mau General* and K. Njama, *Mau Mau from Within*, New York, Monthly Review, 1966.
9. S. A. Gakwandi. *The Novel and Contemporary Experience in Africa*, London, Heinemann, 1977. New York, Africana, 1977.
10. R. Williams, *The Country and the City*, St Albans, Paladin, 1975, p. 344, New York, OUP, 1975.
11. D. Cook, *African Literature*, London, Longman, 1977, pp. 4–5.

Female Writers, Male Critics

Femi Ojo-Ade

We are the victims of our History and our Present. They place too many obstacles in the Way of Love. And we cannot enjoy even our Differences in peace.

We all fall victim.

(Ama Ata Aidoo, *Our Sister Killjoy*)

Introduction: Female Writing, An Art of the Minority

African literature is a male-created, male-oriented, chauvinistic art. An honour-roll of our literary giants clearly proves the point: Ngugi wa Thiong'o, Senghor, Soyinka, Achebe, Mphahlele, and others. Literature being a function of life, fact feeds fiction; the poet meets the politician. Senghor, Toure and others combine the artistic vocation with political position. Male is the master; male constitutes majority. The fact is well documented in our colonial history. The white civilizer, as cunning as ever, carefully chose his black counterpart to run the affairs of the 'Dark Continent'. Woman is considered to be a flower, not a worker. Woman is supposed to be relegated to the gilded cage; she is not the contributor to, the creator of, a civilization. So the new black bourgeoisie, all awash with the off-white paint of civilization, emerged in the arena of inhumanism. Blackish skin, multicoloured masks aglow under the African sun, they croak the national anthem composed by the ex-colonial master, their woman, white teeth glistening with Maclean's, just a step behind.

Man constitutes the majority and woman, the minority. Not a minority of numbers; for it is common knowledge that in spite of the preference for male offspring shown in Africa and elsewhere, females are the dominant sex among newly born babies.[1] Minority should be contemplated in the sense of Dominated, Disadvantaged,

Exploited, Excluded. As far as literature is concerned, the connotation becomes both symbolic, social and numerical. The female counterparts of the Soyinkas are a rare breed.[2] They do exist, however. Nwapa, Aidoo, Njau, Emecheta and Head are names that come to mind. For that rare breed, practising the art of writing poses problems at once similar to, and greater than, those faced by their male 'masters'. First, the situation and circumstances are hardly right. Writing is still largely an esoteric vocation, a haven of an elite, anathema to an illiterate majority faced with the immediate realities of misery and concerned with survival.

> To be a good novelist the writer must operate within a conducive atmosphere. She must have time and space to reflect and indulge in introspective thinking. For many potential writers in this country neither the time nor the space is available. In addition to family drawbacks, the government seems not to appreciate the value of home-produced works. It seems to be doing very little to encourage writers, financially and otherwise.

Those are the words of a female Nigerian novelist living in England.[3] Her observations are poignant and thought-provoking. Unfortunately, African reality hardly provides the 'conducive atmosphere' required by the writer; it may never even provide such an atmosphere in our generation. The consolation is that those writers who are courageous enough, adamant enough, committed enough to tempt and tame fate will always write.

The male writer, like the male social animal, is more fortunate than the female. His presence is taken for granted. The publisher seeks him out, unlike the woman whose silence is also taken for granted. Cultural misconceptions and taboos abound. It is believed that women must keep quiet when men are talking. Woman is woman, mother, child-bearer, supporter of man. If woman talks too much, she is considered uncouth, uncivilized. If she is educated, she is classified as a weird specimen.

Fortunately, taboos die — though slowly — with the times. With the new, warped, so-called luminaries emerging from the colonial roots, even the female deaf and dumb have acquired a voice. It is a voice of confusion, of confrontation, of commitment. The men have had their say; they continue to have it. It is now the women's turn. If we think of the International Women's year we will come to realize the debt owed to western civilization.

In any analysis of a colonial society struggling to de-colonize itself, the woman's role in the struggle cannot be overlooked. There

are militants carrying placards and revolutionaries toting gre-
nades. Male and female, together, live out their agonies, paradoxes
and dilemmas. Woman has a lot to write about and it is a fortunate
phenomenon that she is taking a step out of the womb.

Now, the question may be asked, and it has been asked already:
why write about female African writers at all? Here is one answer:

> The personality and the inner reality of African women have been
> hidden under such a heap of myths, so-called ethnological theories,
> rapid generalizations and patent untruths that it might be interesting to
> study what they have to say for themselves when they decide to speak.[4]

To that statement this critic adds: the female writer, having gone
through the same, or almost the same, experience as the man,
should have something to say about that experience, namely,
Colonialism – Christianity – Civilization. The adopted male and
female children of the white father sing their songs of praise at the
altar of the white God. Blind men and women in a dark alley grope
their way towards the dawn of a new day of decolonization and
independence. Dawn turns into darkness through an unexpected
eclipse. The blind men, having regained their sight, become blind
again, and beg the departed master to come and show them the way
to go home. The new duo of ex-master and ex-servant constitutes
the essence of neo-colonialism.

The literary critic observes the scene with keen interest. Like the
writer, he is aware of his task:

> The most serious task facing our critics is that of relating our writers'
> works to the whole state and condition of our people's existence and
> drawing out the meaning of this literature for the African public by
> demonstrating not only its excellence but also its relevance.[5]

Criticism, like creativity, is a function of a socio–economic and
political reality. Both contribute to the survival of society.
Admittedly sentimentality should be avoided. Indeed, some would
love to have *objectivity* as the watchword of all criticism. But this
critic refuses to accept this notion. It is impossible to eliminate the
human being, the mind, the heart, from life's essential realities,
unless man is killed and replaced with an automaton, or a
computer.

And the echo of the critic's rebuttal fills the land: prejudices,
biases, idiosyncrasies are permitted. But permission is not
permissiveness. Moderation is far from mania. Commitment to a
culture is not acculturation. Consciousness of a race is not racism.

The line between sanity and madness is very thin. The coward vastly outnumber the courageous, and it is a coward that woul institute a law banning a black from criticizing a white, a white from criticizing a black, a woman from criticizing a man, and a man from criticizing a woman. In our critique of the works of Nwapa, Aidoo, Emecheta and Njau, we shall express the ideas of an individual, a man, looking at the works of women, and the notions of a society reviewing the standpoint of her members. That is only natural, just as it is to be expected that the writers under discussion represent individual and group viewpoints. Woman and man exist in harmony, and in conflict. Convergences and divergences are forever present.

Flora Nwapa's Tragic, Traditional Heroine

It is only natural that the female African writer should depict the travails of female characters. The creator exhibits deep empathy for her heroine who, to a large extent, is a mouthpiece for her personal notions on life, a sister in suffering. Autobiography feeds fiction. The original coalesces with the double. Woman weeps with woman; for the life of a woman is filled with worries.

> Tragedy in the Igbo situation is not in the feeling that nothing goes right for the individual, but the fact that any success he attains is followed sooner or later by a bigger and more terrible misfortune. This is a constant reality in Igbo life, which among some Igbo groups is described as the phenomenon of *Ume*.[6]

Another constant in life is fear: fear of the Enemy, fear of the Gods. However, that does not mean that the human being exists like a vegetable, resigned to reacting automatically before the devastating actions of the adversary. Besides, there are always heroic characters during the storm. Such is Efuru, extraordinary daughter of an extraordinary father.

> Efuru was her name. She was a remarkable woman. It was not only that she came from a distinguished family. She was distinguished herself. Her husband was not known and people wondered why she married him.[7]

There lies the first abnormality: a man must hold the position of power. He is father of the family, prince of the populace, breadwinner, lord and master. Efuru is an 'outsider', not one to be excommunicated – no apologies to the catholic congregation – not one to be burnt at the stake. She is a revered, respected 'outsider'.

She is lord and master of her man, Adizua. The man is an 'imbecile', a pauper who cannot pay the dowry, a 'nobody' with whom Efuru decides to run off without performing traditional marriage ceremonies.

Flora Nwapa tries hard enough to make her heroine a positive figure meriting sympathy. But those very qualities that dazzle both family and friends set Efuru up as a victim of tragedy. The first domineering demeanour builds up till the day Adizua disappears. The wife detests farming – 'I am not cut out for farm work. I am going to trade' (p. 5) – so the husband abandons the farm and becomes a trader. The wife cannot bear the boring life of the village, so her husband scurries to town to be at the side of the unique woman that is the cynosure of all eyes – 'After seeing this type of woman, one hisses when one sees one's wife' (p. 8). The wife says it is time to pay dowry to her father, so Adizua obeys.

Efuru flouts the very first laws of tradition and she will pay the price in the end. Unlike Adizua's mother who has accepted woman's traditional role, Efuru refuses to play second fiddle.

People say that Adizua is a nonentity, a nobody, a fool ready to accept his wife's superiority. The posture is perfect: the ever-loving husband vows to stick to his childless wife through thick and thin:

> 'Please don't think that it makes any difference to me whether you have a baby or not. You know I will be the last person to do anything that will hurt you my wife. You know I cannot change you with a wife who would give me twenty sons.' (p. 26)

Efuru has total confidence in him, although she realizes the importance of children to every man and woman: 'Don't you think it will be better if you began to look around for a young girl for a wife?' (p. 26). Soon, she becomes pregnant and has a bouncing baby girl, only to lose her on a day when Adizua is away.

The ever-present, ever-loving, submissive husband disappears. He disproves the belief that a man cannot be a man even when his wife is an Efuru, 'a woman among women'. Adizua reveals new, strange ways; he becomes problematic. He constitutes the first problem for which the extraordinary Efuru has no solution. Beyond every mountain lies a valley. Behind every beauty lurks a beast. The genius is brother to the fool. Efuru the extraordinary is made of ordinary clay. She becomes submissive and sad. Adizua disappears and she goes searching for him. She ends up returning to her father's house.

The heroine's sympathizers would quickly denounce the unfaithful Adizua for leaving Efuru for another woman. The answer to such an accusatory posture would be Tradition. Man marries many wives. Man takes decisions. Man is lord and master. If Efuru had been a loving, submissive wife, maybe she would not have been abandoned. Besides, her problem with children, as she herself asserts, constitutes an inadequacy that could be exploited. A woman that cannot reproduce is not a woman. The richest woman on earth is the poorest without a child:

> What is money? Can a bag of money go for an errand for you? Can a bag of money look after you in your old age? Can a bag of money mourn you when you are dead? A child is more valuable than money. (p. 37)

Now, if that very inadequacy makes a common woman out of Nwapa's heroine, it also enhances her extraordinariness. If her earlier suggestion to Adizua, to take a second wife, seems less than honest, the subsequent efforts are no doubt made in good faith. For all her aggressiveness and uniqueness, in spite of her single-mindedness and rebellious nature, Efuru remains quite attached to the tradition by which the wife participates in the search for a new mate. Polygamy is not a bane:

> 'If he wants to marry a wife I shall be only too happy. In fact, I have been thinking of it for some time for I have not had a second baby, and now I wonder whether a second one will ever come.' (p. 50)

Also:

> 'What is wrong in his marrying a second wife? It is only a bad woman who wants her husband all to herself. I don't object to his marrying a second wife, but I do object to being relegated to the background. I want to keep my position as the first wife, for it is my right.' (p. 53)

The rules are clear: the man 'must go about it in an open and noble way' (p. 57). And that is exactly where Adizua falls flat on his face. Man is mean; man is monstrous. It is even revealed that Adizua resembles his father. Efuru finds out from her mother-in-law – it serves her right for flouting a tradition that demands adequate investigation of the partner's background before the union is approved – that Adizua's father was a vagabond. He ran away from his wife, surfaced six years later with another, wealthier woman, and finally returned to his first wife, sick and tired, to die. So Efuru's exit from the prison of her marriage is deemed glorified by her and her creator. 'To suffer for a truant husband, an irresponsible husband like Adizua is to debase suffering. My own suffering will be noble. I shall leave him' (pp. 61–62). Her father,

her mother-in-law and the latter's sister, all advise her to be patient, but she refuses.

Her new husband is a former childhood playmate named Gilbert. Her father gives his consent to the marriage. For a change, the man is well behaved, accepted and approved of by all. Apparently, Efuru is happy and will forever be happy. An interesting element of the new union is that Gilbert is a Christian. His African name, Eniberi, is offensive to him. His courtship of Efuru is 'civilized'. There are polite exchanges and a long, platonic relationship before any physical contact. Proposal of marriage is made with the woman having time to 'think it over'. The author expresses tacit acceptance of Christian superiority; Efuru's father exults at his child's choice. 'The white men are little gods' and their adopted son, Gilbert, is no less a god among his people. African tradition is stigmatized as backward and the civilized couple seizes every opportunity to prove their happiness in their Christian ways.

However, a close look at the life of our Romeo and Juliet reveals the hollowness of that happiness. Trappings of capitalism, Christian hypocrisy, civilized charlatanism abound. Gilbert and his people recognize Efuru for what she is: 'Her hands make money. Anything she touches is money' (p. 125). What pleases his mother most about Efuru is the fact that 'any trade she puts her hand to is profitable' (p. 136). They are all glad to use her talent. Besides, once Gilbert knows that Efuru is barren, he goes out and has a child by another woman. He keeps the secret from her for two years. It is astonishing that Efuru does not get angry after learning of the secret child; yet she had berated Adizua for his waywardness and infidelity. The reasons are complex, just as her character and her society are complex. Christianity is superior, but tradition dies hard. The mongrel owes allegiance to, and feels love for, both disparate parents. Traditional society prefers children to money but rains abuse upon the poor. Gilbert does not mind a childless wife but has a secret son outside marriage. Efuru reveres the harmonious basis of polygamy yet takes a third wife 'who will compete with the second wife. She thinks she can do what she likes in this house'.

Many myths about Africa need to be eradicated, and Nwapa's novel, to a certain extent, succeeds in doing just that. However, since modernism and tradition cannot be clearly separated, confusion remains and the heroine, like her man Gilbert–Eniberi, symbolizes that very confusion of the new Africa. Efuru is the past, but Efuru is also the present. She repels the sound and fury of the former but cannot stand the silence and frustration of the latter. Gilbert accuses her, falsely, of adultery. Her honour debased, her pride hurt, she leaves him and returns to her father's house.

Her literary sister, Idu,[8] enjoys a similar fate of loneliness and tragic superiority. But Idu's is different from Efuru's. Her two children survive and she is patient, totally devoted to her man. When her husband Adiewere dies, Idu refuses to become his brother's new wife. She remains alone, thus flouting tradition. 'She "died" the day her husband died' (*Idu*, p. 216), and dies physically days after. Indeed, Idu, though tragically struck like Efuru, is a more acceptable personality. She is closer to tradition than the cantankerous Efuru. Her joys are more authentic, more down-to-earth. While Efuru is 'married' to the woman of the lake – the latter chooses her as her worshipper, a reason to which Efuru's childlessness is adduced – Idu remains forever attached to her Adiewere. That fact underscores the paradox pervading the whole of the society under focus. The more *traditional* Idu rebels against tradition while the more *modern* Efuru espouses tradition. In the final analysis, Flora Nwapa's heroines and novels, are quintessential examples of the ironies and contradictions rampant in 'developing' Africa. And womanhood is part of the whole syndrome.

Aidoo and Europe: Lair of Love and Lesbianism

While Nwapa's heroines are attached, no matter now tenuously, to the African soil, other females, feminist offspring of western education, fly away from 'pagan' Africa, in search of the golden fleece. What most only manage to dream of, the chosen few accomplish. The slogans are unforgettable: see Paris and die; London the cradle of civilization; Europe, the nerve-centre of modernism. It is hard to forget the look of pride affixed to the faces of the departing loved ones, on those balmly tropical nights filled with gaiety at our international airports of sub-national standard. Much more poignant still are the memories of the new arrivals – been-to's, Johnnies-come-lately, choking under the heavy tie-knot, suffocating in the three-piece, woollen suit, bowler hat under one arm, a walking-stick umbrella dangling from the other. Male writers, flushed with the personal taste of acculturation and alienation, have beaten the theme almost to death (Ousmane Socé Diop, Camara Laye, John Pepper Clark, Ayi Kwei Armah, and others), and now it is the turn of the women who, it must be emphasized, have not enjoyed, as much as the men, the privilege of dying a living death in a white man's winter.

Sissie is the heroine of Ama Ata Aidoo's *Our Sister Killjoy*[9] – 'reflections from a black-eyed squint'. But let no one be deceived: 'our sister's black-eyed squint at things' is not a story of hate, but of love – and that, indeed, is another oversimplification. We are told that the lady's real name is Mary, and that the common appellation, Sissie, is reserved for one loved by her black brothers and sisters. Sissie is a member of the Ghanaian arm of INVOLOU, an international group of teenagers helping to build schools, dig wells, 'change a fifth rate feeder road into a second rate feeder road' (p. 34). She belongs to a select few in society, budding bourgeois blessed with philanthropic fervour in their dealings with the numberless poor. Sissie is chosen to go to Europe as part of the INVOLOU group. 'Sissie and her companions were required to be there, eating, laughing, singing, and eating. Above all eating' (p. 35). So the ambassadors descend upon Europe, stuffing themselves with a certain calmness that passeth all understanding while working leisurely at a pine-nursery to protect those Christmas trees against winter.

It is during that sojourn in a Bavarian village that Sissie meets Marija. 'To those for whom things are only what they seem, Marija is a young Bavarian woman' (p. 79). Bavaria is part of Germany, and that fact arouses memories of Adolf Hitler, of Nazis exterminating Jews, of the Aryan superman stomping upon the bent bones of the other subhumans. Marija's village has a castle turned into a hostel for the young volunteers from abroad and in such a castle once lived some lord controlling the destiny of many serfs. Moreover, we are told that that particular village used to be the centre of massive chemical plants using human bodies as experimental components. Marija is Bavarian, indeed. Racist to the core, her first interest in Sissie is due to curiosity:

– Mary, Mary . . . and you an African?
– Yes.
– But that is a German name! said Marija. (p. 24)

Marija is Bavarian, no doubt: she met two Indians working some time before. She claims to love them a great deal; she even asks whether Sissie is Indian. Marija is German; she asserts: 'My man is called ADOLF' (p. 23).

It does not matter, however. Sissie sees beyond those superficial trappings. 'Marija was warm, too warm for Bavaria, Germany, *from knowledge gained since*' (p. 27). Those final words constitute a refrain in the novel and they must be of particular importance to the understanding of Sissie's personality and experiences. For there is in her, while she is participating in the events described, a certain naivete that galls the reader, an astonishing stupidity that smirks of bad faith. Sissie is an adult, capable of reasoning; yet she lacks the clearsightedness necessary to see through the sham love of a lesbian.

Marija asks to be her friend; she agrees. Thus begins a series of daily meetings, long walks together, a long stay in Marija's house with big Adolf always absent, and little Adolf forever present and intruding. Marija plays the man from the beginning:

> Marija asked a few questions while Sissie, answering, told her friend about her Mad country and her Madder continent. (p. 40)

Marija selects special plums for her friend, everyday. There are suspicious looks among the village aristocracy about the strange relationship. Perverse is the word they use. 'SOMEONE MUST TELL HER HUSBAND!' (p. 44). But the two women are not deterred. Once, walking hand in hand, they are accosted by an old white couple who curse them. Marija blushes R–E–D, but Sissie just keeps smiling, because she does not understand their mad countenance.[10] Now, before anyone begins to fall prey to Sissie's claim to true naivete, let us quote her very observation on the first evening that her Bavarian friend takes her out:

> There was a certain strangeness about Marija. . . . Her eyes had a gleam in them that the African girl would have found unsettling if the smiles that always seemed to be dancing around her lips had also not been more obviously there. She was flushed and hot. Sissie could feel the heat. (p. 45)

That first night out, Marija states that she would not have been able to bear it if Sissie had been disallowed from accompanying her home. Our dear sister remains unruffled. What is her position in all this? It is not known immediately, nor categorically, although there is a subtle annoyance with their critics. Another curious fact is that Sissie agrees with Marija to put back the time of their meeting to a couple of hours later in the night, to avoid the stare of gossips.

Then it strikes like lightning: the young couple goes to Marija's house; Sissie is asked upstairs to see the rooms: 'I wanted to be alone. To talk with you . . . you know, Sissie, sometimes one wants to be alone. Even from the child one loves so much. Just for a very little time . . . maybe' (p. 49). Then Marija suddenly holds the

African woman tight and kisses her flush on the mouth, right there in the nuptial chamber, with the bed specially made, clean as a virgin's body. One might expect Sissie to slap, scream, spit; to curse, scratch, scurry out of the room. She does not do any of those things. Two pairs of eyes stare at each other, two mouths open wide, in disbelief. Sissie – the novelist, too – definitely feels pity, sympathy, understanding for poor Marija. Her loneliness is constantly emphasized.

The reaction to that sympathy is a series of questions. Who is not alone? Does aloneness extricate the lesbian from the wrath of the heterosexual? How deep is Marija's suffering? Does Big Adolf exist at all? Sissie never meets him but, remarkably enough, Marija says that he will definitely be at the special dinner that she had planned for Sissie who has just informed her of her departure and inability to attend the dinner.

As for Sissie, descriptions of LOVE abound during the period of her affair with Marija. 'Work is love made visible . . . . Love is always better when doomed' (p. 41). In a moment of sheer courage and utter frankness, our dear sister gives away her secret:

> Once or so, at the beginning of their friendship, Sissie had thought, while they walked in the park, of what a delicious love affair she and Marija would have had if one of them had been a man. Especially if she, Sissie had been a man. She had imagined and savoured the tears, their anguish at knowing that their love was doomed. But they would make promises to each other which of course would not stand a chance of getting fulfilled. She could see Marija's tears . . . . That was a game. A game in which one day, she became so absorbed, she forgot who she was, and the fact that she was a woman. In her imagination, she was one of these black boys in one of those involvements with white girls in Europe. Struck by some of the stories she had heard, she shivered, absolutely horrified. (p. 61)

There, indeed, is a revelation. Black woman aspires to play the role of black man. Black boy takes white girl. The revenge of the race, some call it. African literature has several examples of such encounters; so too does real life. We recall the raving madness and neurotic phobia of a failed African man in England, spitting out his abhorrence for the white society. He cries out:

> 'I will fight Powell and probably take him to hell with me. And do you know how I'll do it? I'll do it with his curious sisters. I will infiltrate your society as you have mine.' . . . Sex revenge would be his success.[11]

While the rage subsides, the black man comes to live the myth that he has tried to belie. The myth affirms that white skin is superior, that white woman is the wonder of the world. Now, Sissie is weighed down by a deep-rooted inferiority complex which makes for her contradictions. The movement is multifold: Love–Hate–Revenge–Love. Love between two human beings. Love between man and woman. Hate for racist Europe. Hate for superior man. Revenge against man, against Europe. Love for man, black man. Sissie, with her big mouth and foul temper – she is definitely not the retiring, housekeeping type – seizes every possible occasion to sneer at men. So, with Marija, she feels man's 'inhuman sweet sensation to see another human being squirming'. 'There's pleasure in hurting,' she says. On another occasions, she scolds her friend:

'It is not sound for a woman to enjoy cooking for another woman. Not under any circumstances. It is not done. It is not possible. Special meals are for men. They are the only sex to whom the Maker gave a mouth with which to enjoy eating. And woman the eternal cook is never so pleased as seeing a man enjoying what she has cooked . . .' (p. 77)

The irony of the above statement is too glaring to be misconstrued. It all goes to show how mean man is supposed to be. Like our other dear sisters, Aidoo berates black man for his innumerable low qualities. What stands out in her own attack, however, is the deep love binding black man and woman together. That love-solidarity stands against the lesbian love exhibited by Marija – and, to some extent, responded to by our dear sister – and her Europe. When Sissie looks beyond the individual named Marija (which she does in the long run) what she sees is sick, white Europe for which the African feels pity:

Why weep for them? In fact, stronger in her was the desire to ask somebody why the entire world has to pay so much and is still paying so much for some folks' unhappiness. (p. 66)

Marija's sickness, Europe's sickness, is not to be condemned, says Sissie, but pitied. Therein lies her humanism, her wisdom 'from knowledge gained since'. Such pity is not to be mistaken for acquiescence or complicity. It is simply that Sissie is not a purveyor of hate. Indeed, we cannot forget that, in spite of her militant fire, in spite of her revolutionary ardour, Aidoo's heroine remains a woman. Fortunately, that does not stop her from being frank.

The overall picture of Europe is rather morbid. Europe, 'a land where Black men are forever regarded as children' (p. 125). Europe, 'polished steel. Polished tin. Polished brass. Cut glass. Plastic' (p. 12). Europe, land of white supremacy:

> Trotters, pig-tails, pig-ears. She looked and looked at so many of such skins together. And she wanted to vomit. Then she was ashamed of her reaction. For the rest of her life, she was to regret this moment when she was made to notice differences in human colouring. No matter where she went, what anyone said, what they did. She knew it never mattered. But what she also came to know was that someone somewhere would always see in any kind of difference, an excuse to be mean. (pp. 12–13)

Now, if Europe holds such glaringly negative truths for blacks, why do many go there? Why do many insist on staying? Sissie's quest for love among her own brings her face to face with those truths, and those dilemmas. Like black man, she feels a guilty love for that hellish Europe; she feels a certain pride in being a been-to. We must remember that she is a product of colonial education, a foster-child of Europe, a black bourgeois. The travel programme in which she gladly participates is symbolic of the West's stranglehold on her motherland. Sissie passes through England on her way back home, specifically to prove to those in Ghana that she has really been abroad. 'Germany,' she says, 'is overseas. The United States is overseas. But England is another thing' (p. 85).

Our sister meets many of her (our) brothers in England. They are 'recipients of the leftovers of imperial handouts', sellers of their soul and their motherland:

> For a few pennies a
> Doctoral degree later and
> Tell us about
> Your people
> Your history
> Your mind (p. 86)

All salvation, it is believed, comes from the imperial seat. Little do they know, poor fools, that 'for the slave, there is nothing at the centre but worse slavery' (p. 66). Perhaps Aidoo's biggest coup in her novel is her astute reference to the famous heart transplant carried out in South Africa by the 'good Christian Doctor' (Christian Barnard), on a white man, with the heart of a black woman. The thoughts and implications are overwhelmingly exciting: a great Christian performance by a devout devil; heart knows no race; a black heart in a white body; opposites attract. And the black African scientist from some free nation without a name or norms – Kunle is his name, a seven-year Londoner – zealously basks in the sun of Barnard's genius. Kunle babbles away on the importance of the transplant, while his country, Nigeria, is embroiled in self-destruction. He says with glee: 'Such development can solve the question of apartheid and rid us, "African negroes and all other negroes" of the Colour Problem' (p. 96). The good Christian doctor has said that *niggerhearts* are so easy to come by, since savage blacks kill each other so impulsively.

The aftermath of the great experiment is, that the black donor, nameless, is forever mired in oblivion, while the famous white recipient dies after living for over a year with the black heart. Many more blacks are ensnared in the fangs of the apartheid beast; Kunle the scientist returns home and soon dies, 'killed by the car for which he had waited so long', and the Christian doctor is alive and well, a living legend, transplanting hearts of dogs, cats and human beings. His apartheid land is as foreign to the African as Europe:

> I have been to a cold strange land where dogs and cats eat better than many many children. Where men would sit at table and eat with animals, and yet would rather die than shake the hands of other men. Where women who say they have no time to bear children and spoil their lives would sit for many hours and feed baby dogs delicate food with spoons, and make coats to cover the hairy animals from the same cloth they wear, as sisters and brothers and friends from our village would do on festive occasions . . . , a land where they treat animals like human beings and some human beings like animals because they are not dumb enough. (p. 99)

No mistake about it: the words quoted above can emanate only from the heart of a black woman, multiple victim of life and love, repository of a civilization built upon continuity, indeed, symbol of the survival of a harried race.

Black Man, Black Woman, Black Bourgeoisie: Loneliness

We have verified Sissie's attachment to the bourgeoisie. Indeed, Aidoo's heroine must be one of the most forthright characters in African literature. For, instead of trying to deny, to run away and hide under the cloak of revolution, she accepts her position as one of that compromising, conniving class consituting Africa's shame. For her, it is not a question of us against them; it is us against ourselves, and them, with the shameful knowledge that, to an alarmingly large extent, we have remained part of them. The ultimate objective is clearly set from the start: to free us from ourselves, from them, to love ourselves; for, without that, we cannot love them. The desire is to have love between black man and woman. We may have to pass through a period of hate, real or apparent; at least, there must be sincerity, forthrightness, bluntness, and arguments. Truth is bitter. At the back of laughter we find tears. Truth is often the harbinger of tears. Sissie talks, thinks, all the time, because she is genuinely concerned about us, about Africa, because she loves us. However, her man fails to understand. We perceive remnants of the legendary male superiority complex. Man is master, man is a monster. Sissie's man claims that she lacks 'feminine instincts' simply because she finds it impossible to pretend. 'A concerned type, with some radical political ideas . . . , with lots of naive enthusiasm' (p. 127), Sissie is a rare woman, embarrassing to the chauvinistic man. The latter is convinced that she is the Enemy. And the old sexist dichotomies are once more established. She is sentimental; he, practical (a medical doctor). 'She is so serious'. Radical is pitched against moderate. Human stands against scientist. Indeed, the man is indirectly asserting the woman's savagery against his own civilization. There are echoes of the Christian doctor transplanting hearts, while Kunle the Nigerian is applauding the racist with all his heart. Sissie worries a great deal; she thinks of language, our borrowed language, 'a language that enslaved me, and therefore, the messengers of my mind always come shackled' (p. 112). She thinks of the survival of the race and the re-discovery of human beings. A new language must be created, 'so that we shall make love with words and not fear of being overheard' (p. 116).

The man is not interested in such banalities, however; to his mind, the African woman's virtues of softness and meekness – 'see, at home the woman knows her position' (p. 117) – should be cultivated by Sissie. There again, as in many other aspects, the man is totally wrong. He fails to realize that the woman's position is 'more complicated than that of the dolls the colonizers brought along with them who fainted at the sight of their own bleeding fingers and carried smelling salts around' (p. 117). The fact is, black man needs to be taught how to love, to see beyond the bulging backside, the feminine façade, the buxom bodies. He has had far too much experience of colonial embourgeoisement for his own good. Longevity has caused loss of authenticity. Acculturation has been consequential to colonial apprenticeship. Having suffered less than the woman, having been entrenched in the neo-colonial fortress, he now finds it difficult to dealienate himself. Like an overzealous student, he has over-mastered the game of hypocrisy and the mania of self-agrandizement, laying claim at once to modernity and the privileges of a tradition that he hardly understands and which belongs to a culture overtaken by the times. Individualism. Capitalism. Civilization. For the man, civilization, consciously or otherwise, means aping white ways. He has stopped asking questions, he has adapted himself to, or seeks, the situation affording him the opportunity to 'live and let live'.

Sissie and others like her would not let him be. They keep asking questions, blaming themselves and all those like him, even when, according to the male lackeys of the neo-colonial monster, 'there is nothing the matter with anything':

> There goes Sissie again. Forever carrying Africa's problems on her shoulders as though they have paid her to do it. (p. 118)

So, love sours, loneliness surfaces. Of course, the latter has always been there, hidden away, repulsed, even feared. Sissie knows it; so does her man. Only he is too cowardly to admit that 'there is a kind of loneliness overseas which is truly bad' (p. 119). The cold winter of white Europe bites the black skin. The stony faces stare at the black face, asking in loud silence when he is returning home. He is dogged by companions called silence, rejection, loneliness. Africans overseas are dead, says Sissie, and she is definitely right to say so. For their self-exile, a younger version of the old liquidation of the continent, is not a state of bliss but of bankruptcy, barrenness and blight. The warmth of the woman would be a way of achieving some joy, but the stupid man throws away the chance. Sissie laments:

> They say that any female in my position would have thrown away everything to be with you, and remain with you: first, her opinions, and then her own plans. But oh deliciously naive me. What did I rather do but daily and loudly criticise you and your friends for wanting to stay forever in alien places? (p. 117)

Man never seems to want to learn that he is not god, that, like all beings and things, he is dispensable, even when he is an almighty doctor. Worse still is his habit of being incorrigible. While the Sissies of Africa fail to lure their men away from Europe, these same men end up worshipping at the feet of white women. Our male writers provide us with innumerable examples. They bring their snow-queens home to Africa, vowing hyprocritically to settle down with them in a land where even the established sons of the soil remain aliens.

Africa: Home, Sweet, Bitter Home

Ama Ata Aidoo's heroine, as we have stated, does not run away from problems. She does not seek easy solutions nor does she claim to have all the answers. While preaching regularly to Africa's exiled sons to go home, she agrees that there are pitfalls. In many ways, home is hell. Aidoo's catalogue of Africa's ills reminds the critic of the works of Armah and Awoonor, her illustrious compatriots. The difference is that the female novelist brings a touch of love, commitment and positiveness to her criticism of Africa.

To the man with a weak heart, it would be senseless to return home. Africa is a land of the 'moderate nigger', talking of universal truth, universal art, universal literature, universal nothing. Africa is the land of Power:

> Power, Child, Power.
> For this is all anything is about.
> Power to decide
> Who is to live,
> Who is to die.
> Where,
> When,
> How. (pp. 15–16)

Africa is the land of Christianity. And Sissie recalls that God is 'a rather nice, old European gentleman with a flowing white beard' flanked by 'Western, white, English angels' (p. 26). She also remembers the missionaries' lesson: 'for a child to grow up to be a Heaven-worthy individual, he had to have above all, a Christian name' (p. 25). Africa is the land of the bourgeoisie and their 'zombie dynasties', where the poor feed on air and the glory of rich men that come and go. Our leaders are 'sleepwalkers in a nightmare asleep to all things at all times – conscious only of riches, which they gather in a coma' (p. 34). Africa is the land 'where national problems stay unseen while big men live their big lives within':

> In the capitals
> Ex-convicts from European
> Prisons drive the city buses and
> Black construction workers
> Sweat under the tropical sun, making
> Ice-skating rinks for
> The Beautiful People
> While other Niggers sit

With vacant stares
Or
Busy
Spitting their lungs out . . .
We must sing and dance
Because some African made it . . .
Our representatives and interpreters,
The low-achieving academics
In low profile politics
Have the time of their lives
Grinning at cocktail parties and around
Conference tables (pp. 56–57)

The realistic, black image becomes more and more lurid. Why then all those letters asking the exile to come home? The news is never encouraging: debts, misery, sickness, a dead-end of pointless prayers, and death. Why the agitation when those at home own up to being proud that their loved ones are overseas? Here is one answer given by Kunle's mother: miseries abound, but 'apart from you, who else do we have?' (p. 106). Besides, Sissie notes that the best 'brains' seem to be the ones staying away. The worst, too; for, it is their only way of proving to those at home that they are making something of themselves.

Yet Sissie insists that it is best to return home. There is no point in proving anything to whites with cold blue eyes:

> So please come home, My Brother. Come to our People. They are the only ones who need to know how much we are worth. The rewards are hardly anything. For every successful surgery, they will hail you as a miracle worker. Their faith [will be] in your human touch. (p. 130)

Here the heroine and her creator return to the original faith of a people: love, solidarity; the community supersedes the individual. 'A long time ago, people was all people had' (p. 28). Home has its unavoidable human touch, its warmth, its sweetness mixed with bitterness; its hope aglow, not dead. For all the talk of communalism and a classless society in certain quarters, Aidoo is realistic enough to state categorically that present-day Africa has a middle class, a group that has the potential to become a positive force in leading the society out of the colonial, or neo-colonial, prison. It is such a fact that adds to the reasons for going home. 'The aura of having been overseas at all. Belonging to the elite whatever that is' (p. 107).

Some talk of frustration, and they are right. Others hark upon the protracted stagnation, and they are right. Awooner and Armah underline the 'shit' in the streets, and in our lives, and they paint a picture too real to be denied. Achebe emphasizes the corruption which inhibits progress in the community, and he, too, is right. Nokan, Ouologuem, and others still, describe the reactionary tendencies and there is precision in their observation. However, we need more than criticism. We need direction, we need encouragement, we need to return to certain positive aspects of our existence. We need to return to Africa.

We cannot overlook the fact that, once upon a time, there was sweetness in the land, and Aidoo tells us that there is still some sweetness here:

> If the old people are right, that whatever is sweet has some bitterness in it, then we have to determine the amount of bitterness we take from the sweetness of the present. Otherwise, there'll be so much bitterness, we shall never know there was anything else around. (p. 115)

Conclusion: Criticism, Chauvinism, Cynicism . . . and Commitment

Here then is the message of our women writers: black man ought to respect and love black woman; for we are all victims of the oppression, and of ourselves. Africa is our land and it is for us to stay, or return, and free her. This critic accepts that message as a man, as a fellow-traveller through life, as a brother, and as a human being. However, a rejoinder, or a return-message, has to be sent: the black woman, no matter what her plight through a traumatic history, should stop considering the man as the Other, that is, the Enemy. The writers that we have studied dwell too much upon the malady of male chauvinism, a phenomenon that, in its most famous aspect, is no less a Western way than the notions of feminism espoused by some female writers.

Blackness, Africanness, poignantly exemplified in the work of Ama Ata Aidoo, is almost foreign to others who have let the questions of male domination blind them to the necessary solidarity between man and woman. A case in point is the work of Buchi Emecheta whose description of the life of a Nigerian woman in London[12] often smacks of sour grapes against a society that prevented the young Emecheta (the novelist asserts the autobiographical element of her work) from developing as an individual, like a man. Adah, the compromising heroine, claims that there is no racism in Britain, and easily explains away any sign of it as human stupidity and ignorance. Nevertheless – and we believe, fortunately – she cannot help leaving her cocoon and blurting out her resentment once in a while. She sometimes becomes mad at 'being treated as semi-human' (p. 117). At such rare moments she realizes that the solidarity between her and her neighbours in 'the ditch' is based upon negative, meaningless aspects of life, such as delight in flouting social laws, drunkenness, overeating and its resultant obesity, 'joy in communal sorrow' (p. 68), and the overall camaraderie of those condemned into misery. A neighbour calls Adah 'black savage' (p. 117); another calls her white friend 'nigger lover' (p. 112).

The truth of all our existence, black men and women, is, that:

> everybody would always judge one black person by the way another black person behaved . . . As long as you are black, any other black person is your People . . . (p. 53)

That situation will not change for a long time. The reality cannot be wished away. We cannot escape our blackness, no matter how hard we try. That is why Aidoo's *Our Sister Killjoy* must be placed in the forefront of our literary production. Our past, our present, our future, are all linked together. We cannot run away from them and only a liar will claim that they have not been, are not, will not be, problematic. The task is to evolve from misery to mirth, to change from complicity to consciousness, to find out 'which factors out of both the past and the present represent for us the most dynamic forces for the future' (*Our Sister Killjoy*, p. 116). We cannot afford to fall prey to sham universalism, as some of the female writers seem to be doing.

In her discussion of lesbianism, Aidoo establishes a spurious female solidarity, and the critic is not sure whether the novelist is not in a way giving approval to what is at best an abnormality. On this point, Aidoo meets Rebeka Njau who, in her novel *Ripples in the Pool*,[13] describes the traumatic experience of Selina who, after losing grip on her weak husband, falls in love with his sister. Indeed, the danger in feminine power is sentimentality. Tears flow all the time. Call a man names, put him through hell and he is supposed to maintain his equanimity; for we are told, a man does not cry. But then one might wonder why he should not. Crying, they say, is good for the soul. The tears could even help drought-stricken Africa convince the gods to send the rains to earth. Meanwhile, man and woman cannot avoid the reality of roles, no matter how much effort is made to attain equality.

The destiny of Africa continues to be of concern to many writers. The heroines depicted by the women writers definitely have a contribution to make. We should remember that, in reality, African women have been leaders long before now. Queen Nzingha led a protracted resistance against the Portuguese in Ndongo-Matamba (Angola), in the seventeenth century.[14] Moremi of Ife had beauty, virtue, power and courage.[15] And African literature has women like the heroines of Ousmane Sembène's God's Bits of Wood, who participate gloriously in the workers' strike, forging a total solidarity that puts to shame the male workers' schism in the same struggle.[16] The examples may be proof that women are all we need to save our society.

The desire is that we surpass sexist dichotomies, and that might be asking a great deal of our people. For, just as black and white have difficulty in coalescing into human, so also do man and woman have problems forgetting their sexual distinctions. Some positions and roles have to be accepted. Man courts woman. Man makes babies with woman. Woman becomes pregnant, with man's contribution. It is a reality of complementarity, not contradiction, not competition. In spite of unisex, a woman in trousers need not lose her femininity. A man need not be effeminate. Our female writers know it. Nwapa, Aidoo, Emecheta, Njau and others have stated through their heroines that they cherish being women. Not that the state should be a stigma, but a reality marked with potentialities, allowing for growth, while not preventing man from doing the same. Present-day Africa in particular, and the world at large, have created a chasm between man and woman, have nullified the male's sense of security, the very state of mind that used to enhance female freedom and originality.

The stress is so great, the resentment so strong that some men believe that women have no right to put pen to paper, that criticism of female literature (considered a secondary art) ought to be left to the women themselves. Such men seem to forget that black literature itself, their literature, has been long a victim of such discriminatory attitudes.

Some women may even agree that men should desist from reading and criticizing female writing. They may give the male critic the epithet western feminists have reserved for men: Male Chauvinist Pig. Male would stand for megalomania, media madness, marriage; Chauvinist, for charlatan, cynic; pig, for police, life-insurance policy, politics and prostitution. They may even tell the male critic to shove his pen in his mouth, chew it, digest it and reproduce it after seven months, prematurely. And they may be right. Only, one hopes, they will always remember that

Black People still
Die
So
Uselessly! (*Our Sister Killjoy*, p. 108)

NOTES

1. Could it, indeed, be the rarity of male children that has contributed – at least, partly – to the importance of the boy?
2. A few articles have dwelt upon the matter. For example, see Kolawole Ogungbesan, 'The Cape Gooseberry Also Grows in Botswana: Alienation and Commitment in the Writings of Bessie Head', *Présence Africaine*, no. 109, 1st quarterly, 1979, pp. 92–106. See also, Maryse Conde, 'Three Female Writers in Modern Africa: Flora Nwapa, Ama Ata Aidoo and Grace Ogot', ibid., no. 82, 2nd quarterly, 1972, pp. 132–43.
3. Buchi Emecheta. See 'A Worshipper from Afar', interview by Tunde Obadina, in *Punch* (Nigeria), 17 May 1979. This critic recently saw the novelist's name on the staff list of the University of Calabar. Would that be a definitive homecoming?
4. See Conde, op. cit., p. 132.
5. Adeola James in Eustace Palmer, 'An Introduction to the African Novel', *African Literature Today*, no. 7, 1975, p. 148.
6. Ernest N. Emenyonu, 'Who does Flora Nwapa write for?', *African Literature Today*, no. 7, 1975, p. 31.
7. Flora Nwapa, *Efuru*, London, Heinemann (AWS 26), 1966, reset 1978. p. 7. All further references are to this reset edition.
8. Flora Nwapa, *Idu*, London, Heinemann (AWS 56), 1970.
9. Ama Ata Aidoo, *Our Sister Killjoy*, London, Longman, 1977. All further references are to this edition.
10. It is not clear whether the sneering public condemns the couple for their intra-sexual relationship or for their inter-racial friendship.
11. Yulisa Amadu Maddy, *No Past, No Present, No Future*, London, Heinemann, 1973, pp. 95–9.
12. Buchi Emecheta, *In the Ditch*, London, Barrie and Jenkins, 1972. All further references are to this edition: New York, Schocken, 1980.
13. Rebeka Njau, *Ripples in the Pool*, London, Heinemann (AWS 203), 1978.
14. See Chancellor Williams, *The Destruction of Black Civilization*, Chicago, Third World Press, 1974, p. 84.
15. See O. Johnson, *The History of the Yorubas*, London, Routledge and Kegan Paul, 1969, p. 147.
16. There are several articles on the subject; for example, Frederick Ivor Case, 'Workers' Movement and Revolution in *God's Bits of Wood* by Sembène Ousmane' (forthcoming).

Acculturation and Character Portrayal in Southern African Novels

Norman C. Jones

The twentieth century has witnessed a literary explosion in Africa. Adventurers' tales, anthropologists' reports and conventional novels set in some corner of this vast and varied continent (and all by white authors), no longer make up the bulk of African literature. A glance at the booklist of the African Writers Series (Heinemann Educational Books) alone, with its founding editor Chinua Achebe himself an accomplished West African writer, will reveal a considerable and contemporary indigenous authorship. Southern Africa, focal point of world political interest for many years, and the centre of this article's concern, is rich in Bantu writers producing poetry, short stories and novels in English.

It is interesting to note that in the writings of both black and white South African novelists a new emphasis has emerged; a different theme has been developed. The cultural impact upon each other of the races living in Rhodesia and the Republic of South Africa is depicted and its implications explored in the lives of the principal characters in their novels. Charles Mungoshi's Lucifer, in *Waiting for the Rain*, and Stanlake Samkange's Ndatshana, in *The Mourned One*, are two men whose portraits are drawn as studies in acculturation. Jacobus, the Bantu who manages Mehring's farm in *The Conservationist* by Nadine Gordimer and Moses, the Turners' houseboy in Doris Lessing's *The Grass is Singing*, are also to be seen in this light. Not that this is to be regarded as a one-way process. We are constantly being reminded that no white man can live in Africa and remain unaffected by its all-pervasive influence, its timeless cultures and its lingering air of mystery.

Mr Macmillan's 'wind of change' has continued to blow over Africa during the course of this article's preparation. Stanlake Samkange, Zimbabwe–Rhodesia's notable and prolific novelist and historian, resigned his post as Professor of African History at an American university to become educational adviser to Bishop Abel Muzorewa, the country's first Bantu prime minister early in 1980. How his advice related to the philosophies and sentiments of his novels should prove to be a matter of great interest, for in the final scene of *The Mourned One* he makes Ndatshana say to his brother '. . . either the white man or the black man must rule this land but not both'.[1]

Samkange's own academic career is typical, in its beginnings, of many of his own generation's more fortunate and more intelligent Zimbabwean Bantu sons. Born at Chipata, the then Southern Rhodesia, in 1922, he received his primary and secondary education at a mission boarding school. The Waddilove Institution provided him with much of the material (largely autobiographical?) for his early studies of acculturation, racial prejudice and hypocrisy. Tertiary studies at Adams College and Fort Hare in South Africa were followed by further studies at Indiana in the United States of America.

In *The Mourned One*, he functions as both novelist and historian in depicting for us the emergent 'new Africans', and like Achebe in *Things Fall Apart* points up those elements of western culture that seemed to destroy rather than to build. The whole story is told with a view to promoting understanding of the white man's way, which he calls 'this civilisation which saves to kill', and he sums up the whole sad story in the final paragraph which begins:

I trust that the mourned one's hope and wish that others may benefit from his experience and thoughts and be better able to understand 'this society, this culture, this civilisation' has been fulfilled. (p. 150)

The whole novel might be said to be a portrait – a study of acculturation in a life that is spared by the intervention of white, European, religious values in the shape of a priest and which is terminated by the laws of that self-same culture. Ndatshana is a twin and by Bantu tradition should have been killed at birth. An unusual set of circumstances prevents this happening, but having been spared for several months the infant falls sick and is being taken for burial when the medically minded missionary intercepts the funeral party, misinterprets its errand, treats the sick child and takes it to the mission hospital. Here it is brought up for years as an orphan, ignorant of the existence of home, parents or twin brother.

Samkange writes this absorbing Bantu life-story in first person narrative form, asking us to believe that it constitutes a transcription of a personal document that came into his possession when researching material for a series of articles he was writing for the African Press, Salisbury. We are to read the book, then, as an autobiography written by a condemned prisoner in the death cell in Salisbury jail who seeks to achieve understanding of his own life and in doing so possibly to enable others to attain self-knowledge.

Lazarus Percival Ockenden, as he was named by the Methodist missionaries in honour of his benefactor (or Muchemwa, 'the mourned one', as his mother called him), is the product of one culture's interference in the affairs of another. As one reads the story it is clear that many of the problems or areas of conflict – both personal and inter-personal – arise from misunderstanding. Indeed Ndatshana owed his very life to the misunderstanding of the missionary referred to above. Missionaries themselves were often misunderstood by the Africans as, for instance, when the Reverend Percival Ockenden chose to camp in a tent when spending time visiting outlying parts of his parish. This evidence of his consideration for his parishioners – not wishing to impose on them – was regarded by the villagers as a breach of etiquette and a slight on their traditional hospitality.

Language is always a major problem in the area of inter-racial communications and in the early part of this century there was little help for the European who wished to learn chiShona and very few able native interpreters. Early Christian endeavour suffered much at the hands (and lips) of well-meaning but notoriously unreliable interpreters like the Evangelist Moses Magedi whose rendering of the Reverend Ockenden's address is recorded for us by Ndatshana:

Rev. P. O.	Mr Chairman
Evang. M.	Ano chema nga cheme
	(He who cries let him cry)
	And Secretary
	Ano seka, a sekerere
	(He who laughs let him laugh)
	In a certain village
	Mu musha wa Satani
	(In Satan's village)

A village, surrounded by bushes
Musha waka komberedzwa ne, ah!
Zwino nyadza kutaura!
(This village was surrounded by – ah!
it was not proper to say!)

Was born Jesus Christ, the Son of God
Waka zwarwa Jesu Krestu zuva re Mwari
(Was born Jesus Christ the Sun of God) . . . (pp. 35–7)

This address was delivered by the minister to the crowds who flocked to see and hear this man who had raised Lazarus (Ndatshana) from the dead.

Ndatshana is a shrewd and kindly observer of all that goes on in and around the mission station, pointing out matters pertaining to Bantu culture which may not be familiar to the white reader but which gives special significance to the events in the lives of the people learning to live together there. He is brought up and educated in an environment vastly different from that of his twin brother, Zana. The cultural differences between the Waddilove station and his Bantu birthplace, however, do not cancel out the close spiritual affinity between the twin brothers when they meet as adolescents after Ndatshana discovers that he is not after all an orphan but has a family.

His description of that journey home, of his reception by his family and his own response to the village to which he truly belongs gives a measure of the extent to which he has become conditioned by western cultural values. It is at a material level that it first becomes evident. A mat and blankets on a beaten earth floor prove a poor substitute for a European-style bed. Zana sleeps well, while Ndatshana tosses and turns in great discomfort. Sadza (a coarse mealie-meal porridge which is the staple diet of the Bantu, eaten at all meals with a limited variety of 'relishes' – sour milk, green vegetables and rarely meat) proves unpalatable to one who has acquired a taste for bacon and eggs, toast, butter, jam and coffee!

The smells of a village lacking sanitation, running water and infested with flies, the primitive cooking facilities of his mother's hut – all these things make him long for Waddilove. But what he finds at Mariga and which was lacking at the mission is what the black Americans call 'soul'. He describes it as '. . . a code of behaviour, an attitude to life and to other people; perhaps something embodied in the Shona "hunhu" or the Sindebele "ubuntu" "humanness" or "personness"' (p. 96). The timeless quality of village life with its absence of bells soothes and calms him. On a spiritual plane he still readily identifies with his native Bantu culture.

It is evident during this visit to his home that he is out of touch with much of Bantu custom and ceremony as it relates to such matters as love and marriage. The wedding of his cousin Chibinha to the young Catholic schoolteacher, Mayikoro, is his first experience of a big family occasion and Ndatshana carefully records his impressions of an event that contitutes a peculiar blending of Bantu and Christian traditions. (This present writer recollects another instance of syncretism when he officiated at the funeral of a Bantu child in the Madziwa Reserve some twenty years ago. Beautiful and meaningful elements of both cultures can – and are enhanced by doing so – combine to convey deep meaning.)

Ndatshana is totally unprepared for his first experience of falling in love. Keresiya is a beautiful girl whom he first notices at his cousin's wedding. He is strongly attracted to her but does not know what to do about it, or how to interpret her response to his shy, inexperienced approach. Wooing by sexual conquest, as outlined the following day by one of his friends, is a Bantu cultural tradition for which Waddilove has not prepared him. Ndatshana returns to the institution a sadder and a wiser man!

With manhood upon him, Ndatshana is required to obtain a 'Chitupa' – a document of identification that the then Rhodesian government required all Bantu males to possess and produce on demand. This calls for a visit to the local Native Commissioner's office at Marandellas and here his evident ignorance of what is considered appropriate behaviour for Bantu in contact with white officialdom is readily apparent. Some sense of the equality of men of all races had been instilled in him at Waddilove and although he stands when the 'Nkosi' appears, he does not join the others in hailing him as such. (Nkosi is the Sindebele word for 'Lord' and appropriate for addressing the Supreme Deity, as in 'Nkosi sikelele Afrika' – God Bless Africa; the Bantu national anthem.)

Having gone through the process of securing his Chitupa, not without incurring the wrath of the most junior officer for speaking in English, then quoting his adopted English surname and finally listing all the names of his heritage, he hands over a letter of introduction from his Mission 'mother' which secures him an audience with the Native Commissioner himself. Ndatshana enjoys conversation and tea in the shade of a nearby tree with Mr

Teilsen – an enlightened Scandinavian and a man of strong views and progressive ideas. Waddilove had prepared him for this kind of experience by providing him with a broad-based education which the N.C. recognizes and points out to the crowds of Africans who stand around gazing at this open-air afternoon-tea episode.

This encounter has a profound effect upon Ndatshana and he is never to forget this white man who urged Africans to stir themselves and work in their own interests. Some years later when he has been teaching for some little time and become interested in the political movements (union-activated) that have begun to create unrest in the townships, Ndatshana learns of Mr Teilsen's murder. This fills him with distress, especially when he hears that an African who speaks good English is being sought by the police, a man 'somewhere in the country disguised as a teacher'. Returning that night to St Joseph's Mission, where he teaches, Ndatshana falls on to a bed in a drunken stupor and awakes the following morning to be accused of drunken rape. He goes on to describe his arrest and subsequent trial, the cross-examination of the witnesses and the findings of the Court, pointing out the shortcomings of the case for the prosecution and the passing of the death sentence for attempted rape. The acting chief justice makes much of the fact that it was a crime 'committed by a native of education, a professing Christian, attached, as a teacher, to a native Mission' (p. 141).

In his final autobiographical chapter, Ndatshana writes in some detail of his brother Zana's visit to the jail, comparing and contrasting their lives. Zana is 'a raw native' to arrogant whites. He has seen only two white men before he visited the Salisbury jail, has no English, neither reads nor writes, and feels at ease only with traditional African things. He is a man untouched by the European culture that rules his land – the complete antithesis to his brother in so many ways, yet with strong spiritual ties and close affinities.

Their conversation ranges over a lifestyle of the white city-dwellers of Salisbury – the hazards of their roads, the size of their houses, the pace of their lives, their obsession with money, their fear of fatness and of death. Ndatshana confesses that the widening of his horizons has not brought him greater happiness but has only made him more exposed to snubs and insults. Even the Church, in the form of missionaries, has failed him by its inconsistency. A missionary was chief witness against him in Court:

Who was the main witness against me in my trial? Was it not a missionary? Why? Because the missionary only wants me to be his brother in Christ, not his brother in law. He only wants to sing and preach about Christianity on Sundays, not to practise it. In matters of colour he considers himself a white man first and a Christian second. He forgets that Christianity must not only be practised but must be seen to be practised every minute of the hour, every hour of the day, every day of the week, every week of the year and every year of a lifetime. (p. 145)

He goes on to contrast the caring attitude promoted by the African culture towards one's fellows, a benevolence that knows no discrimination nor looks for any return. Having had an opportunity of evaluating each culture, Ndatshana assures his brother that 'there are many things in African culture that are superior to European ways' and that 'Education will ultimately enable us to meet the white man on his own ground and topple him from his pedestal. Sons of Africa will, one day, arise and recover the rule of our land from the white man.' He continues:

They will do this, Gushungo, because the white man is rejecting brotherhood with the black man. If I hang and die, the brotherhood of man, peace and racial harmony in this land will die with me; because where the white man rejects me – *one, who, except for the colour of his skin, is a European* – black men everywhere will realise that there can be no half measures, that co-operation with these people is impossible and that either the white man or the black man must rule this land but not both. (pp. 146–7)

In his final recorded word to his brother, Ndatshana declares his own assessment of his acculturation – a European in all but skin colour. Less than half a century later there are Africans whose opportunities are greater than the mourned one's and who seek to lead their fellow Zimbabweans, both black and white, in paths of peaceful co-existence.

Charles L. Mungoshi, author of *Waiting for the Rain*, was born in 1947 near Enkeldoorn in the then Rhodesian Midlands and like Stanlake Samkange had a church mission school education. All Saints, Daramombe and St Augustine's Secondary School equipped him for employment as a research assistant with the Forestry Commission and subsequently Text Book Sales in Salisbury. In addition to his collection of short stories and his novel in English, Mungoshi has also published a novel in Shona.

Coming on the scene a quarter of a century later than Samkange, he was to benefit from the vast changes that had taken place in the educational climate of Rhodesia in the mid-1950s. Black political pressure for the revision of Native Education Syllabi for Schools led to the implementation in 1957 by the African Education Department (note the change of terminology) of completely new programmes of study for Bantu students. On the credit side the teaching was less catechistic, there was more creative writing, and better structured vernacular courses were introduced. Increased opportunities for secondary education were made available with a new drive to build more schools on the part of both government and missions. On the debit side, missions lost their practical training schemes in agriculture, building, carpentry and homecraft at a time when the labour force could not accommodate more white-collared workers and the Reserves still needed the practical skills of mission-trained young people to develop their lands and improve living standards.

We are aware of the historian at work in Samkange's novel, but in Mungoshi we discover a poet. Whereas *The Mourned One* is in standard idiomatic English the language of *Waiting for the Rain* owes much to the beauty of chiShona in its form and imagery.

Like Achebe and Samkange, Mungoshi, too, seeks to demonstrate the disruptive, destructive force of white cultural influences upon the African people. But where Samkange shows a system first saving and then destroying a Bantu life, Mungoshi shows the impact of one culturally influenced Bantu life on a small village community – the leaven that leavens the lump. Samkange spends a lot of time on descriptions of life within a mission station's boundaries or some other European-dominated context (Native Commissioner's office, courtroom, cell); Mungoshi focuses on the Bantu village.

There is an immediacy and urgency in the style of this novel, and Mungoshi's use of third person present tense promotes reader involvement. An air of mystery skilfully built up in the first chapter underlines the significant message in its opening lines:

> Things are happening here and there and whether you can see them or not you can't certainly say the Old Man doesn't see them.[2]

In what we later discover to be the Old Man's dream we get a view of the dynamic elemental forces at work in the Bantu world, and his response to them – he awakes with 'the old war chant' in his throat. Storms have been presented in English literature by writers as diverse as Shakespeare and Hardy as reflecting human moods and emotions, but the rest of the symbolism in this chapter is essentially African. Drums convey a variety of messages and moods. They still beat across the bush advising of deaths or inviting to weddings, calling to the dance as once they summoned to war. The noise of the cracked tin toys superimposes itself on the drumbeats; message and meaning are lost. There are the Silence with its images of dust and water, heat and cold, and the Plain which becomes the Bearded Forest and reverts to being the Plain again. One can get lost there, lose all sense of direction. Surrounded by nothingness one finds oneself preyed upon by the great black crow-owl. The Old Man fights off the challenge of death to meet another day.

Life in the village is not regulated by bells or dominated by clocks but by the natural rhythm of night and day. The old folk are the first to stir, before sun-up, and be about their business – the Old Man on patrol to ward off evil influences and Old Mandisa laboriously grinding her peanuts into butter. There being no footprints of enemy prowlers, no bloodstains left by witches, the Old Man feels free to chat with Mandisa, the sweetheart of his youth whom he often regrets he did not marry, as his wife Japi is half-deaf, half-blind and somewhat half-witted into the bargain!

This gentle beginning to a new day, with its reference to the significance of cattle to this cattle-culture people, turns the Old Man's thoughts in the direction of his three remaining sons, Kuruku, Magaso and Tongoona. His hopes for the future lie with Tongoona – the youngest – and his family. The drum he is busy making is for his grandson Garabha, Tongoona's first-born. With painstaking attention to detail, Mungoshi builds up the scene against which the action is to take place and introduces the characters with due deference to age and status. A vividly portrayed early morning scene in Tongoona's hut reveals the thirty-year-long misery of his marriage and hints at conflict over the son who is about to visit them and who wishes to go overseas. The father approves but the mother bitterly opposes the boy's desire. Tongoona has attained the fourth standard at school and has served with the British South African Police at Cape Town in the mid-1940s; his wife Raina has neither education nor experience of the vast world beyond the borders of their immediate neighbourhood. This is a major factor in their diversity of viewpoint; Tongoona is influenced by his contact with European culture while Raina's reactions are pure Shona.

The conventions and courtesies of daily life in the village are faithfully portrayed, the Shona pattern of greetings being preserved in translation. 'Mangwanani!' (Good morning!) is invariably followed by 'Marara here?' (Have you slept?). No conversation or questioning can precede this preamble. The first thirteen chapters gradually build up the scene as people go about their work, discuss the arrival later in the day of the one who is going away, and greet John, Kuruku's second son who has come to see Lucifer and give him a going-away gift of a transistor radio.

The Old Man is unfamiliar with radio, suspicious of its voices — are they gossips or spies? — and sounds out John on his revolutionary inclinations. Grandfather may not know much about modern inventions and innovations but there are some things that he is still well informed about and his philosophies sometimes surprise the younger members of the family who think they are the only ones ever to have entertained progressive ideas or contemplated fighting for ideals.

The last stage of Lucifer's bus journey home takes him through the rolling ranches of the fertile Hampshire Estates to the featureless, barren Manyene Tribal Trust Land. An absence of two years sharpens his perception of his home territory — a funeral in the distance, a halt for refreshments at the township where he looks out from the bus at faces vaguely familiar but nameless. 'He is ashamed. He is supposed to know their names but he doesn't. An uneasiness — a feeling of not belonging — assails him . . .' (p. 40).

This is the first indication of the distancing that acculturation has effected in Lucifer's attitude towards home.

Greeted by his father, who waves the bus down on the seemingly endless dusty road, Lucifer stands 'confused between embarrassment and pity, resentment and guilt — his eyes fixed on the dirt-matted hairs on his father's stone-wall chest' (p. 42). His father's questions about his luggage and the contents of his single valise cause him further discomfort and he has to confess that he hasn't done much reading lately. Tongoona cannot quite see the role of art in western society and the idea of making a living from drawing or painting is hard for him to comprehend. Books and reading are a different matter altogether; he understands them. When his father challenges him about the letters he didn't write, both Lucifer and Tongoona feel ill at ease in this new adult father-and-son relationship. 'They finish the last part of their short trip in total silence: Tongoona ahead and Lucifer behind, like a man and his shadow.' (p. 44).

His first encounter with his mother is no more auspicious. His feelings for her are of pity; she declares that he looks half-starved. He is embarrassed as he perceives himself to be a source of conflict between his parents and feels uncomfortable at his grandparents' questions. There is tension in the air when Lucifer's sister, Betty, greets him in his room where he has withdrawn with a book. He feels threatened by her, unable to relax and behave naturally under her searching scrutiny. The smells of the place, the vermin, the return of childhood fears of nightmares – those dreams of witches – all crowd in on him. His reading in modern psychology has not helped him to uproot himself completely from the soil out of which he sprang.

An urge to express himself in verse produces a telling comment on his reaction to 'home' and he links it with a sketch of the funeral procession he saw as he entered the tribal trust lands earlier that day:

Home . . .
Aftermath of an invisible war
A heap of dust and rubble
White immobile heat on the sweltering land
Home . . .
The sharp-nosed vulture already smells carrion –
the ancient woman's skirts
give off an odour of trapped time
Home . . .
Return science to its owners
The witch demands a ransom for your soul
Your roots claim their rightful pound of clay
Home . . . ?
Home sweet home?
muffled thuds
of soft earth
on dead wood
on the nailed
despair within
Home . . .
Eternal creak-crack of ox-carts against gravel
along the shortest road to the village
– a road that goes nowhere –
The Earth takes back its gift. (pp. 52–3)

Having written this he returns to the family and their questions, their accounts of the misfortunes that have befallen them, their superstitious fears and the scandal surrounding his sister. He listens without comment. The arrival of his uncle Kuruku enlivens the proceedings but even his liquor-loosened lips draw little response from Lucifer, whether the topic be native charms and medicines or the Old Testament curse of Ham.

John's presentation of the radio triggers off the customary courtesies, but when Lucifer hears the comments about the present of food brought by Rhoda he walks out angrily. He seeks out his grandfather and speaks freely with him about his overseas study trip and items of family news. Grandfather's reference to Garabha's possible coming and his caring for Lucifer sets him reflecting on what he had learned of Christianity. Devotion and jealousy, conceit and pride – what a confusion of conflicting emotions and spiritual values had existed within him! His mission school experience had led him to reject his belief in God. He now questions the nature of love, feels the falsity of his own position, the danger of his own pride:

> And he knows it's partly because of his lack of belief, his own uncertainty and restlessness that's helping to create this tension in the family. Somehow, when he is around, everybody begins to panic, everybody seems to be measuring his or her actions in the light of Lucifer's silent criticism. And Lucifer can't help feeling he is letting them down. It's them who put him in a false position. (p. 72)

The interview with his father and subsequently with both parents leaves Lucifer with no option but to accept the fact that he alone can decide whether he goes overseas or not. They want him to be happy, and he must make his own choice. His juvenile rebellion at being confronted with personal responsibility subsides and he accepts one of the inevitabilities of adulthood.

Garabha, the wandering drummer and brother to Lucifer, is brought into the story at this point as a contrast, a sharp reminder that brothers, as they grow up, often grow away from each other.

Garabha's portrait is sensitively drawn. He is in tune with nature, responsive to the rhythm of life, from from ties or responsibilities and welcome as a musician at any village celebration. It was this that occasioned his late arrival home. The description of his journey home is full of music and poetry; nightfall is 'like a sad song', and as his heart beat quickens he proceeds 'down the cattle-and-rain-deepened stony path to the river'. He is able to distinguish between a person's real feelings and his pose; he knows his father as a man and as a father and husband before his family.

There is a strange restlessness about him, for his hands are everlastingly playing invisible drums. Through them he is linked with the ancestral past – the race-memory of long ago. He too feels that his parents regard him as having failed them; he hasn't settled down in the traditional manner. Unlike Lucifer he relates well to his sister Betty and in his conversation with her – the first member of the family he meets – he reveals a perceptive and sympathetic understanding of her.

We begin to realize that although on the surface life in the Old Man's village seems to go on according to age-old Bantu custom and tradition, we can see things fall apart even here: Paul in prison for his revolutionary and rebellious ideas, Lucifer seeking foreign travel and a career in art, John assimilating the white man's culture and bringing the first radio to the village, Betty pregnant, unmarried and unashamed!

Garabha is uneasy at home, too. Conversation with his mother is painful – he perceives her to be hysterical and ugly and almost a stranger to him. She fails to understand this son also. Garabha is disappointed that he and Lucifer are unable to communicate, for he still cares for him. He is concerned that his father, Tongoona, fails to understand him and even orders him to leave the village and never return. The Old Man's intervention and assessment of the true situation is splendid. Turning to Tongoona, he says:

> You are a very fine father, aren't you? Is there anyone else in the whole world who has got it hanging in a bunch between his legs except you? Who else has fathered children except you? Who knows the pains of childbirth but you? Is that it? Is that the way you see it? Talking to the boy like that in my face! Because I am not your father and what you know about everything came from your mother? To you I am just another fool doing you out of your food? I sit here all day long doing nothing but telling the boy to disobey you? Is that the way you see it? Well, go on. Talk to him. Talk to him and tomorrow he is going to bring you a daughter-in-law and he will get a job in the city and all your troubles and misery will just vanish as if they had never existed. Go on! Talk to him! You! Your mouth should have been made longer than your mother's – for extra talking power. Talk to him all day, all night, for a hundred years – and make him change – because you have been told that it's talking that brings about change. You! There he is, talk to him, Father of Millions! (p. 112)

Tongoona's problem is that he cannot reconcile his experience of the sophisticated world outside with life in his village and this inner conflict is constantly spilling over.

Tensions build up in the closing stages of the story when the doctor is called in to the assembled household and sorcery, witchcraft and native medicines are invoked to resolve the evils of this troubled home. Lucifer rises to his feet and walks out of this sinister scene, rejecting the whole business of Bantu *nhanga* and *muroyi*. The medicine-man (or woman) has no place in his philosophy. He rejects the responsibility of the family which they attempt to thrust upon him. Rejecting the protective medicines offered for his safety, he joins in the prayers of the white priest who has come for him. Even the traditional gift of the peanut butter is spurned as the car begins to roll forward. The final break is made:

> 'Let's go, Father,' Lucifer says.
> Like a false skin, the people peel back as the car moves forward. Looking at them in the rear-view mirror, Lucifer sees them in this order: his mother sitting down in the sand, his father's hand frozen in the air above him, Old Mandisa's hands cupped over her failing eyes, and Betty's turned back – going away with the tin of butter in her hands. (p. 179)

Father Williams' comments on the beautiful country and the charming manners of the people sound strange to the ears of one whose attention has been taken by a vulture in the sky. He watches 'the leprous skin of his country slough off and fall back dead behind him' and then, becoming more relaxed 'tries to look at his country through the eye of an impartial tourist'. (p. 180). For him, acculturation has produced total alienation. Lucifer can no longer identify with his home, his family or his Bantu culture. Like Ndatshana he has come to feel himself, except for colour of his skin, a European.

The novel offers no solutions to the problems it raises, the questions it asks. What will become of the village in the reserve and on the tribal trust lands? What of the shadows, superstition, sterility and fear? What future is there for the Lucifers of today? Aware of the impotence of the old beliefs, suspicious of the new, will they find a faith to live by?

Before moving on to consider the works of two white novelists of southern Africa I would suggest that Ezekiel Mphahlele's short stories, *In Corner B*,[3] serve as good follow-up reading to *The Mourned One*. African traditions and white law are woven into compelling stories by this Bantu academic. Complementary to Mungoshi's *Waiting for the Rain* is Credo Mutwa's *My People*,[4] the writings of a Zulu witchdoctor whose stated aim in writing is to promote understanding among whites of the ways and culture – the heritage – of black Africans. Both these books are compelling reading.

Doris Lessing was born of English stock in 1919 and spent her childhood on a large farm in the then Southern Rhodesia. Exactly thirty years later she brought the manuscript of her first novel to London. It was immediately accepted and in 1950 Michael Joseph published *The Grass is Singing*. She has since written short stories, plays and poems as well as a journalistic report on Rhodesia which she visited in 1957. Her work has been widely acclaimed.

The Grass is Singing is essentially a story of white people in Rhodesia – and in particular the settlers or farmers – drawn from Lessing's shrewd observations of country life. It reveals the variety of reactions to the environment, lifestyle and presence of Bantu in that small community but also contains some interesting studies of the African. Samkange and Mungoshi look through African eyes and see first their fellow Bantu; Lessing perceives the whites in this acculturational process, sometimes referred to as the 'colonial experience'.

The story opens with a brief newspaper report of the murder of a farmer's wife by her native houseboy and goes on to examine the reactions and responses of the locals to this tragedy. The Turners were never popular in the district, keeping themselves to themselves and never gracing a social occasion of any kind with their presence. Their squalid little house is despised; their incompetence and poverty nearly earns them the label of 'poor whites', but they are not Afrikaners and do not have a family of children.

The news of the murder evokes sympathy for Dick Turner but seems to arouse anger towards Mary, who has, according to her neighbours, received her just deserts. A mystery is hinted at, but first the background is filled in. The first character portrayed in any detail is Charlie Slatter. The Turners' nearest neighbour (his farm is some five miles away), he has for a long time cast a covetous eye on the Turners' place.

It is Slatter to whom the farmboys bring news of the killing and who organizes the police investigation. This one-time London grocer's assistant has been twenty years in Africa but is still essentially a Cockney. He farms to make money and rules his farmhands with the *sjambok*. Hard on his own wife and family, he despises gentleness, especially in men, yet spends money to ensure that his sons become 'cultured' gentlemen.

This hard, insensitive man stands in sharp contrast to Tony Marston, the softly-spoken young Englishman who had recently come from England to be Dick Turner's assistant. In the presence of death he is fearful, tense, unsure and in conversation with Slatter uncertain of his ground. He has his suspicions as to the motive for murder but is afraid to speak his mind. He is denied the opportunity of expressing his opinion to the police sergeant who is dealing with the case as a routine matter with a minimum of enquiry. Tony is of little consequence here – he is new, doesn't know the country, and was even by-passed by the farm hands in reporting the murder. His pride is injured, he feels angry, resentful at their unconscious patronage, but is well aware that no simple case of black and white confrontation can explain away this killing. One needs to probe behind the scenes, seek an understanding of the problems of relationships between the Turners before any true light can be shed or any just judgement passed.

In these brief hours Tony had come to see the colour bar at work seeking to cover up this 'failure'. He would need to learn that ' . . . to live with the colour bar in all its nuances and implications means closing one's mind to many things, if one intends to remain an accepted member of society.'[5] He must be prepared to adapt or be rejected. Nauseated by his experience and its implications he left the farm, eventually drifted to the Copperbelt and ended up as a mine manager and was written off by the district as having 'no guts'.

Doris Lessing now proceeds to relate the origins and background of the murdered woman and the events which led up to her death. Mary's is the most detailed.

Starting work at sixteen, she soon establishes herself as a successful secretary. Shorthand, typing, book-keeping and secretarial duties come like second nature to her. At twenty, she is in a good position when her mother dies, to be followed five years later by her father with whom she had not had any contact for years. Free of all family ties she becomes a member of the smart set – part of the social scene. A slim thirty-year-old blonde, she is private secretary to her employer and still lives in rooms at the girls' club, while many of her contemporaries have married and settled down.

Inclined to be sentimental and offering a sympathetic ear and a shoulder to lean on, Mary is, however, completely turned off by sex in any form, due in the first instance to childhood memories she has long since sought to submerge. Overhearing gossip about herself she seeks to change her image, starts looking for a marriage partner but provides the locals with plenty to talk about when she runs away, outraged, from a fifty-five-year-old widower who attempts to kiss her as part of his courtship of her.

Mary meets Dick Turner, a shy young farmer, by chance at the cinema. Hating towns, he longs to be settled on his farm with a wife and family and after a period of uncertainty proposes to Mary and is accepted. A special licence marriage is arranged and Dick takes his bride straight back to the farm.

It is dark when they reach their primitive home. Dick is both excited and embarrassed by it all; he senses that nothing is really good enough for Mary and that he had no right to bring her there. She tends to feel trapped in a situation reminiscent of her own childhood. Dick's timid adoration saves the day in the moment of their first sexual encounter:

> It was not so bad, she thought, when it was all over: not as bad as that. It meant nothing to her nothing at all. Expecting outrage and imposition, she was relieved to find she felt nothing. She was able maternally to bestow the gift of herself on this humble stranger, and remain untouched. Women have an extraordinary ability to withdraw themselves from the sexual relationship, to immunise themselves against it, in such a way that their men can be left feeling let down and insulted without having anything tangible to complain of.[6]

She embarks upon the task of improving the home, encounters problems in handling domestic servants, is overcome by the heat, refuses to socialize and begins to antagonize Dick. As Dick's enterprises fail one after another – the bees, the pigs, the store – Mary longs more and more to be away from it all. She does summon up courage, packs a suitcase and leaves for town. Things have changed there, however, and so has she. The farm and the veld, the ubiquitous natives have dragged her down; even her old employer will not take her back.

Dick follows her and persuades her to return with him to the farm. Shortly after this he falls ill and Mary has to try and keep things going. Attempting to exercise some 'authority' over the servants on the farm, she strikes one who has spoken in English and asked for water. The *sjambok* in her hand cuts open his face. Some two years are to elapse before she sees him again. Dick has sent him up to the house to train as houseboy, since domestic staff have been virtually impossible to secure for some time.

Her attitude towards natives has not changed in all this time. She still regards them as inferior, fit only to be bossed about, and repulsive in their animal lusts and appetites. Although she is afraid of this big man, Moses, she continues to train him, and he proves to be the best worker she has had. He has a pride and a certain dignity – a personality; something she had not found in a Bantu before. This angers and embarrasses her but she cannot dispense with his services. Gradually her mind begins to go – how can she see blacks as human beings? It goes against all her previous concepts of master and servant races.

At this point in the story our attention is focused on the attitude and actions of Moses. He is kind, firm, courteous and deferential in his dealings with this sick white woman; he helps her to bed, takes her a tray of food and encourages her to eat, anxious to please and looking for approval. When she is a little better and they occasionally talk he asks about the war and what Jesus thinks about people killing each other. This prompts Mary to ask Dick where Moses came from, and she learns he was a mission boy.

It is interesting to note Dick's attitude to the products of missions. Like many farmers he feels 'they should not be taught to read and write: they should be taught the dignity of labour and general usefulness to the white man' (p. 164).

Moses invades her dreams, questions her fear of him when he is prepared to relieve her of her vigil at her sick husband's bedside. Her fear and fascination become an obsession. Slatter becomes concerned at the tone she adopts to Moses when she speaks to him – 'flirtatious coyness' is the phrase. Charlie recognizes the implications and makes urgent attempts to persuade the farmer to get out before it is too late. Dick, under a great deal of pressure himself, acquiesces and plans are made. Tony comes in to run the place, stumbles across this servant–mistress relationship and Moses leaves the house in an atmosphere fraught with terrible tensions.

The murder on the verandah is Moses' way of depriving Tony, whom he mistakenly believes to be his rival, of triumph in winning Mary's love away from him. Having done this he is satisfied and prepared to allow the inevitable consequences of this action to take their course.

Doris Lessing faithfully depicts the African scene and the cultural values of the white farmers in the first half of the twentieth century. Her characters are convincing as the products of their environment, but none of them conveys a message of hope. Mary is destroyed by her cultural encounter across the racial lines even before her murder, and Moses is doomed. Turner is a broken man, and only Slatter whose god is money and who seeks to preserve the cultural dichotomy seems to get anywhere.

Nadine Gordimer is a South African writer born in that land and still living there. Her home is in Johannesburg, but her writing covers the African landscape from Zaïre to the Kalahari. She writes of Africa in the twentieth century, and has been doing so for about thirty years. She was co-winner of the Booker Prize for *The Conservationist* in 1974 and received the French international literary prize, the Grand Aigle d'Or, in the following year.

Nadine Gordimer's new novel, *Burger's Daughter*,[7] concerns Rosa, daughter of Lionel Burger, a successful doctor and communist fighter against apartheid. She takes up her father's cause when he dies in prison in his middle years. Rosa visits Europe and while on the Côte d'Azur becomes the mistress of a French schoolteacher who has left his family in order to work on his thesis on *the cultural effects of the colonial experience* (my emphasis). According to Claire Tomalin, Nadine Gordimer is implying in this book 'that it is not really possible for the European mind to meet the South African experience, to encompass the nature of what is going on there'.[8] Speaking of Nadine Gordimer's style she says she 'nails detail so that it speaks its own moral'. Within this new story sexual beauty and clear laughter become banners for the cause of freedom.

In *The Conservationist*, Nadine Gordimer portrays in Mehring a wealthy white industrialist-cum-weekend-farmer and the philosophies by which he lives.[9] A forty-minute drive in his Mercedes gets Mehring from his executive offices to the 400-acre Transvaal farm he has bought as an investment, because it is the fashionable thing to do, because at heart he is a conservationist, but primarily because it would be a good place to bring a woman. To satisfy him the farm has to become productive – beauty in a farm as well as in other areas of life has to be functional to please Mehring. Divorced from his wife, and with a teenage son in boarding school, he lives a bachelor-type existence.

A popular figure with the ladies, Mehring is always in demand at parties and never without a partner. One relationship seems significant to him – a long-standing affair with Antonia, the grass-widow wife (and ultimately leftist defector) of a university professor obsessed with anthropology and linguistics. Sophisticated yet sensuous, Mehring takes his sex where he can find it – the

Portuguese girl on the plane, the African prostitute. For such a man it is hard to discover that his only son has marked homosexual inclinations.

Bilingual, as all South Africans are expected by their government to be, Mehring reserves Afrikaans for his dealings with officialdom although his farm workers know he doesn't like the Dutch. He addresses his 'hands' in English, generally through Jacobus, his Bantu farm manager, and takes his farming very seriously.

He is distressed to find plovers' eggs removed from their nests by children on a visit one Sunday morning, but this concern is overridden by the news that the body of a dead man – a Bantu stranger – has been found on the farm. He is even more put out when he learns that the police have not removed the body but have simply put it in a shallow grave on his farm. His plans for the farm are long-term (his planting programmes include eucalyptus and oak and Spanish chestnut). While seeking to preserve the *status quo*, he yet jokes about the Africans using the wood in years to come when they would have taken over.

Mehring is on easy terms with his farm manager, whom we first meet on that first Sunday morning, clad in overalls and rubber boots, looking for Mehring to tell him about the discovery of the body. Jacobus is always anxious to please – obsequious even – speaking in broken English through broken and decaying teeth. He is possessed of a strong sense of duty and bears his delegated authority well towards the other workers. He knows just how far he can go in putting Mehring's tractor or phone to personal use, or what supplies he can divert to his own purposes. He is fond of his master and thinks a great deal of young Terry who readily identifies with both the Africans on the farm and the Indians at the store. Though misunderstanding prevents him seeing in the New Year with Mehring over a bottle of Scotch, he appreciates the perks of the job, the occasional drink, the cigarettes.

Jacobus stands as a mediator between the simple, uneducated farmhands and their white boss. His interpretations of what he is told are often subject to modification, as in his account of the fruit of the nut trees they are planting and the time they would wait for harvest. One sees a touch of Samkange's Evangelist Moses Magedi in him at such times. Neither Mehring nor Jacobus could run the farm without the other. Perhaps their mutual need underlines the need for co-operation and teamwork, on the part of all the races, so that instead of stagnation there might be growth, peace, prosperity and progress.

NOTES

1. Stanlake Samkange, *The Mourned One*, London, Heinemann (AWS 169), 1975, p.147. All further page references are to this edition.
2. Charles Mungoshi, *Waiting for the Rain*, London, Heinemann (AWS 170), 1975, p. 1. All further page references are to this edition.
3. Ezekiel Mphahlele, *In Corner B*, Nairobi, East African Publishing House, 1967.
4. Credo Mutwa, *My People*, Harmondsworth, Penguin, 1971.
5. Doris Lessing, *The Grass is Singing*, Harmondsworth, Penguin, 1961, p. 27. All further page references are to this edition. New York, New American Library,. 1976.
6. Ibid., p.57.
7. Nadine Gordimer, *Burger's Daughter*, London, Cape, 1979.
8. Claire Tomalin, review of *Burger's Daughter*, *Punch*, 27 June 1979.
9. Nadine Gordimer, *The Conservationist*, Harmondsworth, Penguin, 1978: New York, McGraw-Hill, 1976.

New Writing from Zimbabwe: Dambudzo Marechera's *The House of Hunger*

Mbulelo V. Mzamane

Introduction

Very little has been written about literature in Zimbabwe.[1] Yet like everywhere in Africa, there exists in Zimbabwe toway an old tradition of largely unrecorded oral literature, as old as the Mhondoro cult. For instance many legends are still told about Chaminuka, the Shona seer, who prophesied before Lobengula, the Ndebele conqueror-king, the arrival of men without trousers (*vasina mabvi* in Shona), men reputedly more powerful than the Ndebele or the Zulu. Chaminuka's vision, wisdom and fearlessness in the face of death are still celebrated in literature by both the Shona and the Ndebele. As Lawrence Vambe points out, Chaminuka has also provided blacks in Zimbabwe with 'an inexhaustible emotional theme for their political poetry, platform stunts and poster slogans'.[2] But this rich oral tradition has largely gone unrecorded and has been little exploited by creative writers, though some attempts have been made in the indigenous languages, notably by writers like M. Shamuyarira whose collection of Shona traditional poetry first appeared in 1959.[3]

A considerable body of written literature, largely missionary-inspired, also exists in Shona and Ndebele on historical and traditional subjects or on the rather overworked theme, first used by South African writers, of the corrupting influence of city life.[4] So far this literature has been designed for African schools and to that extent has been associated with the white Rhodesian government, which controlled African education. But with independence, the growth of literature in the indigenous languages, like further research into oral tradition, is a distinct possibility, even if only to replace biased textbooks which were produced under the tutelage of whites and tended, as a result, to pander to white supremacy. The position in Zimbabwe is now different from the situation that still prevails in South Africa where literature in the indigenous languages continues to be produced under the auspices of the white minority regime and to be mixed up with the government's policy of Bantu education and Bantustans. Unlike many other states in Africa, Zimbabwe has been further blessed by having only two major indigenous languages to contend with.

Outside the oral tradition and literature in the indigenous languages, Doris Lessing's *The Grass is Singing* is probably the best-known work in fiction to use a purely Rhodesian setting.[5] But modern fiction in English by blacks in Zimbabwe began with the translation of Solomon Mutswairo's *Feso*,[6] a novel about life in Zimbabwe before the arrival of whites. The English translation unfortunately bears little resemblance to the Shona original. However, the leading literary figure in Zimbabwe has probably been the historian Stanlake Samkange with the appearance of his *On Trial for my Country*,[7] which is based on an imaginary confrontation between King Lobengula and Cecil John Rhodes. Samkange's latest novel, *Year of the Uprising*,[8] is also set in the turbulent period of 1896/7, when the people of Zimbabwe made an unsuccessful last-ditch stand against the white invaders. Lawrence Vambe, one of the country's first black journalists, ranks with Mutswairo, Samkange and a few others as Zimbabwe's pioneer writers in English. Vambe's *An Ill-Fated People*, which cannot strictly be termed a novel, is a curious mixture of legend, family chronicle, national history, contemporary politics and African customs. But Vambe's book, together with another work in prose by Samkange, *Origins of Rhodesia*,[9] represent the first serious efforts by Africans to piece together their history from oral sources and thus strip it of all the usual distortions and insulting insinuations, efforts that have been carried out more successfully by a younger generation of historians like Alec Mashingaidze, Hoyini Bhila, Ngwabi Bhebe and Stan Mudenge. The deployment of history for literary purposes in the works of all these writers had another revolutionary purpose. Their historical writings, emerging as they did during the intensification of efforts to oust Smith's regime, were also designed to forge an accessible myth in order to sustain the people in their heroic struggle for emancipation. Thus the theme of resistance to white settlement is prominent in the works of all these early writers.

A new generation of writers, among whom the most celebrated is probably Dambudzo Marechera, author of the prize-winning *The House of Hunger* and *Black Sunlight*, is less pre-occupied with early historical themes.[10] They are more concerned with the contemporary state of affairs, namely the recent war situation in Zimbabwe. An unpublished short story, 'To Be Free', by Evuray Daka Zhakata, who until recently has been resident in Lesotho, deals with the feeling of duplicity that assails an African member of the Rhodesian armed forces, until he decides to join the ranks of the guerrillas. The poetry of Polycarp S. Chimedza is concerned with the oppressive conditions, the rotten quality of life among blacks under Smith's regime and the liberation struggle.[11] All these themes are prominent in the writings of Dambudzo Marechera, with which the rest of this essay is concerned.

The House of Hunger

Though Marechera's work is written against the background of pre-independence Zimbabwe, it represents a considerable development in African literature. His work is not pure anti-colonial protest, as one might have expected from pre-independence Zimbabwe. He writes in a deeply introspective vein and shows a keen interest in unveiling the psychic responses of his protagonists. There is an almost total absence of celebration, romanticizing the African past or glorifying the African personality such as one finds in the literature of the negritude movement; none of the exclusive pre-occupation with the iniquities, as such, of the white racist minority regime or the guerrilla struggle, as in South African literature or in the early fiction of East Africa. Marechera's work also differs in tone from the gentle prodding irony and satire (largely corrective or reconstructive in intention) of the post-independence novel, especially in West Africa. His expression of disillusionment in his work is deeper even than Ngugi's or Armah's; its cynicism more complete than anything Soyinka has ever been accused of. There is an element of resignation and a devil-may-care type of attitude in his work. But on closer examination this apparent resignation and the frivolity and recklessness of his characters mask their extreme sensitivity and vulnerability. Their perverse behaviour also manifests a kind of assertiveness that can be seen as some form of defensive mechanism against life's utter senselessness and brutality, against all the chaos in their families and the disarray in the nation, which threaten Marechera's characters and infect their whole personalities.

What might probably be described as Marechera's creed as a writer is set out in 'The Writer's Grain'. The first part of this story deals with the agony of a writer who finds his creative efforts scoffed at by experts in whose laboratories his grain is analysed and found wanting. To compound his problems his personal life is in disarray – his marriage is on the point of breaking up as a result of his wife's unfaithfulness. The experience unhinges his mind and leaves him drifting and raving like a lunatic, full of bitterness, especially against the white establishment. Presumably the writer in this story has been frustrated to a very considerable degree by 'experts' on African literature, a problem that is brought up again in 'Are There People Living Up There?'. This story shows how writing to a publisher's prescription can lead to insincerity and distortion. In this story the writer enters for a literary competition on the subject of the ideal modern African family. The situation of affluence and success evoked in the story he actually writes to meet the requirements of the competition, is a far cry from the bleak conditions of life among Africans as he knows them. In both these stories Marechera wants to assert his artistic independence. The second part of 'The Writer's Grain' portrays an outrageous and absurd situation involving a boy, a warthog, which is the boy's mentor, and two dinosaurs, which are highly contemptuous of modern man. This Kafkaesque story, which is also reminiscent of Eugene Ionesco's work, insists on the primacy of the imagination and of creative freedom to which Marechera is pledged as a writer:

> . . . to insist upon your right to go off at a tangent. Your right to put the spanner into the works. Your right to refuse to be labelled and to insist on your right to behave like anything other than anyone expects. Your right to simply say no for the pleasure of it. To insist on your right to confound all who insist on regimenting human impulses according to theories psychological, religious, historical, philosophical, political, etc. . . . Insist upon your right to insist on the importance, the great importance, of whim. There is no greater pleasure than that derived from throwing or not throwing the spanner into the works simply on the basis of whims . . . (p. 122)

This passage, which reads like Marechera's own crusade for freedom of self-expression, is a statement of his personal philosophy as well as his literary creed. The non-conformist views he expresses in the passage also explain his delight in shocking, horrifying and baffling his readers, and in depicting eccentric and iconoclastic characters. His commitment is first and foremost to his art, which nonetheless captures human foibles and frailty, the human condition at its most sensitive and vulnerable point. The above extract also provides an answer to his detractors, represented by the Nigerian student in 'Thought-tracks in the Snow':

> He had, he said, read my stories and found them quite indigestible. Why did I not write in my own language? he asked. Was I perhaps one of those Africans who despised their own roots? Shouldn't I be writing within our great tradition of oral literature rather than turning out pseudo–Kafka–Dostoyevsky stories? (pp. 142–3)

Without agreeing with this estimate of Marechera's work on every point, this essay will also attempt to show that there is some substance in such criticism against Marechera.

The title story of *The House of Hunger*, which is the main focus of this study, is written against the background of discontent. It is an expression of disillusionment with both the past and the present, and is written without any illusions about the future. The novella deals with the misery and the sordidness of life in his home and in Rhodesia in general, which is dubbed 'the House of Hunger' and from which the central character of the story seeks to escape, as Marechera himself was to do. The opening paragraph of this quasi-autobiographical story expresses the major character's desire to escape the soul-destroying clutches of poverty, squalor, starvation, brutality, frustration and oppression:

> I got my things and left. The sun was coming up. I couldn't think where to go. I wandered towards the beerhall but stopped at the bottle-store where I bought a beer. There were people scattered along the store's wide verandah, drinking. I sat beneath the tall msasa tree whose branches scrape the corrugated iron roofs. I was trying not to think about where I was going. I didn't feel bitter. I was glad things had happened the way they had; I couldn't have stayed on in that House of Hunger where every morsel of sanity was snatched from you the way some kinds of bird snatch food from the very mouths of babes. And the eyes of that House of Hunger lingered upon you as though some indefinable beast was about to pounce upon you. (p. 1)

After this strained beginning, conveyed by means of the staccato movement of the prose, the author delves into the psychic experiences and responses of his characters under such devastating conditions. 'Soul-hunger' and 'gut-rot' are expressions used throughout the work to refer to the physically and mentally crushing conditions. What the author does in the rest of the story is expressed in the words of the central character when he speaks of reviewing 'the foul turd which my life had been and was even at that moment' (p. 1). To this end the narrative proceeds through flashback and reminiscence.

Various minor characters who appear and disappear early in the work illustrate the physical insecurity that leads to spiritual agony. The desperation that often sets in under such conditions normally culminates in tragedy and violent reaction, as the characters whose lives are dealt with in the following extract illustrate:

> The old man who died in that nasty train accident, he once got into trouble for begging and loitering. And then Peter got jailed for accepting the bribe from a police spy. When he came out of jail Peter could not settle down. He kept on talking about the bloody whites; that phrase 'bloody whites' seemed to be roasting his mind and he got into fights which terrified everyone so much that no one in their right mind dared cross him. And Peter walked about raging and spoiling for a fight which just was not there. And because he hungered for the *fight* everyone saw it in his eyes and liked him for it. That made it worse for him until his woman got pregnant and the schools inspector said she couldn't teach in that state, and Peter threatened to crush the sky into nothing and refused to marry her because he wanted to be 'free'. It was during that disgrace that father took something mildly poisonous and sickened visibly before our eyes and didn't speak a single word, though we knew he knew it was all to pressure Peter into marriage. (p. 2)

These scenes set the tone for the rest of the action in the story.

As the problem in Rhodesia was then largely political, it is not surprising that the mainspring of the action in the story is political. Political activity and insurrection are espoused by the people, especially the youth, as a means of self-expression and self-realization. But for the central character politics proves to be a blind alley, as he himself acknowledges when he describes his political involvement at high school:

> It was at this time my sixth form like other sixths rushed out into the streets to protest about the discriminatory wage-structure and I got arrested like everybody else for a few hours: which meant fingerprints and photographs and a few slaps on the cheek 'to have more sense', though the principal restrained his bile and only gave us a long sermon of how necessary it was to get qualified before one deigned to put up the barricades. At this time I was extremely thirsty for self-knowledge and curiously enough believed I could find that in 'political consciousness'. All the black youth was thirsty. There was not an oasis of thought which

we did not lick dry; apart from those which had been banned, whose drinking led to arrests and suchlike flea-scratchings. (p. 2)

As this passage shows, there is a certain cynicism towards politics throughout Marechera's work, a measure perhaps of his own frustration and bitterness. This cynicism is paralleled by his seemingly vulgar attitude to sex, 'an irreverent disgust for women' (p. 3) – it isn't really that, as I hope to show – which reflects on the depravity of their ailing society. But sex, like drugs and alcohol, also serves as a form of release from the maddening world. Some of the main character's experiences in the 'House of Hunger' are concerned with his sordid sexual activity, which results in the boy contracting venereal diseases very early in life.

Despite the sexploitation in which most of his male characters gloat, Marechera himself seems to hold strong feminist views. The central character in the 'House of Hunger' paints grim pictures of wife-beating, rape and other crimes against women which are rampant in the ghetto. In what is most certainly Marechera's own voice he expresses women's grievances in an otherwise male-dominated world in the following terms:

> But the young woman's life is not at all an easy one, the black young woman's. She is bombarded daily by a TV network that assumes that black women are not only ugly but also they do not exist unless they take in laundry, scrub lavatories, polish staircases, and drudge around in a nanny's uniform. She is mugged every day by magazines that pressure her into buying European beauty; and the advice columns have such nuggets like 'Understanding is the best thing in the world, therefore be more cheerful when he comes home looking like thunder.' And the only time the *Herald* mentions her is when she has – as in 1896/7 – led an uprising against the State and been safely cheered by the firing squad or when she is caught for the umpteenth time soliciting in Vice Mile. (p. 50)

Marechera's 'irreverent disgust' is really directed against the attitudes that deny women, who are the most vulnerable members of society, their dignity; attitudes that perpetrate suffering and exploitation, while paying lip-service to the African cause. This is the true cause of Marechera's seemingly cynical attitude even towards supposedly revolutionary politics; it is also an answer to Julia's accusation – 'You hate being black' (p. 45), because it illustrates how some unscrupulous politicians appeal to African solidarity as a pretext for dominating and inflicting suffering on others. The book, which appeared at a time when Muzorewa and

Smith had already reached their internal settlement, a settlement seen by many as a manifestation of opportunism by self-seeking African politicians, can be regarded as an expression of the author's disillusionment with such African leaders. However, Marechera's disillusionment is so complete that he fails to discriminate between self-seeking opportunists and selfless dedicated revolutionaries in the struggle for independence in Zimbabwe.

Far from hating himself for being black, Marechera harbours contempt for characters who are ashamed of their colour. 'Black Skin What Mask', as the title suggests, is Fanonian in conception. The story is about a black Oxford undergraduate who is embarrassed by his shabby, drunken friend, also a student at Oxford. The student who is ashamed of his blackness is forever making an ass of himself by chasing white women, who find him an utter bore. In terms of Marechera's analysis, by aspiring to be accepted by whites this student is really striving to run away from his individuality, to obliterate his own identity as a black man. He has a psychological minus value of himself; he looks upon himself in negative terms and is motivated by self-hatred. A careful reading of 'Black Skin What Mask' suggests that it would be inconsistent with the facts to say that Marechera himself hates being black, no matter how much one may disagree with his views on Zimbabwean politics or disapprove of his apparent flippancy, his cynicism, defeatism and so on.

In 'House of Hunger' the central character's excruciating ordeals include his experiences as a student at university and his experience of the heavy-handed treatment meted out by Smith's regime to their opponents, whether they are students, workers or guerrillas. Workers on strike are arrested; African guerrillas when caught are executed and their bodies publicly displayed even before schoolchildren. Under such conditions everybody is seized by a deep yearning for freedom, for fulfillment and an elusive peace:

> There was, however, an excitement of the spirit which made us all wander about in search of that unattainable elixir which our restlessness presaged. But the search was doomed from the start because the elixir seemed to be right under our noses and yet not really there. The freedom we craved for – as one craves for dagga or beer or cigarettes or the after-life – this was so alive in our breath and in our fingers that one became intoxicated by it even before one had actually found it. It was like the way a man licks his lips in his dream of a feast; the way a woman dances in her dream of a carnival; the way the old man

ran like a gazelle in his yearning for the funeral games of his youth. Yet the feast, the carnival and the games were not there at all. This was the paradox whose discovery left us uneasy, sly and at best with the ache of knowing that one would never feel that way again. There were no conscious farewells to adolescence for the emptiness was deep-seated in the gut. We knew that before us lay another vast emptiness whose appetite for things living was at best wolfish. Life stretched out like a series of hunger-scoured hovels stretching endlessly towards the horizon. One's mind became the grimy rooms, the dusty cobwebs in which the minute skeletons of one's childhood were forever in the spidery grip that stretched out to include not only the very stones upon which one walked but also the stars which glittered vaguely upon the stench of our lives. Gut-rot, that was what one steadily became. And whatever insects of thought buzzed about inside the tin can of one's head as one squatted astride the pit-latrine of it, the sun climbed as swiftly as ever and darkness fell upon the land as quickly as in the years that had gone. (pp. 3–4)

A tragic sense of discrepancy between the people's aspirations, mainly political, and the attainment of their ideals thus character- ized life under Smith's regime in Rhodesia. Marechera's language is richly poetical. Use of expletives and the imagery of excretion and putrefaction – linguistic traits that have been called 'verbal acid' by one reviewer and dubbed 'uninhibited' by another – reflect, as in Armah's case, the debilitating and the disgusting nature of his characters' experiences.

Marechera also depicts acts of violence against defenceless women. Peter constantly beats Immaculate, the woman he has impregnated and refused to marry; he beats her just as he has seen his own father beat his mother. In the words of the blurb, 'he behaves with his tender young woman in a precise repetition of the model he knows'. The children in the streets also evince a violent streak by taking sadistic delight in murdering a cat and smashing up everything. Such sadistic pleasures are the common pass-time of ghetto children the world over. Marechera's analysis of the senseless violence among the oppressed is also Fanonian, like his description of self-negation in 'Black Skin White Mask'. He shows how oppression brutalizes by examining the relationships that have been so affected: between his parents, between Peter and Immaculate and so on.

As an escape from the House of Hunger, the boy in the story seeks to recreate for himself 'a labyrinthine personal world which would merely enmesh [him] within its crude mythology' (p. 7). Here the boy's propensity for fantasy has an anaesthetic effect against all the pain inflicted on him; fantasy becomes a panacea against a diseased universe. Physical disease is actually a characteristic of the quality of life in the House of Hunger and reflects the inner corrosion of the mind, of family life and society:

> In the House of Hunger diseases were the strange irruptions of a disturbed universe. Measles or mumps were the symptoms of a maligned order. Even a common cold could become a *casus belli* between neighbours. And add to that the stench of our decaying family life with its perpetual headaches of gut-rot and soul-sickness and rats gnawing the cheese and me worrying it the next morning like a child gently scratching a pleasurable sore on its index finger. (p. 7)

Women, his mother in particular, become sacrificial figures, manifestations of life's batterings and sufferings. 'Her face,' the boy says of his mother, 'was long and haggard, scarred by the many sacrifices she had taken on our behalfs' (pp. 8–9). She resorts to excessive drinking and then to adultery as a result of life's frustrations – the same frustrations that attend college dropouts, like her son, who have been rendered useless by an inappropriate educational system. When his mother complains about his uselessness despite his university education, his brother, Peter, answers for him: 'Tell that to Ian Smith. All you did was starve yourself to send this shit to school while Smith made sure that the kind of education he got was exactly what has made him like this' (p. 9). Later in the story the devastation of life in Rhodesia upon the womenfolk in particular is again illustrated through the experience of Nester, who is discussed later.

From pondering about his failure at university, the boy's thoughts then shift to some of his school associates like Harry. By contrast Harry has become materially successful, perhaps in the way the boy's mother would like her son to be. But Harry has achieved his success through opportunism and betrayal. He is a cheap impressionist whose triumphs, over which he gloats, appear very hollow. Easy white pick-ups and flashy clothes constitute the sum total of his achievement:

> At school he had always tortured me about my lack of 'style' – and lack of money. In the sixth form he had the cubicle next to mine and was forever recounting harrowing stories about 'where he was at with the chicks'. He knew all the city slang, all the slick scenes, and at the throw of a dice could name every name worth knowing in 'Showbiz'. But when we found out that he had been working for the Special Branch in its infiltration of student organizations we one stormy night gagged him, bound him like a crumb of stale toast, and after a rather dramatic

journey out of the dormitory area beat him up so thoroughly that he took
to his bed and for at least three hours did not open his mouth to boast
about where he was at. (p. 10)

As a traitor he remains unrepentant and unreformed as in another
of Marechera's stories from the same collection, 'The Transformation of Harry'. Everything about him is painted 'Bloodred' – his
coat, handkerchief and tie (p. 15) – to imply that he thrives on blood
money. Yet he remains so vainglorious that he is described as the
kind of person who 'must have made a lot of photographers rich' (p.
11) by constantly taking photographs of himself to minister to his
vanity.

Photography is used in the story, as in Fugard's *Sizwe Banzi is
Dead*, to reflect people's dreams for a better life. In the photographic studio they can pose as what they would like to be. The
squalor of their reality is, as it were, 'obliterated in an explosion of
flash-bulbs' so that afterwards one can say, ' "That's me, man – me!
In the city" ' (p. 11). All this points to the people's material
aspirations, which in Smith's Rhodesia cannot be realized unless
one turns into a traitor like Harry; it reflects their 'cruel yearning
which can only be realized in crude photography' (p. 11). Fantasy
is again presented as a means of playing out people's dreams in
society, dreams that are otherwise unattainable. The need to
fantasize is so acute that Solomon, like Styles in *Sizwe Banzi is
Dead*, has become wealthy as the township's photographer.

The influences of Athol Fugard's theatre on Marechera are many
and varied. Echoes of Fugard in *The House of Hunger* include the
photograph of the man, 'ankle over knee, grinning, holding in each
hand a cheap cigar and a rolled cigarette. A price-tag pinned to his
cheek read: 'Fugard" ' (p. 37). Another of Marechera's stories from
the same collection, 'Are There People Living There?', takes its title
from another Fugard play, *People Are Living Up There*, which is
also about the fantasy world of the poor, the dispossessed and the
loveless. These associations in Marechera's work reinforce the
concept of fantasy as a basic survival kit for his characters.

'House of Hunger' attempts to give a close-up view of black
townships in the former Rhodesia. The keynote of such descriptions is squalor and what the author calls 'gut-rot:

barbed wire, whitewashed houses, drunks, prostitutes, the angelic
choirs of god-created flies, and the dust that erupted into little clouds of
divine grace wherever the golden sunlight deigned to strike . . . the
stinking public lavatory. (p. 11)

These 'angelic choirs of god-created flies' described above 'sing' Handel's 'Hallelujah Chorus'. Although we realize that Marechera is trying to capture the buzzing noise made by the flies, the reference to Handel's music sounds somewhat incongruous; there certainly must be a more appropriate metaphor to evoke the atmosphere of the ghetto. Similarly Marechera's literary allusions, based on Greek mythology or the European literary tradition, occasionally misfire. In this respect it can be said that his literary analogies owe very little to the African tradition, and rob his work of a Zimbabwean authenticity. Indeed there is a sense in which Marechera could try to write within the 'African tradition' – and that doesn't necessarily imply churning out conformist or imitational work – instead of scoffing at such suggestions as the Nigerian student makes in 'Thought-tracks in the Snow'. Marechera could strive to be even more ingenious by delving deeper into his environment, especially for his images and metaphors. Yet such literary allusions, images and metaphors as he uses can be illuminating in portraying too, especially the fantasy world of the central character in 'House of Hunger', who, is, in a sense, alienated from his people and environment by his university education. Peter sarcastically calls him Shakespeare and dismisses him as 'bookshit' (pp. 11–12); and the barman is mesmerized by the boy's conversation with Harry on Homer, T. S. Eliot, Blake, Yeats and others – only Harry, true to his pretentious nature, through his ignorance, attributes a jumble of quotations from different sources to the same author. The barman considers the boy to be a person set apart. The boy's learned talk thus becomes a measure of his estrangement from ordinary people like the barman.

But the boy painfully finds out that with all his learning he cannot transcend his environment. Immaculate's attempts to instill renewed zeal and a new drive for success into him fall like seed on infertile soil, further reflecting his despondency, dejection and spiritual sterility, the complete absence of any zest for life, any willingness to drag himself up from the quagmire of squalor, deprivation, misery and oppression. 'She made me want to dream, made me believe in visions, in hope,' the boy recalls. 'But the rock and the grit of the earth denied this' (p. 12). The boy also reflects on other aspects of life in the House of Hunger 'where the acids of gut-rot had eaten into the base metal of [his] brains' (p. 13) – a reference to his personality disintegration.

In a moment of impotent rage the boy tears up his books in protest, after his mother has beaten him for addressing her in

English. He foregoes his dinner, in silent protest, which is then gobbled down by his mother. When the matter is reported to his father he is given another bashing, more violent than the first, his front teeth being knocked clear out. The child-battering that follows the boy's mute, ineffectual protests at home parallels his beating by the police for political involvement. In fact, all political protest is met with brutal treatment in the same way as the boy's protests are cruelly stiffled at home. His home is in this sense a microcosm of Rhodesian society; the violence at home is merely a fraction of the violence employed outside.

The physical and spiritual battering he receives from all sectors of the community creates grave misgivings in the boy about his aptitude for anything positive. So that when Harry says to him, 'You literary chaps are our only hope,' the boy almost chokes on his drink and tells himself that the situation must be really hopeless if someone as helpless as himself appears to offer others a lifeline (p. 16). This is evidence of low self-esteem. Marechera's characters often indulge in considerable self-abasement and flagellation, which almost verge on self-pity, masochism and defeatism. A sad, mournful tone informs his writing. As earlier suggested, his characters are vulnerable inconoclasts whose sensitivity has been violated by the system. Their eccentricity is a measure of their sensitivity and the violation they have suffered. As a recluse, the boy lives in a world of private grief. Just how private his grief is, is evidenced by Harry's other ironic statement in the pub, 'You look well!', when the boy is actually struggling to suppress vomit (p. 16). The fact that he wants to vomit suggests more than mere physical sickness from over-indulgence; it shows 'gut-rot' or spiritual sickness, which has been induced by his utter helplessness and his disgust with conditions in the House of Hunger.

Treachery, which becomes a characteristic of life in the House of Hunger, is shown not only through Harry's traitorous activities but also through the boy's 'disinterested intervention', whereby he takes Immaculate from his brother, Peter, and Julia from his friend, Philip, who has entrusted her to his care. It is the physical conditions and the political situation in general that have infected individual personalities with their poison and affected loyalties and relationships in this way. The chaos that is manifested on the political level is also reflected on the personal level; the prevailing physical destitution breeds psychic disorder. The totality of the oppressive conditions in the House of Hunger creates corrosive bitterness in the central character of the story. The situation breeds hatred in him:

> I found a seed [he says], a little seed, the smallest in the world. And its name was hate. I buried it in my mind and watered it with tears. No seed ever had a better gardener. As it swelled and cracked into green life I felt my nation tremble, tremble in the throes of birth – and burst out bloom and branch. (p. 17)

In addition to hatred, the symptoms of psychic disorder which, as already suggested, reflects a disorderly universe are already in evidence early in the book. For instance, while in the pub with Harry the boy imagines he has been reciting poetry when in fact he's 'just been sitting there like someone in a trance', as Harry observes (p. 18). He cannot even recall the lines of the poem which have merely flitted through his mind. The poem itself expresses dejection and despondency in a chaotic and purposeless world:

> Fragment of this huge emptiness
> Whose pulses sparkle in man's eyes
> What excavation discovered you so rudely into the light? (p. 18)

It is the boy's own life and the lives of others around him that are like 'fragments' in a void. He sees life as living death and ceases to worry even about his own health because, as he tells himself, 'dead souls have no worries' (p. 19). He has also ceased to worry about his own safety, despite the appearance of his picture in the newspapers in connection with anti-government activities for which he is wanted by the police.

In the pub we also meet Julia, an underground agent of the liberation movement, who works under the cover of her other profession, prostitution. With her cheap make-up she resembles 'a beer-hall doll' and behaves like one (p. 20). Her appearance and conduct bear all the unmistakeable signs of havoc wrought by the conditions of life among black women in Rhodesia; for example, the skin-lightening cream that has eaten deep into her skin and left her face a sickening red, like raw meat.

The coarse nightclubs ('all garish colours and lights and a band of half-naked girls dressed up in leopard skin and gyrating some coarse smanje-smanje'), the vulgar music ('not so much singing as farting out in an unnatural base voice'), the obese pickups – all these evoke a feeling of revulsion inside him (p. 25). He feels caught in a rathole; he feels, he says, 'like a cat thrown without extreme unction into a deep well' (p. 25). There seems to be no escape from it all, and this drives the boy crazy. He indulges in sexual intercourse with the fat singer from the nightclub as if his very life depends on it, as if to seek release, to purge himself of all the pent-up emotions wrought by hunger, deprivation and oppression:

> The skin-lightened dancer – she was burning, burning the madness out of me. The room had taken over my mind. My hunger had become the room. There was a thick darkness where I was going. It was a prison. It was a womb. It was blood clinging closely like a swamp in the grass-matted lowlands of my life. It was a Whites Only sign on a lavatory. It was my teeth on edge – the bitter acid of it! It was the effigy [that is, Ian Smith] swinging gently to and fro in the night of my mind. And the pain of it flared into flame, flickering like a match; for a moment it lit up the room, making the shadows of the naked dancer and me leap quickly across the ceiling and fuse into an embrace. Leaping like ecstasy grown sad – a violence slowly translating into gentleness. (p. 25)

But even after burning himself up in this way he still feels unfulfilled, like a 'blackened twig' (p. 25). Sex, like politics, offers a false lifeline.

Reminiscing about his political involvement once more, the boy recalls being beaten up after addressing a political gathering during which he supposedly 'harangues' his audience (p. 26). Nonetheless, the violent reaction from his audience appears grossly disproportionate to the provocation. It is somewhat senseless, too, as the audience next turns upon his tormentor with whom they appeared to sympathize at first. The other man is beaten up so brutally that he ends up in a lunatic asylum, to which conditions in the country would seem to be leading everybody. This is also the reason for Marechera's preoccupation with lunacy in his work. The boy himself in 'House of Hunger' experiences a nervous breakdown on several occasions, the consequence of his feeling of insecurity and of being pursued by everyone. This is the significance of the three men and the woman in his hallucinations during one of the periods when he flips out:

> There had been four of them; three men in threadbare clothes and the woman of the faded shawl. This had happened a few weeks before my sixth-form examinations – which I then had to write with the assistance of a massive dose of white triangular pills. At first the three men and the woman merely followed me about the school saying nothing but just being *there*. Crudely there. I would be talking to friends and then become intensely aware of *them* standing close to my friends. I would be in the history classroom listening to the history master and as usual taking notes and things when I would with a leap of the heart-beat

> realise that they were in the room, moving about, following the teacher, sitting down when he sat, and aping his every gesture. Or after our football practice when we were in the showers they would appear standing stiffly watching my nakedness. One day this so terrified me that I rushed stark naked out of the showers screaming my head off. (p. 29)

As in Bessie Head's *A Question of Power*,[12] Marechera presents lunacy in the form of evil beings conspiring against and willing evil on him:

> I had only been in the room for a few seconds when I began to hear the tiny maddening sound. I shifted my weight, listening. It was the sound of distant footsteps coming and going in all the other rooms that pressed against my room. Feet exactly taking step in time with each other; coming and going. Trudging and turning just behind a point midway between my eyes. (p. 38)

Paranoia begins to assail the boy, so that he suspects friends and foes alike of undermining his sanity. He hears imaginary voices shouting obscenities about his mother's loose morals. At this stage of the story the author is trying to show that it is in large measure the breakdown of morality within the boy's own home, where the air reeked of guilt, shame, outrage and scandal, that leads to the disintegration of his own personality. The boy is exposed to perverted behaviour of all kinds at an early age. He has his first experience of drunkenness from alcohol supplied by his own father, who ends up quarrelling with his enraged mother before the children on this and other occasions; he learns about his mother's adultery and promiscuity at the age of four, when she lets in a strange man through the window in the middle of the night and the boy has to listen all night long to their groans and grunts in bed; as a young boy he is also treated to a demonstration of masturbation by his elder brother, Peter; and he also follows prostitutes with other boys in the streets to see how they do it; finally he learns about rape, which is very widespread in his environment. His education both at home and in the streets has been a series of excruciating ordeals and sordid experiences. Given this background, his escapist world of books and his university education are but ineffectual shields against the onslaught of his environment, against life's brutal thrusts. It is a matter of time before he becomes submerged in the world of drugs, alcohol and sexual orgies, no longer as an observer (as in his youth) but as an active participant. And when the mask of intoxication wears off he flips out completely.

His recuperation from his first nervous breakdown symbolically follows a particularly violent storm during which he and Harry wrestle in the mud. After the storm and the fight, he feels cleansed. The mystical quality of this experience invites a comparison with St Paul's conversion on the road to Damascus. 'It was a new clarity,' the boy says, 'the kind of madness that overcomes Pauline travellers on the road to Damascus' (p. 34). The storm-fight is his own baptism by fire and may be related to the violence that is necessary to purge and free Rhodesian society.

The impurities in this society are also manifested in the religious order. Immaculate's father, who is a Roman Catholic priest, illustrates both the widespread moral turpitude and the reactionary nature of certain religious zealots. It could very well be Marechera's mistake (it is hard to tell), but Roman Catholic priests do not marry as Immaculate's father does. Marechera most probably has in mind the Anglican priests at St Augustine's in Rhodesia where he went to school. It is the Anglican church in Rhodesia that has been accused of conniving with Ian Smith's minority racist regime, whereas the Catholic establishment is said to have come out strongly against it. In politics Immaculate's father, who represents the reactionary elements within the church, connives with the oppressor by preaching unquestioned obedience to authority and a rejection of African culture, which he considers atavistic. The boy and his schoolmates violently resist this false gospel from Immaculate's father, who is really trying to ingratiate himself with the authorities. They pummel him with ink and sadza (hard porridge made from maize meal). But the boy suffers another relapse as a result – his reaction has been too violent – which is conveyed, as in Bessie Head's *A Question of Power*, by a great deal of obscurity and disjointedness in the narrative. Insanity here and elsewhere acts as some kind of built-in shock absorber, some form of emotional cotton wool to cushion the soul against certain deadly knocks. In moments of great emotional stress nature provides its own anaesthetic, as it were. However, it is also such experiences that leave lasting scars on the boy's soul.

The boy's reminiscences then switch to his student days. He recalls their frustrated efforts as university students to establish a creative writing magazine and to involve themselves in the Zimbabwean struggle for liberation. To this end the blacks cultivate uneasy alliances with white students like Doug, the artist, and Citre who is 'worried about being drafted into the army' (pp. 66, 67). They are drawn together by art and politics, but in practice they resort to dagga and sex orgies because, as already suggested, they are unable to transcend their environment. Here Marechera's fatalism surfaces again. The boy even starts an affair with a white crippled girl called Patricia, but it is also doomed to failure because of the racial malady in their society. Patricia and the boy are even beaten up by a group of white rightwing students.

The fight with the rightwing students has a wider significance. It represents intolerance from the supporters of the regime as well as the inescapable confrontation between those who are truly committed to the struggle and the supporters of the system who believe that white is might. As in the fight itself, the boy's lone efforts and those of a few others who think like him are rendered hopeless by the extreme brutality of their encounter with rightwing forces. 'No one would intervene to try and help us,' he says of the time he and Patricia were beaten up, 'because she and I had dared to flaunt our horns and hooves to our racial groups' (p. 72). The fatalism involved in Patricia's affair with the boy is reminiscent of Peter Abrahams' treatment of the theme of love across the colour line in *The Path of Thunder*.[13]

Patricia ends up roaming aimlessly through the African continent, after her troubles with the Rhodesian authorities over her paintings – another example of stifled self-expression. She returns home ill, never recovers her speech and the boy is debarred from seeing her at the Whites Only hospital. Like Peter Abrahams, Marechera generally shows sympathy for those whites like Doug, Citre and Patricia who are themselves victims of racial bigotry. Of Patricia he even says that she was one of those people 'whom our country either breaks or confines in prison and lunatic asylums' (p. 71). But their actions against Rhodesian authoritarianism can only be, as the boy says, an exercise in futility:

> We were whores; eaten to the core by the syphilis of the white man's coming. Masturbating onto a *Playboy* centrefold; screaming abuse at a solitary but defiant racist; baring our arse to the yawning pit-latrine; writing angry 'black' poetry; screwing pussy as though out to prove that white men do not in reality exist – this was all contained within the circumvention of our gut-rot. (p. 75)

Like the hippie cult of the 1960s, the lifestyle of the radical youth at the university represents rebellion against a representative order. Marechera himself, at least as a writer, is a rebel and a nonconformist rather than a revolutionary.

The decadent social order among the students and the community at large manifests itself through permissiveness on campus as well as in the crude sexism of Marechera's work in general. The young students even make pornographic films of the boy having sexual intercourse with Patricia, and Citre with Julia. While talking to the boy at the pub, Julia can hardly restrain herself from fondling his penis unobserved by the others. At another stage in the story another prostitute, Nestar, relates her harrowing sexual experiences to the boy. She reveals the existence of considerable sex mania among the whites, which further underlines the decadent social and political order under which they live. Some of Nestar's clients have been very important personages in the land. The symptoms of sickness in Rhodesian society manifest themselves among people of all races and in all ranks of life.

Rhodesia's history and the political system under which the people live have greatly contributed towards all this decadence. To illustrate this point, the boy relates the treachery and intrigue whereby Lobengula is tricked into signing the Rudd Concession, ceding large tracts of land to the British South Africa Company under Rhodes. This is the cause of the struggle in Rhodesia. 'Lobengula finally agreed to be eaten by Rhodes,' the boy reflects. 'My generation had all but been consumed by gut-rot' (p. 44). The Shonas come off worse than the Ndebeles, as both Jameson in the name of Rhodes' company and Lobengula claim sovereignty over them. 'Mashonas are servants of the white man,' Jameson says. 'To whom do the Mashona belong if they do not belong to the king?' Mtshete, Lobengula's *induna*, asks (p. 42). In this way the book shows that there have been instances in history of black as well as white tyranny. Marechera is even deeply suspicious of the double standards evinced by contemporary African politicians. 'Actually, class consciousness and the conservative snobbery that goes with it,' the boy in the story argues, 'are deeply rooted in the African elite, who are in the same breath able to shout LIBERATION, POLYGAMY without feeling that something is unhinged' (p. 44). The boy's disillusionment, which reflects Marechera's own, thus extends to the modern African elite whose lives are fraught with contradictions and hypocrisy. He is critical of the exploitative tendency and the opportunism of some African politicians. 'Sometimes freedom's opportunity is a wide waistline,' he says, commenting on self-seeking African leaders. African society, according to Marechera, has disintegrated, largely as a result of oppression and powerlust, going far back into history, to a point where there must be serious doubts about the integrity of the new leaders whose ineffectiveness and inefficiency he likens to that of 'senile gods' (p. 46).

The brutalizing effects of Rhodesian society are also shown through Nestar's family. Nestar begins to solicit in the streets for her survival at the age of twelve. The products of her sexual adventures are two children, a boy to whom she gives birth in the bush and a girl named Ada. The girl falls into the decadent company of the radicals among whom the central character of the story moves. (In 'The Transformation of Harry', a story that uses some of the characters from 'House of Hunger', Ada is used as bait to catch Harry, and his attempts to seduce her and recruit her to spy on the political activities of her boyfriend, Peter, backfire.) Nestar has brought up her children under very difficult conditions. 'The pain, blood and emptiness,' she explains about the painful birth of her first child, 'made [me] there and then decide to fight into the thick of money' (p. 51). She has mastered all the techniques necessary for her survival and can be violent too when occasion demands it, as is demonstrated when she thrashes Philip and the central character of the story after they have beaten up her son for raping Philip's sister. Nestar's children evince the characteristics of growing up in a slum environment. The language of Nestar's son, for instance, when we first meet him, is very coarse. 'What do you want with my mother, munt?' he asks the central character in the story when he finds him with Nestar. 'Begging for arse? You fucking stinking nigger' (p. 63). Although he is described by Philip as a mere kid and is himself a product of sexploitation, he is involved in a case of rape, and he so manhandles Philip's sister that she ends up in hospital. As with the central character's brother, Peter, Nestar's son has obviously been affected by his upbringing and reacts 'in a precise repetition of the model he knows'.

The House of Hunger switches again to the subject of race relations. In an incident that is reminiscent of Alex La Guma's 'Coffee for the Road', [14] Philip and the main protagonist arrive at a white-owned coffee-shop, which has separate counters for blacks and whites. Like the Indian lady in La Guma's story, they are met with open hostility by the white proprietor:

> Sunlight bounced off a grimy phone booth and noiselessly splintered into the glass front of a drowsy coffe shop. I rapped on the counter with a coin – the way Harry does. A white old age pensioner's face slowly rotated into view. It stared hard at us as if we were something shameful like doubtful foreign coins. The pink mouth embedded in meagre

strings of pink fat twitched, sticking with saliva like stalagmites and
stalactites. It said:
  'Kaffirs at the back. Kaffirs . . .' (p. 56)

For retaliating against such discriminatory treatment they are
immediately identified by the police as agitators, which is also the
fate of the Indian lady in La Guma's story. Inevitably they are
accused of terrorist activities and communist subversion. The boy
is subsequently arrested and while he is in prison attempts are
made by the authorities to force him to reveal his political associates,
but he stubbornly refuses to. Like La Guma in *In the Fog of a
Season's End*, Marechera describes the boy's prison experiences
and the sadistic torture to which he is subjected, the type of
atrocities the Rhodesian authorities have to resort to in a desperate
effort to crush black resistance:

> There was only a bench in it. And with the questions and the questions
> and the blows, the bench began to grow and grow with my life and
> bruises, with my breath and the stains of my blood. Something had gone
> out of me and into the bench which had come alive with it. Someone
> was saying 'Leave me with the fucking cunt for five minutes and he'll
> talk like never-never.' Something exploded inside my head. (p. 57)

The boy's friend who shares most of his experiences with him is
Philip. Philip illustrates the attitudes and the values for which the
gang of radical youth stands. His poems express the 'discontent,
disillusionment and outrage' they all feel. He feels very strongly
about white injustice and ugliness in the world. 'There's dust and
fleas and bloody whites and roaches and dogs trained to bite black
people in the arse,' he says to his friend (p. 59). Marechera's
cynicism and pessimism are again extended to the African
politicians. Philip is disgruntled with leaders who are basically
white-oriented, with all the sell-outs who infiltrate the liberation
movement:

> There's white shit in our leaders and white shit in our dreams and white
> shit in our history and white shit on our hands in anything we build or
> pray for. Even if that was okay there's still sell-outs and informers and
> stuck-up students and get-rich-fast bastards and live-now-think-later
> punks who are just as bad, man. Just as bad as white shit. There's a lot of
> these bastards hanging around in London waiting to come and become
> cabinet ministers. (p. 59)

He warns that the future may remain as bleak for black Rhodesians
as long as the leadership, even that of the Patriotic Front, is sold out
to materialistic ends.

But without being really aware of it, Philip has joined the ranks of the very African middle class he despises, even as he is expatiating his revolutionary ideals to the boy. It is all very well to condemn the African leadership for some of its excesses, but what of Philip's own exploitation of women? His values have begun to alter and the irony of his position is not lost upon the boy. He observes that Philip now has a cosy office and smokes cigars instead of the rolled cigarettes they used to smoke together.

In his office Philip then hands his friend a newspaper with a picture of Edmund, a former boyhood friend of theirs, who is reported to have died in the fierce guerrilla struggle then raging between the Patriotic Front and Smith's forces. When they see Edmund's picture they remember their school days, especially one rather eventful day when little Edmund fought with the big bully, Stephen. In the words of the blurb, 'School is brutalizing too'; so that the central character in the story remembers the beating of Edmund, 'the weakest yet most obstinate of boys', when he sees a picture of his corpse in the paper. Marechera has been a witness to the tragedy of Zimbabwe's guerrilla struggle. Stephen is also a representative of those self-proclaimed revolutionaries who mouth radical slogans that are not matched by their lifestyles.

In a passage that is reminiscent of Ngugi's description of Chui as a schoolboy in *Petals of Blood*,[15] Stephen speaks Pan-Africanism and advocates Africanizing their school curriculum and the teaching staff. Yet his behaviour to Edmund, a child from an underprivileged background, is extremely insulting, as when he tells everybody at school that Edmund's mother is a prostitute, by which means she manages to keep Edmund at school – something the rest of the students in Edmund's class know, though none of them would ever be so insensitive as to say it to Edmund's face. Contradictory sides of Stephen are effectively juxtaposed in a particularly vivid description of his character:

> Stephen was an avid reader of the Heinemann African Writers Series. He firmly believed that there was something peculiarly African in anything written by an African and said that therefore European tools of criticism should not be used in the analysis of 'African literature'. He had also gleaned a few nuggets of thought from E. Mphahlele's *The African Image*. And he had a life style to go with it: he was nearly expelled for refusing to go to mass and to prayers – he said 'Christianity is nothing but a lie; seek ye the political kingdom and everything else will follow'; he was always taking the geography master to task about his ironic comments about the primitive state of Africa's roads; he was

always petitioning for African history to be taught – the only history we were taught was British and European, with the United States for dessert. He took dagga; he believed that there is a part of man which is permanently stoned and that this was beautiful . . . Stephen also had nightmares, great bouts of them; and he was ashamed of this one 'weakness'. (p. 64)

Stephen's character resembles that of many self-proclaimed revolutionaries whose double standards Marechera attacks.

Summarizing his life history towards the end of the story, the boy again attributes his personality disintegration to his sordid family background in highly evocative passages, which are worth reproducing at some length:

It was the House of Hunger that first made me discontented with things. I knew my father only as the character who occasionally screwed mother and who paid the rent, beat me up, and was cuckolded on the sly by various persons. He drove huge cargo lorries, transporting groundnut oil to Zambia and Zaïre and Malawi. I knew that he was despised because of mother, and because he always wore khaki overalls, even on Sundays, and because he was quite generous with money to friends and enemies alike. The only thing was that he was an alcoholic.

He once got Peter and I so drunk that mother thrashed the three of us and then shoved him out of the house for the night. The only time he came close to hitting mother was when she discovered in his travelling bag a quite elaborate set of anti-VD paraphernalia: injections, pills, penicillin, which she threw out into the dustbin . . .

But mother was more feared than respected. She was a hard worker in screwing, running a home, and maintaining a seemingly tight rein over her husband; she was good in fights, and verbal sallies, never losing face; and, more important for me, she had nothing better to do than to throw her children into the lion's den of things white. Peter took after her, while I was more my father. Certainly father could never control Peter – only mother could do that; and therefore father handled me severely.

Peter, of course, early became the enemy of all fathers and mothers who had daughters. He and mother gave to the house a whiff of scandal strong enough to be detected throughout the whole region. When Peter became twenty-one father gave him for a present a new anti-VD set. Mother merely warned Peter not to get involved with married women. And I – rather grudgingly, for I was extremely jealous – gave my dubious blessing. (pp. 77–8)

The boy in the story receives his final lessons from the old tramp with whom he sits around a fire roasting maize. The old man tells the boy stories that are 'oblique, rambling and fragmentary' (p. 79). But a coherent line of thought holds the old man's narrative together. His stories are about the struggle for survival among outcasts – like the hunter of women who gets 'cast out of village, town and country' (p. 79); they are about the indestructible quality of man's soul even in the most adverse of conditions – 'the brain only dies at its own behest,' the old man says to the boy; they are also about people's dreams and frustrations – which is really what the whole story is about. In the final analysis the old man's advice to the boy is to clear out of Rhodesia before Smith's soldiers, who are already on the lookout for him, catch him and beat him to pulp. 'I think Trouble is knocking impatiently on our door,' he tells the boy (p. 82). This statement, which is the old man's parting shot to the boy and the novella's final statement, in what is basically a quasi-autobiographical story, can also be read as an explanation of the reasons for Marechera's own decision to flee from Rhodesia into exile in England. His reasons are explained at greater length in 'Thought-tracks in the Snow'.

Marechera's work, for which he received the 1979 Guardian prize for fiction is, like Edmund's poetry in 'House of Hunger', 'a painstaking exploration of the effects of poverty and destitution on the "psyché" ' (p. 61). His narrative technique resembles the old man's at the end of the story; it is 'oblique, rambling and fragmentary'. However, the story is told in a coherent pattern that highlights the plight of the ordinary people in Rhodesia who were caught on the wrong side of Smith's regime. Marechera's stand as a writer and a person is that of a rebel rather than a revolutionary. His voice is a significant addition and a unique contribution to African literature. His *avantgarde* experiments with form are proving very interesting – and increasingly unintelligible, as his latest work, *Black Sunlight*, illustrates.

As a writer of quasi-autobiographical work Marechera is more readily comparable to Bessie Head. He does what Bessie Head, in an address to the Writers' Workshop of the University of Botswana, says she does in her novels:

> I have found that the novel form is like a large rag-bag into which one can stuff anything – all one's philosophical, social and romantic speculations. I have always reserved a special category for myself, as a writer – that of a pioneer blazing a new trail into the future.[16]

NOTES

1. The most comprehensive survey to date of black Zimbabwean literature in English is G. P. Kahari's *The Search for Zimbabwean Identity: An Introduction to the Black Zimbabwean Novel*, Gwelo, Zimbabwe, Mambo Press, 1980. But Marechera falls outside the scope of the survey.

2. Lawrence Vambe, *An Ill-Fated People*, London, Heinemann (AWS 112), 1972, p. 70; Pittsburgh, University of Pittsburgh Press, 1973.

3. Musa Shamuyarira et al., *Madetembedzo*, Cape Town, Longmans, Green, in association with the Southern Rhodesia African Literature Bureau, 1959.

4. Albert S. Gerard, 'African Literature in Rhodesia', *African Report*, vol. 13, no. 5, Washington D.C., May 1968. This essay provides a concise survey of literature in Zambabwe in the indigenous languages. Another, though less complete, survey appears in Oscar Dathorne's *The Black Mind*, Minneapolis, University of Minnesota Press, 1974.

5. Doris Lessing, *The Grass is Singing*, London, Michael Joseph, 1950. This novel has since been reissued by Penguin (1961) and Heinemann in the African Writers Series (1973); New American Library, 1976.

6. Solomon Mutswairo, *Feso*, Cape Town, Oxford University Press, 1957.

7. Stanlake Samkange, *On Trial for My Country*, London, Heinemann (AWS 33), 1967.

8. Stanlake Samkange, *Year of the Uprising*, London, Heinemann (AWS 190), 1978.

9. Stanlake Samkange, *Origins of Rhodesia*, London, Heinemann, 1968.

10. Dambudzo Marechera, *The House of Hunger*, London, Heinemann (AWS 207), 1978 (all further page references are to this edition); New York, Pantheon, 1979. *Black Sunlight*, London, Heinemann (AWS 237), 1980.

11. See my article, 'The Poetry of Polycarp S. Chimedza', *Review of African Political Economy*, no. 18, Sheffield, 1980.

12. Bessie Head, *A Question of Power*, London, Heinemann (AWS 149), 1973.

13. Peter Abrahams, *The Path of Thunder*, London, Faber, 1952.

14. Alex La Guma, *A Walk in the Night and Other Stories*, London, Heinemann (AWS 35), 1968.

15. Ngugi wa Thiong'o, *Petals of Blood*, Heinemann (AWS 188), 1977.

16. Bessie Head, 'Some Notes on Novel Writing', *New Classic*, no. 5, Johannesburg, 1978, p. 32.

Reviews

E. N. Emenyonu, *The Rise of the Igbo Novel*, Ibadan, Oxford University Press, 1978, 400pp.

In this book Emenyonu traces the origin of the Igbo novel – starting with the oral tradition (especially the folk tale), through the Onitsha Market group of writings, to the modern Igbo novel where his main point of focus is on Cyprian Ekwensi and Chinua Achebe.

The book reads quite well, and helps to document certain fundamental views about such novels as Ekwensi's *People of the City* and *Jagua Nana*, as well as Achebe's *Things Fall Apart*, *No Longer at Ease*, *Arrow of God* and *A Man of the People*. Unfortunately Emenyonu's review of Igbo novels ends with these two novelists, while such prominent Igbo novelists as Onuora Nzekwu, Flora Nwapa, Elechi Amadi, John Munonye, Nkem Nwankwo and others are grouped together in the penultimate chapter. A striking omission is the book's failure to offer a definition of the controversial term 'Igbo literature'. And this is a serious omission in a book that discusses the rise of the Igbo novel.

The crux of Emenyonu's treatise is that the Igbo novel as we know it today originated from oral tradition, as can be deduced from the ensuing quotations: 'Contemporary Igbo novel, poetry or drama is an extension of Igbo oral literature' (p. 2), 'Achebe's literary art derives from Igbo narrative tradition' (p. 155). In fact Emenyonu sophistically tries to trace the development of the Igbo novel through Igbo pioneer writers like Pita Nwana, and the Onitsha Market pamphleteers to Ekwensi and Achebe. In spite of his acknowledgement of the fact that Pita Nwana's *Omenuko* and Leopold Bell-Gam's *Ije Odumodu Jere* were modelled after western novels, he still insists on a quasi-organic link between the different stages of the Igbo literary history and development.

As far as his statement that the contemporary Igbo novel derives from oral tradition is concerned, I can only refer Emenyonu to Eustace Palmer's preface to his *Growth of the African Novel* (London, Heinemann, 1979) in which he rightly points out that:

> A number of African novelists incorporate elements of the oral tradition in their novels, but these are not therefore outgrowths of the oral tale. Much as we would like to think so for nationalistic and other reasons the novel, unlike poetry and drama, is not an indigenous African genre . . . The African novel grew out of the Western novel and writers like Achebe, Laye and Ekwensi were much more influenced by Conrad, Hardy, Dickens, Kafka, and George Eliot than by the African oral tale. (p. 5)

Emenyonu overstresses the importance and contribution of the Onitsha Market group of writings to the development of modern fiction as is evident from the following quotation:

> It is this intimacy with both material and audience, perhaps more than anything else that will remain the greatest contribution of the Onitsha writers in the course and development of modern Igbo fiction. (p. 86)

To begin with, the Onitsha Market literature, though being the forerunner of modern Igbo fiction, has contributed little to the development of this class of writings. The Onitsha stories were narratives modelled after popular European romances, Shakespearean drama and biblical stories, while often making use of local characters and setting. With the exception of Ekwensi, no Igbo novelist has any significant connection with the Onitsha writings. Emenyonu refers to the 'Onitsha literary movement' as 'an important segment of modern Igbo literature', adding that 'its true significance lies more in its sociological than literary relevance' (p. 84). Clearly this class of writings does not have the rhetorical and stylistic merits that should recommend them for classification as literature; they are popular romances and nothing more.

The section on Pita Nwana's narrative, entitled 'Omenuko: An Example of Mixed Literary Forms', should have been pursued further and expanded to include Bell-Gam's *Ije Odumodu Jere*, for in spite of the disparity in language, there is a closer connection between this type of narration and modern Igbo fiction than there is between the latter and the Onitsha pamphlets.

Emenyonu has nothing but praise for Ekwensi. There is no reference to any of the numerous stylistic and rhetorical deficiencies of his novels, and such an omission (especially from a renowned critic) is as dangerous as it is misleading to prospective students of Igbo literature. Unfortunately, when Emenyonu decides at length to find a slight fault with Ekwensi, it is for the wrong reason:

> One could disagree with the author in his concept that the big city with all its crookedness and degeneration, does corrupt the individual. It is possible to argue that nothing can corrupt a person unless he wants to be corrupted or there is some weakness or flaw in his character . . . (p. 99)

From the above it is clear that Emenyonu has misunderstood the most central theme of Ekwensi's city novels. Ironically it is the second sentence of the quotation that clearly states Ekwensi's concept of the city and its people. This is manifest in such characters as the uncorrupt city girl Beatrice II, the good lorry driver Kofi, in the fate of Sango, the hero of *People of the City*, and even in the final episode of *Jagua Nana*.

On the whole Emenyonu's observations about the novels of Ekwensi and Achebe constitute no more than a documentation of well-known views; they have no additional information to contribute to the study of Igbo literature.

There are a few serious flaws in this study; Emenyonu sometimes juxtaposes antithetical terms like the reference to the Onitsha writers as a 'non literary group' and to their writings, at the same time, as 'literature' (p. xiv); he refers to *Omenuko* and *Ije Odumodu Jere* as novels; there are grammatical errors such as the use of present and past tenses in the same phrase – 'it was not only the city which corrupts Jagua . . .' (p. 100); on page 8 the Igbo word 'odu' is wrongly written thus:

Taa isi ya piarara   Anugoro
Taa odu ya piarara   Anugoro

As has been stated earlier, Emenyonu's study is a good documentation, a useful students' reference book, but I still look forward to a more comprehensive and thorough study of the Igbo novel.

Catherine O. Acholonu

Chukwuemeka Ike, *Sunset at Dawn*, A Novel about Biafra, London, Collins and Harvill Press, 1976, 255pp.

> We are Biafrans
> Fighting for our freedom,
> In the name of Jesus
> We shall conquer.
>
> We are Biafrans
> Marching to the war
> In the name of Jesus
> We shall conquer. (p. 9)

Thus sang the young volunteers ready to defend the young republic's capital, Enugu, in September 1967 (p. 9). Without modern weapons but with matchetes and their bare bodies. Without resources but with an ideology called Biafra. And with an Old Testament faith:

> . . . We shall not be moved,
> We shall not, we shall not be moved;
> Just like a tree that's planted by the water,
> We shall not be moved. (p. 11)

The originator of this epic children's crusade was Biafra's Director of Mobilization, Dr Amilo Kanu. Again and again his raw young recruits of the Civil Defense Corps, aroused by his infectious optimism in the face of overwhelming odds, would break into song:

> Armour'd-u car,
> Shelling machine,
> Heavy artillery,
> Ha enwegh ike imeri Biafra!
> [They can't overrun Biafra]

A few days later Enugu falls to the Federal army. No resistance worth the name is offered. Few lives are lost. The matchete attack on Nigeria's armoured columns – 'a crazy idea', as its originator fully realizes – has been cancelled by His Excellency the Commander-in-Chief at the last moment.

The actions of Amilo Kanu, one of the main characters in Chukwuemeka Ike's fourth novel, *Sunset at Dawn*, seem to be motivated by an initial political handicap: being married to a non-Igbo and envisaging a brilliant medical career at the University of Ibadan, the young doctor refuses to return to the east when his native region is about to break away from Nigeria; only a fake telegram announcing his father's death brings the wayward son home. The fact that he has befriended two of the Biafran officers subsequently shot as leaders of the anti-Ojukwu coup attempt after the Midwest débâcle hardly helps matters. A forward strategy of bold commitment to the cause is the only answer. His Biafranism is finally consecrated by his military heroism in the frontline, where he has volunteered to fight as a common soldier: 'His uniform carried nothing but the Biafra sun, on both sleeves' (p. 213). While convalescing in a concealed hospital he is picked off mysteriously, and rather unbelievably, by a lone Nigerian aerial bomb.

His wife Fatima, a Hausa, whose uncle is a former Federal minister involved in organizing the 1966 massacres of eastern Nigerians in the then Northern Region, finds herself on the Biafran side much against her will. Estranged and embittered at first by the loss of her elder son, killed by a Nigerian shell, and the quaintness of Igbo village life after her flight from the comfort of Enugu, she becomes involved in work for the refugees, especially kwashiorkor cases ('Harold Wilson's children'), and ends up deeply committed to the Biafran cause.

While this marital relationship, surveying and evolving under the strains of war, despite the husband's occasional cavalier infidelities, is the most interesting aspect of the novel from a psychological point of view, its sociological import lies in the interaction of a group of characters to which Amilo Kanu belongs, united by bonds of friendship.

There is Professor Ezenwa, the Nsukka historian, forever mourning the loss of his research papers occasioned by the *vandals'* premature arrival on the campus, often finding new developments 'difficult to conceptualize', harbouring an innate scepticism that sometimes casts a shadow of doubt on his political loyalty, but outwardly a true Biafran intellectual:

> Having forgotten to include his shaving set among the few belongings he took out of Nsukka, he had decided to join the band wagon and sport a beard. It made you look like a revolutionary, Cuban style. It identified you with His Excellency. (p. 35)

There is a Barrister Ifeji, 'wearing his usual three-piece suit of dark, striped, woollen material, complete with gold chain across his waistcoat and black bowler hat' (p. 22). In a heroic age in which *agbadas*, the flowing robes of the Yoruba, emblematic of Nigerian oneness, are often ripped off the wearer's back and burned on the spot by a fanatic populace, this London outfit is a remarkable survival of the past. But if Barrister Ifeji changes to the 'Biafran suit' towards the end of the war, it is only because the collar of his only remaining shirt has got frayed beyond repair.

Mr Ikem Onukaegbe, a civil servant, is depicted as somewhat frivolous; he is keenly interested in 'shelling' operations, not those on the war-front, to be sure, but the type involving 'cradlers' — Chinua Achebe's 'Girls at War' — unattached female undergraduates unable to make both ends meet on their meagre secretarial salaries and ready to stand in, to use a vertical metaphor, for the absent wives of top administrators or military officers. He is one of those about whom a medical doctor complains bitterly:

> They strut about like peacocks, calling themselves Director of one thing or other and enjoying more amenities in wartime than ministers did in the political days, while professionals like us slave away without recognition. (p. 125)

Mr Ndubuisi Akwealumo, the youngest permanent secretary in the civil service, is as close to Dr Kanu as 'palm kernel to fried breadfruit'. He does not share his friend's enthusiasm for carrying arms but is genuinely convinced that in his job as Director of Procurement he is making his best possible contribution to the war effort. A young scientist, Dr Osita, who has devised Biafra's first rocket, belongs to the group only marginally. The saga of Biafra's technological miracle still remains buried in some recondite mind.

The most moving figure in the group is a non-academic, Duke Bassey, nicknamed 'Indigenous', the only non-Igbo among them. Formerly the prosperous owner of a chain of supermarkets, he loses all of them one by one through the enemy's advance, is rejected and betrayed by his own people in Annang Province, narrowly escapes extermination, and then almost gets lynched by overzealous Civil Defenders on the Igbo side. Despite his many reverses and the disappearance of his family he remains undaunted in his loyalty, seeking solace in religion.

Despite glimpses of village life showing the sufferings of the common people, despite the graphically described horrors of air-raids and refugee camps, this novel deals primarily with the wartime problems of the Biafran elite, its resilience, inventiveness and zest for survival. It's most striking characteristic is a rigid status consciousness that places the holders of titles like Dr,

Professor, Permanent Secretary or Barrister in an unassailable position with which the author, despite gentle ironies, seems to identify, and which is no whit different from the pride of position of the post-war national bourgeoisie. Witness the heartfelt sob of a loving wife in an obituary notice appearing in a leading Nigerian newspaper: Rest in Perfect Peace, Dear Lawyer.

Caught in bed with a teenager by his irate wife, the Director for Mobilization piously exhorts his spouse not to make a scene since he has 'an image to protect'. Fatima herself, although on the way to national integration as a true Biafran, asserts her claim to preferential treatment on the social level:

> . . .If secondary school girls could be chauffeur-driven just because they made themselves available to boys who, thanks to the war, had become army officers the day after leaving secondary school, how much more right had she, Fatima, fully qualified X-ray technologist, and wife of a lecturer in medicine, member of the War Services Council and Director for Mobilization for Biafra? (p. 97)

Apart from Professor Ezenwa's Cuban-style beard, there is little or none of the 'Little Green Book' type of socialism propounded in the Ahiara declaration (Ojukwu's ideology of the Biafran people) discernible in the group. Unlike Soyinka's 'interpreters', Ike's young 'elites' are actually old bottles bubbling with new wine; they are part and parcel of a politico–social system whose inner contradictions they fail to see.

Even though he may be unaware of some of the hidden ironies in a society that views itself as essentially new, as 'the first truly independent African country' (p. 191), embodying freedom from fear and persecution and a more equitable social order, Chukwuemeka Ike has not quite lost the satirical bite of his earlier novels. The main characters in Sunset at Dawn, being essentially civilians, are critical of the army. If nothing else, the DMI (Directorate of Military Intelligence), for example, has quite a reputation for producing the best whisky in the republic. Says Enzenwa:

> Someone ought to tell the DMI to face their assignment and leave distilling spirits to the chemists. If they had done so all this time maybe we would have had fewer tactical withdrawals. (p. 170)

Wartime Biafra to the author is not a scene of unrelieved horror, but often enlivened by flights of optimism and humour in the midst of defeat:

No attempt had been made to capitalize on those natural defences of Enugu which soldier and civilian had talked about with so much confidence. Even the famous herbalist brought all the way from Anambra had not been given the opportunity to save Enugu. Everyone had talked about the efficacy of his mysterious medicine pot. Take it to the war front, and place it in position in front of the forward trenches. Every enemy bullet would whistle past its target, mowing down the surrounding vegetation instead of Biafran soldiers. The medicine pot had not performed its wonders on this occasion because there had been no war front and no forward trench. (p. 74)

The Nigerian–Biafra war: a war of ideologies, of religious or ethnic rivalries, of economic interests? A transmuted class-struggle? A war to restore the injured dignity of man? This book gives only partial answers to too many questions. It is a welcome addition to the growing body of literature on a dark chapter in Nigerian history. But the great novel on the conflict still remains to be written.

Willlfried F. Feuser

Stephen Gray, *Caltrop's Desire*, London, Rex Collings, 1980, 136pp.
Es'kia Mphahlele, *Chirundu*, London, Panafrica Library, Nelson, 1980, 220pp.

Both *Caltrop's Desire* and *Chirundu* are by South African writers, but with that said, we exhaust all points of similarity between the two novels. In fact, despite their shared origin and contemporaneity, the two books could scarcely be less alike. *Caltrop's Desire* is by a white South African while *Chirundu* is by a black; *Caltrop's Desire* is set in the colonial era that spans the Boer War to the Second World War, while *Chirundu* is set for the most part in a post-independent African state; *Caltrop's Desire* strains after a rather brittle, self-consciously clever satire while *Chirundu* deftly combines epic, lyrical and tragic elements in a manner that recalls Ngugi's *Petals of Blood*. And, finally, *Caltrop's Desire* amounts to little more than a pretentious failure, while *Chirundu* is a compelling, if slightly uneven, success.

Gray's novel takes the form of a dying man's apologia. John Martin Caltrop, a South African journalist who has lived through, reported and been fundamentally changed by all his country's cataclysmic conflicts from the Matabeleland Campaign of 1896 through the British victory in Benoni in the Second World War, is expiring during election week in 1948. He is departing this life, in fact, precisely at the moment when all the battles he has witnessed will be irrevocably lost as the British colonial age is defeated by Afrikaner apartheid. Like Tolstoy's Ivan Ilych or Browning's Bishop Blougram, Caltrop takes an unblinkered retrospective survey of his life and tries to make some sense of it, tries to determine if it has been worthwhile. As his life ebbs out in a dreary Johannesburg nursing home, he obsessively and at times incoherently reviews his past. The central question the novel poses is: Has history answered or crushed Caltrop's desire?

By his own estimation, Caltrop has been crushed. But one of the many problems in this exasperating novel is that we are never quite clear what it is that Caltrop sought. He narrates his life story as that of an impassioned odyssey, with himself a heroic, lonely questor. Much of the action recounts his one-man trek north from Capetown, bound for Cairo ('like the Empire-builders') in the 1890s, and the adventures and characters he encounters before he comes to a halt, marries and settles down in Kimberley. He says of this quest, 'I was before my time, being a mounted one-man international, in quest of reconciling the nations within me into a greater whole'. Caltrop's identity, then, would seem somehow to be bound up with that of his country. Both are fractured, diffuse and deeply troubled. But the conflicting nations Gray depicts in the novel are incomplete because entirely white: British and Afrikaner. Except for two stereotyped black menials in the nursing home, Caltrop's South Africa is an uncontaminated white preserve. It is impossible, then, for us to believe in the historical veracity of Gray's South Africa, or in the hero-spokesman he has chosen to embody it. Caltrop seems an historical curiosity, a colonial anachronism for whom we can scarcely feel any nostalgia or sympathy.

Nor can we take much interest in the 'desire' that is supposed to be the linchpin of his personality and story. Here at the very heart of the novel is its greatest muddle. Various historical figures traipse through Caltrop's Desire, including Kruger, Baden-Powell and Mary Kingsley. But it is in connection with the nineteenth-century South African novelist Olive Schreiner that Caltrop comes as close as he ever does to disclosing his *raison d'être*. 'Her desire was as thwarted as mine,' he says, 'and by whatever name we called it, I think we were trying merely to be decent South Africans'.

Such is the rather anti-climactic and indefinite claim of Caltrop's deathbed harangue. But even more damning than the feebleness of its message are the terms in which it is couched. *Caltrop's Desire* is an earnestly experimental novel consisting of disjointed utterances, fragments of memory, pompous observations. Chronology is exploded, causal connections severed, motivation obliterated. In short, it is a difficult novel, which is not a valid criticism *per se*, but certainly is highly objectionable when the effort the reader must exert goes largely unrewarded. Gray has read his Joyce and Faulkner and perhaps his Barth and Pynchon as well, but to little beneficial effect. Though brief, *Caltrop's Desire* is a tedious, derivative production, which despite its verbal fireworks remains curiously devoid of life.

Es'kia Mphahlele's *Chirundu* is another matter altogether. The author of several previous works of fiction and of one of the earliest critical studies of African literature, Mphahlele is a mature as well as gifted writer, and *Chirundu* is the sort of powerful, ambitious novel one hopes for from an established writer. The book adroitly and sensitively explores the public and private experience of one Chimba Chirundu. It is the history of his rise as an African leader and recounts the subtle stages by which he evolves from a fervent nationalist revolutionary to a power-hungry minister in a new African state, complete with all the standard paraphernalia of his station – the Mercedes, the London tailored suits, the house with the swimming pool. This, of course, is hardly a new story in the African novel. But what makes *Chirundu* so fascinating is that the familiar tale is told from within, largely from Chirundu's own point of view, so that it becomes a psychological as well as political account.

In addition, Mphahlele is concerned with the private, emotional toll that such a transformation brings in its wake. For Chirundu this means the disintegration of his first marriage, his illegal marriage to a second woman, and the breakdown of his relationship with a beloved nephew. The plot of the novel – the structure upon which all these emotional problems are hung – involves Chirundu's trial on charges of bigamy brought by his first wife, and a transport strike engineered by his nephew against Chirundu, the Minister of Transport and Public Works.

But interwoven with this dominant theme of Chirundu's

political and personal development is a cluster of other crucial concerns: the conflict between traditional and western ways of life, personified by Chirundu's two wives (one for the 'country' who is loyal, brave, sensitive, and one for the 'city' who is sophisticated, materialistic, vacuous), the role of education in contemporary Africa, the breakdown of family bonds, the role of women, and most persistently, the drive for power. Because of Mphahlele's use of first-person narrative and the depth of his characterization, we become very close to Chirundu himself so that his fate, his corruption, seems not only frighteningly believable but also inevitable. In the end, he appears a figure of almost Shakespearian proportions, and our response to him is close to the classic one of fear and pity.

It is through his technical assurance and dexterity that Mphahlele is able to bring off his ambitious conception. The novel consists of three extended first person narratives – Chirundu's, his first wife's, and his nephew's – interspersed with dramatic scenes of dialogue spoken by secondary characters. This complicated use of point of view is made even more complex by Mphahlele's treatment of time. The novel is narrated from a 'present' of April 1969 – during Chirundu's bigamy trial – but the three first person narratives move backward and forward in time so that we have a vivid picture of how and why things have reached the political and personal crisis at the heart of the novel.

There is only one way in which Mphahlele's control of the story falters and that is in his rather awkward and heavy-handed use of python symbolism. From the earliest pages of the book, Chirundu is insistently associated with the 'nsato' or python which crushes his victims to death. The python image fails to function as the objective correlative Mphahlele intended and instead is a useless gilding of the lily, distracting rather than illuminating. The python is trotted out at every conceivable moment and we too clearly see Mphahlele gesturing in the wings on behalf of his symbol, unnecessarily apprehensive that we shall miss his point.

But the creaking of the python is the only major flaw in this impressive and deeply moving novel. And at the very end, on the last page, the symbol suddenly springs to life. Like a dangerous caged snake, Chirundu is jailed after he is convicted of bigamy – of breaking the marriage law of the western way of life that he in all other respects so slavishly imitates. Chirundu, however, is only temporarily constrained – not vanquished. As one of the minor characters observes of Chirundu and his kind, 'What bothers me is that they never let go once they have tasted power'.

Caltrop's death certificate reads 'Cause of Death: Despair'. Mphahlele's conclusion to *Chirundu* is equally bleak. The crucial difference between the two novels is that we are unmoved by Caltrop's death and unconvinced of his world. But we are frightened by Chirundu's promised survival, and Chirundu's world is the same one we live in and see all around us, a world from which Mphahlele so eloquently shows us there is no deliverance.

Katherine Frank

Robert Fraser, *The Novels of Ayi Kwei Armah, A Study in Polemical Fiction*, London, Heinemann, 1980, 128pp.

Robert Fraser's highly commendable book offers us instances of trailblazing exploration of theme and style: it is readable, illuminating and provocative.

The rather generous reception of *The Beautyful Ones Are Not Yet Born* by some reviewers is endorsed, but attention is drawn to 'a much larger pattern of betrayal' (p. 15) that undergirds Armah's treatment of the ruling class. Flashes of searching critique balance the delineation of thematic configurations in *Why Are We So Blest? Two Thousand Seasons* is lifted out of 'the domain of realist art', planted 'in an altogether different terrain . . . that appropriate to myth, legend, and racial memory' (pp. 72–3), and given its fair share of a shower of patronage. Fraser's piece on Armah's historical novel, *The Healers*, is surcharged with a clear perception of the motivation of his characters, and a scholarly appreciation of the historical process that he gives expression to in fiction.

The chapter on *Fragments* raises interesting issues but leaves Armah's second novel still underrated: it is a chapter that may disappoint readers. The paucity of cogent literary criticism is brought into sharp relief by the near parity of comments and quotations from the novel. There are other issues. Commenting on a statement attributed to Naana in the last section of the novel, Fraser writes: 'the "thousand . . . pieces" here are the fragments of the title; the extra thirty pieces are perhaps redolent of the thirty pieces of silver for which Judas Iscariot betrayed Christ' (p. 30). The fact that the tone of intense personal anguish supersedes Naana's earlier reminiscences is significant, because long before Naana's statement we are introduced to a scene in a bar, where we are told of 'the noise of splintering glass . . . the glass and the bottle . . . shattered on the floor'; three men, we are further informed, try 'to pick out the larger pieces of glass' imbedded in the face of the man who has caused the mess, Bukari. Fraser ignores (misses?) the connection, isolates the 'thirty' of 'a thousand and thirty useless pieces' for special significance, and brings in Judas's betrayal of Jesus, which, at one level, is tied up with the undue emphasis he places on the 'quasi-religious' (p. 46) motif in *Fragments*. What is obvious is that the impact of the shattering 'into a thousand and thirty useless pieces' of 'the larger meaning which lent sense to every small thing and every momentary happening years and years ago' has been, and is being, felt by individuals (Naana, Baako, Bukari, etc.), a whole people, and society at large. The falling apart of things, the fragmented individual (the splintering glass is expressive of Bukari's shattered life) in a fragmented society, are issues that are not Armah's exclusive preserve. What is pertinent to Armah's art is the tendency to posit the general in the particular. The name of a town that appears in *Fragments*, 'Bibiani' (i.e., 'this is everywhere'), sums up this important aspect of Armah's work.

These identifiable slips can be glossed over: the author talks of 'Kofi Awoonor's novels' (p. 38), when we know of, and he himself refers to, only one; he suggests that 'Baako's family would seem to be Ashanti' (i.e. Asante) (p. 39), when names like Araba, Ekua, Efua, Kwesi – though Akan – are obviously Fante, not Asante; earlier on reference is made to Kwame Nkrumah's 'Congress People's Party' (p. 3), when the party referred to is the Convention People's Party. However, the piece on Akan custom that makes 'Baako [bear] a more fundamental responsibility than Kwesi, the father' (p. 39) is not only slightly exaggerated but also beclouds the link Armah establishes artistically between Baako and his sister's child. (Admittedly the Akan, particularly the Asante, believe that blood is transmitted exclusively by females and spirit by males, but it is also true that procreation itself is believed to involve mixing a woman's blood, 'mogya', with a man's spirit, 'ntoro',: a father, while alive, has as much responsibility as any uncle for his child's welfare.) The child is premature: it comes unexpectedly like Baako's arrival from abroad. Its outdooring is pushed forward to the fifth rather than the customary eighth day after its 'homecoming'; Baako changes his mind about staying in Paris for 'a week or so', and takes 'the earliest flight to Accra'. The child's mother, Araba, has been pregnant five times but on each occasion, after months of pregnancy, 'everything would pass away in . . . a river of bad blood'. This is not surprising, since Araba considers her genital organ her 'secret weapon' – a coercive 'weapon' she uses to manipulate her husband. Reciprocity and the creative potential of the sexual union between husband and wife are subverted. Significantly, Baako's hands are washed of Araba's blood before he donates his blood to save Araba and her child. Thanking her brother for offering her his blood, Araba says: 'It wasn't the blood alone . . . The child too. You gave him to me . . . if you had not come back yourself, I would have lost this baby also.' Baako's commitment to a life-giving, health-restoring, creative essence isolates him from a people committed to the negation of the ideals he stands for. His affinity in the novel is with the old, blind, weak Naana, and the innocent child who is sacrificed by the cargo-cult devotees.

Fraser offers some valuable criticism of Armah's *Two Thousand Seasons*. The links he tries to establish between André Schwartz-Bart's *Le Dernier des Justes*, Yambo Ouologuem's *Le Devoir de Violence* and *Two Thousand Seasons* – however tenuous – are nonetheless justified by his laudable effort to draw attention to the literary ancestry of Armah's 'novel'. In some few instances (limited almost exclusively to the chapter on *Two Thousand Seasons*) Fraser adopts a rambling tone, and his language predictably becomes too insistent and heavy-handed. 'It is pointless, I think, to beat about the bush by talking of racial "overtones" ' (p. 72) and 'In the context of the massive communal inferiority complex . . . there is only one antidote, a heightening of self-respect, and we need fear no over-dosage' (p. 73) both appear in paragraphs that tend to digress and dawdle.

The merits of Fraser's book on Armah are too obvious to warrant reiteration. If he makes extravagant claims that are not adequately sustained, we are, I think, faced with the usual problem of any such 'brief study' – a setback anticipated by the author in his preface. The book's richness is sufficiently variegated, and the issues raised challenging enough, to sustain our interest in the first-ever study of the whole of Armah's output to date. Fraser's 'Conclusion' is perhaps the most profound piece written on Armah's art and its relation to African and world literature.

Kofi Owusu

Syl Cheney-Coker, *The Graveyard Also Has Teeth*, London, Heinemann, 1980, 128 pp.

The Graveyard Also Has Teeth is a very edifying and interesting collection of poems of even texture and yet multifarious themes. This is the second book by the author of *Concerto for an Exile* (1973). The title derives from the Creole. In Sierra Leone, when mourners are deeply shocked by the death of a beloved, they show their sorrow and pain at the graveyard by shouting hysterically: 'Eh, the grave yard bet (bites) me, eh, it bet (bites) me!' This title thus implies artistic creations of sadness, of agony, of pain full of cryptic and folded meanings.

The collection may be profitably viewed as a panorama of verse brilliantly folded with layers of diverse meanings, perceptions and sensibilities expressed within compressed images. The author obviously regards his poems as enigmas to be solved by the reader. These attributes might make the work appear too exacting but once the right intellectual effort is made, understanding comes easily and the reader sees the poet's landscape, shares in his creativity and in his experience.

Syl Cheney-Coker is a senior lecturer in the Department of English, University of Maiduguri, Nigeria, where he teaches the poetry of the Maghreb, oral narratives and Carribbean/Afro-American literature. Bursting with creative energy, he is sensitive and serious, bold and imaginative, speaking the voice of laughter through tears, of mourning, of anger, wisdom and truth. The collection consists of verse with familiar themes, situations and characters. The poems in this group, which include 'Song for the ravaged country', 'Talons in the flesh of my country', 'The executed', 'Haemorrhage' and 'Putrefaction', seem to be fairly direct descriptions or narratives with a delightful but modest poetic complexity. The themes and situations are easily reflected in the titles, making elaborate comments unnecessary. But lurking behind the paradoxical simplicity of the lines are strong, complex images of birth, initiation, growth and death.

These recurrent images, which help the poems in the collection to achieve an organic unity, seem to symbolize the human life cycle (including the poet's), its genesis, vicissitudes, fear, aspirations, and the search for the meaning of life or eternal good. It is in response to this that the poet embarks on his search, probing himself, the reality of his environment as well as that of our collective unconscious.

'On being a poet in Sierra Leone', 'Song for the ravaged country', 'Portrait' and 'Agony of the lost poets' seem to deal with various aspects of the poet's manifesto. The poet serves as the conscience of the society and defends truth with courage and sincerity. The poet should not be swayed by abuse, threat or adverse criticism. Rather, such negative tendencies in others should serve to spur him on to greater achievements. That is the inspiration the poet gets from being castigated.

Syl Cheney-Coker is a fascinating poet who blends theme, idiom and syntax delightfully. The poems exude an admirable intricacy of language ordering. Significance is given to commonplace statements, events and situations through ironic emphasis. Over the years, the poet has tightened up his style and expression. His present collection is in places fierce, fluent and tense. He is a nationalist, a poet of anger: he is angry with cheats, fakes, dupes, dictators, with life and death; angry with the world and with himself.

Coker's poems are very strongly influenced by Pablo Neruda, Vallejo and the Cuban Padilla. From them, he has borrowed the themes of grief, betrayal, honesty, knowledge and death. Cheney-Coker is in a hurry to confront death, to return to his God. For him, death is as welcome as it was for Christ. The poet as Christ figure is strongly expressed in 'The prodigal son'. He rounds up his philosophical chants to death with 'Funeral dance', where death is celebrated with the beating of conga music and the dance of the fireflies:

> Let them bring my coffin I made panting with joy
> Having no regret leaving the life that I have lived
> To return animal without that heart
> Pissing out its oxidised blood
> Let the gypsy woman play me my final concerto
> Because I weep no more dressing in haste
> For my flight to the graveyard which has teeth.

Cheney-Coker's verse is powerful. Indeed, he is one of the best, if not the best poet that has come out of Africa in the last decade and is one of the most original and gifted African poets alive today.

Segun Dada

Index